INSIGHT GUIDES

KOREAN

PHRASEBOOK & DICTIONARY

Contacting the Editors

Every effort has been made to provide accurate information in this publication, but changes are inevitable. The publisher cannot be responsible for any resulting loss, inconvenience or injury. We would appreciate it if readers would call our attention to any errors or outdated information. We also welcome your suggestions; if you come across a relevant expression not in our phrase book, please contact us at:
hello@insightguides.com

First Edition: 2015
Printed in China

Cover & Interior Design: Pawel Pasternak
Production: AM Services
Production Manager: Vicky Glover
Picture Researcher: Slawek Krajewski
Cover Photo: all iStockphoto

Interior Photos: all iStockphoto

CONTENTS

INTRODUCTION

GETTING STARTED

EXPLORING

ACTIVITIES

HEALTH & SAFETY

FOOD & DRINK

GOING OUT

DICTIONARY

PRONUNCIATION

This section is designed to make you familiar with the sounds of Korean using our simplified phonetic transcription*. You'll find the pronunciation of the Korean letters and sounds explained below, together with their 'imitated' equivalents. This system is used throughout the phrase book; simply read the pronunciation as if it were English, noting any special rules below.

BEGINNING CONSONANTS

Letter	Approximate Pronunciation	Symbol	Example	Pronunciation
ㄱ	g as in girl	**g**	감	*gahm*
ㄴ	n as in no	**n**	나	*nah*
ㄷ	d as in dog	**d**	돈	*dohn*
ㄹ	between English r and l**	**l**	나라	*nah • lah*
ㅁ	m as in moon	**m**	물	*mool*
ㅂ	b as in book	**b**	불	*bool*

*The Korean Ministry of Culture and Tourism has its own Korean romanization system, which you will see on road signs, place names and certain legal documents.
**In Korean, the sounds l and r are pronounced similarly. The position of the tongue when pronouncing the letter ㄹ is somewhere between the position of the tongue when pronouncing r and l in English. It is pronounced more like l when it appears at the end of a syllable, as in 물 mool, and like an r when it is between two vowels, as in 머리 muree. For the sake of simplicity, this sound appears as 'l' in the pronunciation.

Letter	Approximate Pronunciation	Symbol	Example	Pronunciation
ㅅ	s as in sand	**s**	산	*sahn*
ㅇ	silent		이	*ee*

ㅈ	j as in jam	**j**	줄	*jool*
ㅊ	ch as in chin	**ch**	춤	*choom*
ㅋ	k as in kite	**k**	콩	*kohng*
ㅌ	t as in table	**t**	탈	*tahl*
ㅍ	p as in park	**p**	팔	*pahl*
ㅎ	h as in hill	**h**	한	*hahn*
ㄲ	sharp k as in sky	**kk**	꼬리	*kkoh • lee*
ㄸ	sharp t as in stop	**tt**	또	*ttoh*
ㅃ	sharp p as in spy	**pp**	빵	*ppahng*
ㅆ	sharp s as in sun	**ss**	밥	*ssahl*
ㅉ	tz as in pretzel	**tz**	찐	*tzeen*

FINAL CONSONANTS

Letter	Approximate Pronunciation	Symbol	Example	Pronunciation
ㄱ, ㄲ, ㅋ	k as in pick	**k**	목	*mohk*
ㄴ	n as in pin	**n**	산	*sahn*
ㄷ, ㅌ, ㅅ, ㅆ, ㅈ, ㅊ, ㅎ	t as in pot	**t**	빛	*beet*
ㄹ	l as in pool	**l**	풀	*pool*
ㅁ	m as in jam	**m**	곰	*gohm*
ㅂ, ㅍ	p as in top	**p**	집	*jeep*
ㅇ	ng as in ring	**ng**	공	*gohng*

Besides the basic final consonants listed above, there are also complex final consonants made by combining two basic consonants. If a complex final consonant is used at the end of a syllable or before a consonant, only one basic consonant of the two is pronounced.

VOWELS

Letter	Approximate Pronunciation	Symbol	Example	Pronunciation
ㅏ	a as in father	**ah**	안	*ahn*
ㅑ	ya as in yacht	**yah**	야구	*yah•goo*
ㅓ	u as in nut	**uh**	섬	*suhm*
ㅕ	yu as in yum	**yuh**	여자	*yuh•jah*
ㅗ	o as in no	**oh**	소	*soh*
ㅛ	yo as in yoga	**yo**	표	*pyo*
ㅜ	oo as in boot	**oo**	줄	*jool*
ㅠ	like the word you	**yoo**	유리	*yoo•lee*
ㅡ	a short u as in put	**u**	은	*un*
ㅣ, ㅢ	ee as in feet	**ee**	비	*bee*
ㅐ, ㅔ	e as in end	**eh**	새	*seh*
ㅒ, ㅖ	ye as in yes	**yeh**	예	*yeh*
ㅘ	wa as in watt	**wah**	사과	*sah•gwah*
ㅙ, ㅚ, ㅞ	we as in wet	**weh**	왜	*weh*
ㅝ	wo as in won	**wuh**	원	*wuhn*
ㅟ	wi as in twig	**wih**	쥐	*jwih*

There are ten basic vowels in Korean. There are also additional compound vowels made by combining basic vowels. The compound vowels are supposed to be distinguishable in pronunciation, but in casual Korean speech, the distinction between ㅐ/ㅔ, ㅒ/ㅖ and ㅙ/ㅞ/ㅚ has been lost.

HOW TO USE THE APP

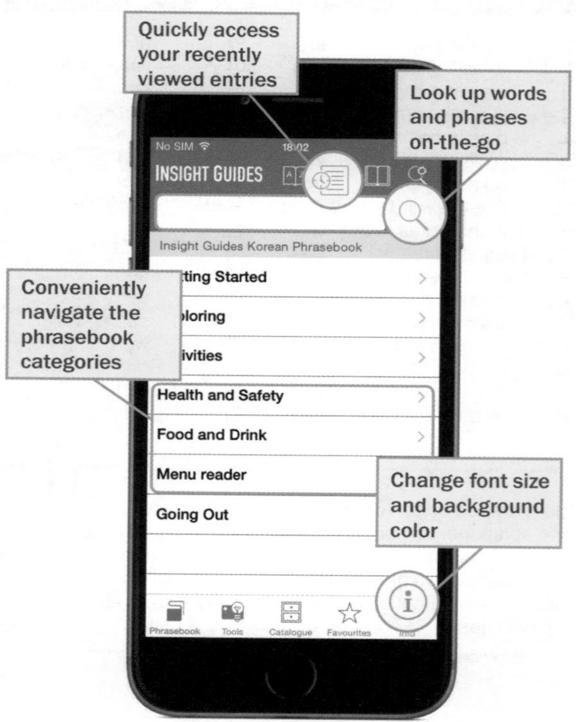

Save the most useful everyday words and phrases to your Favorites

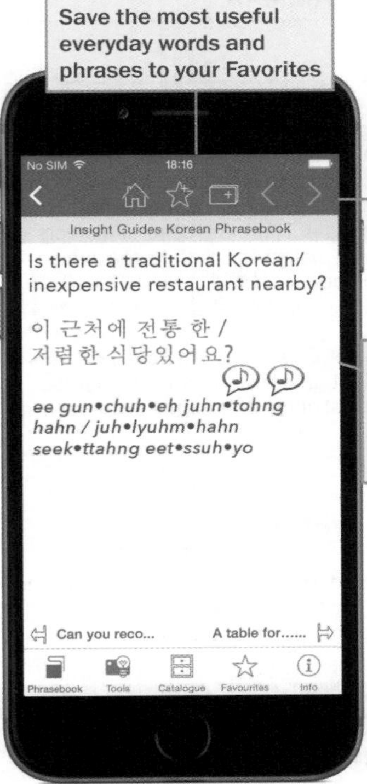

Use the Flash Cards Quiz to learn and memorize new words easily

Take all digital advantages of the app: listen to words and phrases pronounced by native speakers

To learn how to activate the app, see the inside back cover of this phrasebook.

THE BASICS

GRAMMAR

Korean is the official language of both North and South Korea. There are about 80 million Korean speakers worldwide. In South Korea, Korean is referred to as 한국어 *hahn • goo • guh*. In North Korea, Korean is most often called 조선말 *joh • suhn • mahl*. There are several dialects of Korean, but the standard dialect in South Korea, which is featured in this phrase book, is 서울 *suh • ool* (Seoul), and in North Korea, it is the dialect of 평양 *pyuhng • yahng* (Pyongyang).

Korean has formal polite, informal polite and casual forms. The form used is dependent on the situation. This phrase book applies both the formal polite and informal polite forms, as dictated by the context.

VERBS

Korean verbs are conjugated to indicate tense, formality, mood and other aspects. There are three types of speech styles in Korean: formal polite, informal polite and casual.

FORMAL POLITE STYLE

(used in the media, business meetings, speeches, formal interviews, etc., and used more frequently by men than women)

With verb stems ending in a vowel: add ㅂ니다 *(m • nee • dah)*.

With verb stems ending in a consonant: add 습니다 *(ssum • need • dah)*.

INFORMAL POLITE STYLE

(used in daily conversation where formality is not necessary, and used more frequently by women than men, even in some formal situations)
When the final vowel of verb stem is ㅏ or ㅗ : add 아요 *(ah • yo)*.
With other stems: add 어요 *(uh • yo)*.

CASUAL STYLE

(used with children and close friends)
Drop 요 from informal polite style.
There are also honorific endings, which indicate high-level respect and politeness: 으십니다 *u • seem • nee • dah*/으세요 *u • seh • yo* and 십니다 *seem • nee • dah*/세요 *seh • yo*. The former is used when the verb stem ends in a consonant and the latter is used when the verb stem ends in a vowel.

THE PAST TENSE

When the final vowel of the verb stem is ㅏ *ah* or ㅗ *oh*, add 았 *aht*, and when the final vowel of the verb stem is other than ㅏ *ah* or ㅗ *oh*, add 었 *uht*. When the verb ends with 하다 *hah • dah*, add 였 *yuht* after 하 *hah* and final form is 했 *heht*.

THE FUTURE TENSE

For the simple future, add ㄹ 것/거 *guht/guh* when the verb stem ends in a vowel, and add 을 것/거 *ul • guht/guh* when the verb stem ends in a consonant (for the causal form, add 야 at the end). For the intentional future, which is used to express the speaker's strong will or intention, add 겠 *geht* at the end of the verb stem.

IRREGULAR VERBS

There are many irregular verbs in Korean that do not follow a pattern. Following are few examples of irregular verbs.

	FORMAL FORM	POLITE FORM	CASUAL FORM
to help	돕습니다 *dohp • ssum • nee • dah*	도와요 *doh • wah • yo*	도와 *doh • wah*
to walk	걷습니다 *guh • ssum • nee • dah*	걸어요 *guh • luh • yo*	걸어 *guh • luh*
to call	부릅니다 *boo • lum • nee • dah*	불러요 *bool • luh • yo*	불러 *bool • luh*

IMPERATIVES

Unlike English, in which the infinitive form of a verb indicates a command, Korean uses verb endings to form an imperative expression. An example of the formal polite imperative is the verb ending -십시오 *-seep • ssee • yo*; the informal polite is the verb ending -세요 *seh • yo*.

WORD ORDER

Basic word order in Korean is generally subject-object-verb. When there is additional information, word order can be flexible as long as the predicate is placed at the end.

SIMPLE QUESTIONS

To form simple questions, change the 다 *dah* ending of the statement into the 까 *kkah* question ending and add rising intonation.

피터가 시내에 갑니다. *pee • tuh • gah see • neh • eh gahm • nee • dah* (Peter is going to town.)
피터가 시내에 갑니까? *pee • tuh • gah see • neh • eh gahm • nee • kkah* (Is Peter going to town?)

NEGATION

안 *ahn* (no/not) is added in front of verbs and adjectives to indicate negation.
시내에 갑니다. *see • neh • eh gahm • nee • dah* (I'm going to town.)
시내에 안 갑니다. *see • neh • eh ahn gahm • nee • dah* (I'm not going to town.)

NOUNS

Nouns in Korean include particles (see below). Plural forms are not often used in Korean. Whether the noun is singular or plural is judged from the context, or by a number modifying the noun:
표 *pyo* (ticket)
표 세 장 *pyo seh jahng* (three tickets)

PRONOUNS

Pronouns are rarely used; names and titles are used instead. Pronouns have no gender nor case markings (subject, object, etc.). Instead, particles are used to indicate case; these appear after the noun to which they refer.
When the subject of the sentence is a pronoun and the subject is understood through context, then the subject pronoun is often omitted.

PARTICLES

Korean has various particles. For example, subject particles 이/가 *ee/gah* are attached to a noun to indicate the subject of the sentence. The topic particles 은/는 *un/nun* are attached to a noun and are used to introduce someone or something, to compare or contrast and for emphasis. The object particles 을/를 *ul/lul* are attached to a noun to indicate the object of the sentence. When honorific subject particle 께서 *kkeh • suh* is used, it shows special respect towards the subject of the sentence.

ADJECTIVES

An adjective usually precedes the noun to which it refers, as in English: 차 *chah* (car); 좋은 차 *joh • un chah* (nice car).

WORD ORDER

To form a comparative, 더 *duh* is added in front of an adjective.
좋은 차 *joh • un chah* (nice car), 더 좋은 차 *duh joh • un chah* (nicer car)
To form a superlative, 제일 *jeh • eel* is added in front of an adjective.
제일 좋은 차 *jeh • eel joh • un chah* (the nicest car)

ADVERBS & ADVERBIAL EXPRESSIONS

Adverbs are placed in front of a verb or an adjective. Commonly used adverbs include:
아주 *ah • joo* (very)
또 *ttoh* (again)
가끔 *gah • kkum* (sometimes)
자주 *jah • joo* (often)
빨리 *ppahl • lee* (quickly)
많이 *mah • nee* (a lot)
너무 *nuh • moo* (too)
항상 *hang • sahng* (always)

GETTING STARTED

THE BASICS

NUMBERS

NEED TO KNOW

	Sino-Korean*	Korean*
0	영/공 *yuhn/gohng*	
1	일 *eel*	하나 *hah•nah*
2	이 *ee*	둘 *dool*
3	삼 *sahm*	셋 *seht*
4	사 *sah*	넷 *neht*
5	오 *oh*	다섯 *dah•suht*

* Sino-Korean numbers are used for years, months, days or money. Korean numbers are used with particles or counters.

6	육 *yook*	여섯 *yuh • suht*
7	칠 *cheel*	일곱 *eel • gohp*
8	팔 *pahl*	여덟 *yuh • duhl*
9	구 *goo*	아홉 *ah • hohp*
10	십 *seep*	열 *yuhl*
11	십일 *see • beel*	열하나 *yuhl • hah • nah*
12	십이 *see • bee*	열둘 *yuhl • ttool*
13	십삼 *seep • ssahm*	열셋 *yuhl • seht*
14	십사 *seep • ssah*	열넷 *yuhl • neht*
15	십오 *see • boh*	열다섯 *yuhl • ttah • shut*
16	십육 *seem • nyook*	열여섯 *yuhl • yuh • suht*
17	십칠 *seep • cheel*	열일곱 *yuhl • eel • ghop*
18	십팔 *seep • pahl*	열여덟 *yuhl • yuh • duhl*
19	십구 *seep • kkoo*	열아홉 *yuhl • ah • hohp*
20	이십 *ee • seep*	스물 *su • mool*
21	이십일 *ee • see • beel*	스물하나 *su • mool • hah • nah*

22	이십이 *ee • see • bee*	스물둘 *su • mool • dool*
30	삼십 *sahm • seep*	서른 *suh • lun*
31	삼십일 *sahm • see • beel*	서른하나 *suh • lun • hah • nah*
40	사십 *sah • seep*	마흔 *mah • hun*
50	오십 *oh • seep*	쉰 *swihn*
60	육십 *yook • sseep*	예순 *yeh • soon*
70	칠십 *cheel • sseep*	일흔 *eel • hun*
80	팔십 *pahl • sseep*	여든 *yuh • dun*
90	구십 *goo • seep*	아흔 *ah • hun*
100	백 *behk*	
101	백일 *beh • geel*	
200	이백 *ee • behk*	
500	오백 *oh • behk*	
1,000	천 *chuhn*	
10,000	만 *mahn*	
100,000	십만 *seem • mahn*	
1,000,000	백만 *behng • mahn*	

There are two numbering systems in Korean: Sino-Korean numbers and pure Korean numbers. Sino-Korean numbers are used to count years, months, days, minutes and currency; Korean numbers are used mostly for counting people or things. For 100 and greater, only one counting system is used. Arabic numbers are usually used for written forms.

ORDINAL NUMBERS

first	첫째 *chuht • tzeh*
second	둘째 *dool • tzeh*
third	셋째 *seht • tzeh*
fourth	넷째 *neht • tzeh*
fifth	다섯째 *dah • suht • tzeh*
once	한 번 *hahn buhn*
twice	두 번 *doo buhn*
three times	세 번 *seh buhn*

TIME

NEED TO KNOW

What time is it?	몇 시입니까? *myuht ssee • eem • nee • kkah*
It's noon [midday].	정오입니다. *juhng • oh • eem • nee • dah*
At midnight.	자정에요. *jah • juhng • eh • yo*
From one o'clock to two o'clock.	한 시부터 두 시까지요. *hahn see • boo • tuh doo see • kkah • jee • yo*
Five after [past] three.	세 시 오 분요. *seh see oh boon • nyo*
A quarter to four.	네 시 십오 분 전요. *neh see see • boh boon juhn • nyo*
5:30 a.m./p.m.	오전/오후 다섯 시 삼십 분요. *oh • juhn/oh • hoo dah • suht ssee sahm • see ppoon • nyo*

DAYS

NEED TO KNOW

Monday	월요일 *wuh • lyo • eel*
Tuesday	화요일 *hwah • yo • eel*
Wednesday	수요일 *soo • yo • eel*
Thursday	목요일 *moh • gyo • eel*
Friday	금요일 *gu • myo • eel*
Saturday	토요일 *toh • yo • eel*
Sunday	일요일 *ee • lyo • eel*

DATES

yesterday	어제 *uh • jeh*
today	오늘 *oh • nul*
tomorrow	내일 *neh • eel*
day	일 *eel*
week	주 *joo*

month	월 *wuhl*
year	년 *nyuhn*

MONTHS

January	일월 *ee • lwuh*
February	이월 *ee • wuhl*
March	삼월 *sah • mwuhl*
April	사월 *sah • wuhl*
May	오월 *oh • wuhl*
June	유월 *yoo • wuhl*
July	칠월 *chee • lwuhl*
August	팔월 *pah • lwuhl*
September	구월 *goo • wuhl*
October	시월 *see • wuhl*
November	십일월 *see • bee • lwuhl*
December	십이월 *see • bee • wuhl*

SEASONS

spring	봄 *bohm*
summer	여름 *yuh • lum*
fall [autumn]	가을 *gah • ul*
winter	겨울 *gyuh • ool*

HOLIDAYS

South Korea

January 1: 신정 *seen • johng* New Year's Day
March 1: 삼일절 *sah • meel • tzuhl* Independence Movement Day
May 5: 어린이날 *uh • lee • nee nahl* Children's Day
June 6: 현충일 *hyuhn • choong • eel* Memorial Day
August 15: 광복절 *gwahng • bohk • tzuhl* Liberation Day
October 3: 개천절 *geh • chuhn • juhl* National Foundation Day
December 25: 성탄절 *suhng • than • juhl* Christmas

In addition to the holidays listed above, there are also three public holidays in South Korea that are based on the lunar calendar and, so, fall on different days every year: 구정 *goo • juhng* (Lunar New Year, in January or February), 석가 탄신일 *suhk • kkah tahn • see • neel* (Buddha's Birthday, in May) and the 추석 *choo suhk* (Harvest Moon Festival, in September or October).

ARRIVAL & DEPARTURE

NEED TO KNOW

I'm on vacation [holiday]/business.	휴가로/일 때문에 왔습니다. *hyoo • gah • loh/eel tteh • moo • neh waht • ssum • nee • dah*
I'm going to…	…갑니다. *…gahm • nee • dah*
I'm staying at the … Hotel.	…호텔에 머물고 있습니다. *…hoh • teh • leh muh • mool • goh eet • ssum • nee • dah*

BORDER CONTROL

I'm just passing through.	통과 여객입니다. *tohng • gwah yuh • geh • geem • nee • dah*
I'd like to declare…	…신고하고 싶습니다. *…seen • goh • hah • goh seep • ssum • nee • dah*
I have nothing to declare.	신고할 것이 없습니다. *seen • goh • hahl kkuh • see uhp • ssum • nee • dah*

YOU MAY HEAR...

여권 좀 보여주십시오. *yuh • kkwun johm boh • yuh • joo • seep • ssee • yo*	Your passport, please.
방문 목적이 무엇입니까? *bahng • moon mohk • tzuh • gee moo • uh • seem • nee • kkah*	What's the purpose of your visit?
어디에 묵으실 겁니까? *uh • dee • eh mook • gu • seel kkuhm • nee • kkah*	Where are you staying?
얼마나 계실 겁니까? *uhl • mah • nah geh • seel kkuhm • nee • kkah*	How long are you staying?
누구하고 같이 오셨습니까? *noo • goo • hah • goh gah • chee oh • shut • ssum • nee • kkah*	Who are you here with?

YOU MAY HEAR...

신고하실 물건이 있습니까? *seen • goh • hah • seel mool • guh • nee eet • ssum • nee • kkah*	Anything to declare?
이것은 관세를 내야 합니다. *ee • guh • sun gwahn • seh • lul neh • yah hahm • nee • dah*	You must pay duty on this.
이 가방을 열어 보십시오. *ee gah • bahng • ul yuh • luh boh • seep • ssee • oh*	Open this bag.

YOU MAY SEE...

세관
seh • gwahn
customs

면세품
myuhn • seh • poom
duty-free goods

자진 신고
jah • jeen seen • goh
goods to declare

면세
myuhn • seh
nothing to declare

입국 심사
eep • kkook seem • sah
passport control

경찰
gyuhng • chahl
police

MONEY

NEED TO KNOW

Where's...?	…어디 있습니까? *...uh • dee eet • ssum • nee • kkah*
the ATM	현금 인출기 *hyuhn • gum een • chool • gee*
the bank	은행 *un • hehng*
the currency exchange office	환전소 *hwahn • juhn • soh*
When does the bank open/close?	은행 언제 엽니까/닫습니까? *un • hehng uhn • jeh yuhm • nee • kkah/ daht • ssum • nee • kkah*
I'd like to change dollars/pounds into Won.	달러를/파운드를 원화로 바꾸고 싶습니다. *dahl • luh • lul/pah • oon • du • lul wuhn • hwah • loh bah • kkoo • goh seep • ssum • nee • dah*
I'd like to cash traveler's checks [cheques].	여행자 수표를 현금으로 바꾸고 싶습니다. *yuh • hehng • jah soo • pyo • lul hyuhn • gu • mu • loh bah • kkoo • goh seep • ssum • nee • dah*

AT THE BANK

I'd like to... …싶습니다.
...seep • ssum • nee • dah

change money	환전하고 *hwahn • juhn • hah • goh*
change dollars/ pounds into Won	달러를/파운드를 원화로 바꾸고 *dal • luh • lul/pah • oon • du • lul wuhn • hwah • loh bah • kkoo • goh*
cash traveler's checks [cheques]/ Eurocheques	여행자 수표를/유로체크를 현금으로 바꾸고 *yuh • hehng • jah soo • pyo • lul/ yoo • loh • cheh • ku • lul hyuhn • gu • mu • loh bah • kkoo • goh*
get a cash advance	현금 서비스 받고 *hyuhn • gum ssuh • bee • su baht • kkoh*
What's the exchange rate/fee?	환율이/환전 수수료가 얼마입니까? *hwahn • yoo • lee/hwahn • juhn soo • soo • lyo • gah uhl • mah • eem • nee • kkah*
I think there's a mistake.	착오가 있는 것 같습니다. *chah • goh • gah een • nun guht gaht • ssum • nee • dah*
I lost my traveler's checks [cheques].	여행자 수표를 잃어버렸습니다. *yuh • hehng • jah soo • pyo • lul ee • luh • buh • lyuht • ssum • nee • dah*

Banks are open Monday through Friday, 9:30 a.m. to 4:30 p.m. At some banks, cash can be obtained from ATMs with many international bank and credit cards. Keep in mind, though, that most banks allow ATM transactions only if the user has an account at a Korean bank. For cash withdrawals only, 현금 인출기 *hyuhn • gum een • chool • gee* (automatic cash dispensers) are available at some public transportation terminals and convenience stores.

My card…	제 카드를… *jeh kah • du • lul…*
was lost	잃어버렸습니다 *ee • luh • buh • lyuht • ssum • nee • dah*
was stolen	도난당했습니다 *doh • nahn • dahng • heht • ssum • nee • dah*
doesn't work	쓸 수 없습니다 *ssul ssoo uhp • ssum • nee • dah*
The ATM ate my card.	현금 인출기가 제 카드를 먹어버렸습니다. *hyuhn • gum een • chool • gee • gah jeh kah • du • lul muh • guh • buh • lyuht • ssum • nee • dah*

For Numbers, see page 20.

YOU MAY SEE...

Korean currency is the 원 *wuhn* (**Won**, abbreviated as **W**).
Coins: 십 원 *see bwuhn* (10 **Won**), 오십 원 *oh • see bwuhn* (50 **Won**), 백 원 *beh gwuhn* (100 **Won**), 오백 원 *oh • beh gwuhn* (500 **Won**)
Bills: 천 원 *chuh nwuhn* (1,000 **Won**), 오천 원 *oh • chuh nwuhn* (5,000 **Won**), 만 원 *mah nwuhn* (10,000 **Won**)

YOU MAY SEE...

카드를 넣어 주십시오 *kah • du • lul nuh • uh joo • seep • ssee • oh*	insert card here
취소 *chwih • soh*	cancel
확인 *hwah • geen*	enter
비밀번호 *bee • meel buhn • hoh*	PIN
출금 *chool • gum*	withdrawal
당좌 계좌에서 *dahng • jwah keh • jwah • eh • suh*	from checking [current] account
저축 계좌에서 *juh • chuhk keh • jwah • eh • suh*	from savings account
영수증 *yuhng • soo • jung*	receipt

CONVERSATION

NEED TO KNOW

Hello.	안녕하세요. *an • nyuhng • hah • seh • yo*
How are you?	잘 지내십니까? *jahl jee • neh • seem • nee • kkah*
Fine, thanks.	네, 좋습니다. *neh joht • ssum • nee • dah*
Excuse me!	실례합니다! *seel • leh • hahm • nee • dah*
Do you speak English?	영어 하십니까? *yuhng • uh hah • seem • nee • kkah*
What's your name?	이름이 어떻게 되십니까? *ee • lu • mee uh • ttuh • keh dweh • seem • nee • kkah*
My name is…	제 이름은…입니다. *jeh ee • lu • mun…eem • nee • dah*
Nice to meet you.	만나서 반갑습니다. *mahn • nah • suh bahn • gahp • ssum • nee • dah*
Where are you from?	어디서 오셨습니까? *uh • dee • suh oh • syuht • ssum • nee • kkah*
I'm from the U.S./U.K.	저는 미국에서/영국에서 왔습니다. *juh • nun mee • goo • geh • suh/ yuhng • goo • geh • suh waht • ssum • nee • dah*
What do you do?	무슨 일 하십니까? *moo • sun neel hah • seem • nee • kkah*

I work for...	저는…에서 일합니다. *juh • nun...eh • suh* *eel • hahm • nee • dah*
I'm a student.	저는 학생입니다. *juh • nun* *hahk • ssehng • eem • nee • dah*
I'm retired.	저는 은퇴했습니다. *juh • nun* *un • tweh • heht • ssum • nee • dah*
Do you like...?	…좋아하십니까? *...joh • ah hah • seem • nee • kkah*
Goodbye. (to someone leaving)	안녕히 가세요. *ahn • nyuhng • hee gah • seh • yo*
See you later.	나중에 뵙겠습니다. *nah • joong • eh* *bwehp • kkeht • ssum • nee • dah*

In formal Korean, 씨 *ssee* (Mr., Mrs. or Miss) is said after a colleague's or subordinate's full name and 님 *neem* (an honorific form added to a kinship term, a job title or a personal name) is used for one's superiors or distant adults to show respect. Also note that the last name precedes the first name.

LANGUAGE DIFFICULTIES

Do you speak English?	영어 하십니까? *yuhng • uh hah • seem • nee • kkah*
Does anyone here speak English?	여기 영어 하시는 분 계십니까? *yuh • gee yuhng • uh hah • see • nun boon geh • seem • nee • kkah*
I don't speak (much) Korean.	한국어 (잘) 못 합니다. *han • goo • guh (jahl) moh tahm • nee • dah*
Can you speak more slowly?	더 천천히 말씀해 주시겠습니까? *duh chuhn • chuh • nee mahl • ssum • heh joo • see • geht • ssum • nee • kkah*
Can you repeat that?	다시 말씀해 주시겠습니까? *dah • see mahl • ssum • heh joo • see • geht • ssum • nee • kkah*
Excuse me?	뭐라고 하셨습니까? *mwuh • lah • goh hah • syuht • ssum • nee • kkah*
What was that?	뭐라고요? *mwuh • lah • goh • yo*
Can you spell it?	철자가 어떻게 됩니까? *chuhl • tzah • gah uh • ttuh • keh dwehm • nee • kkah*

Please write it down.	좀 써 주십시오. *johm ssuh joo • seep • ssee • yo*
Can you translate this into English for me?	이거 영어로 번역해 주시겠습니까? *ee • guh yuhng • uh • loh byuh • nyuh • keh joo • see • geht • ssum • nee • kkah*
What does this/that mean?	이거/저거 무슨 뜻입니까? *ee • guh/juh • guh moo • sun ttu • seem • nee • kkah*
I understand.	알겠습니다. *ahl • geht • ssum • nee • dah*
I don't understand.	모르겠습니다. *moh • lu • geht • ssum • nee • dah*
Do you understand?	아시겠습니까? *ah • see • geht • ssum • nee • kkah*

YOU MAY HEAR...

영어 조금 밖에 못 합니다. *yuhng • uh joh • gum bah • kkeh moh tahm • nee • dah*	I only speak a little English.
영어 못 합니다. *yuhng • uh moh tahm • nee • dah*	I don't speak English.

MAKING FRIENDS

Hello!	안녕하세요! *ahn • nyuhng • hah • seh • yo*
Good afternoon.	안녕하세요? *ahn • nyuhng • hah • seh • yo*
Good evening.	안녕하세요? *ahn • nyuhng • hah • seh • yo*

My name is...	제 이름은…입니다. *jeh ee • lu • mun...eem • nee • dah*
What's your name?	이름이 어떻게 되십니까? *ee • lu • mee uh • ttuh • keh dweh • seem • nee • kkah*
I'd like to introduce you to...	…께 소개시켜 드리겠습니다. *...kkeh soh • geh see • kyuh du • lee • geht • ssum • nee • dah*
Nice to meet you.	만나서 반갑습니다. *mahn • nah • suh bahn • gahp • ssum • nee • dah*
How are you?	잘 지내십니까? *jahl jee • neh • seem • nee • kkah*
Fine, thanks. And you?	네, 좋습니다. 잘 지내십니까? *neh joh • ssum • nee • dah jahl jee • neh • seem • nee • kkah*

Politeness and etiquette are valued in Korean society. When greeting someone or departing, Koreans nod or bow their heads. Try to use both hands when you hand something (e.g., a business card or gift) to someone, for it shows respect.

TRAVEL TALK

I'm here...	여기…왔습니다. *yuh • gee...waht • ssum • nee • dah*
on business	일 때문에 *eel tteh • moo • neh*
on vacation [holiday]	휴가로 *hyoo • gah • loh*

studying	공부하러 *gohng • boo • hah • luh*
I'm staying for...	...동안 머물 겁니다. *...ttohng • ahn muh • mool kkuhm • nee • dah*
I've been here...	여기...동안 있었습니다. *yuh • gee...ttohng • ahn eet • ssuht • ssum • nee • dah*
a day	하루 *hah • loo*
a week	일주일 *eel • tzoo • eel*
a month	한 달 *hahn dahl*
Where are you from?	어디서 오셨습니까? *uh • dee • suh oh • syuht • ssum • nee • kkah*
I'm from...	...에서 왔습니다. *...eh • suh waht • ssum • nee • dah*

For Numbers, see page 20.

PERSONAL

Who are you with?	누구하고 같이 오셨습니까? *noo • goo • hah • goh gah • chee oh • syuht • ssum • nee • kkah*
I'm here alone.	여기 혼자 왔습니다. *yuh • gee hohn • jah waht • ssum • nee • dah*
I'm with my...	...하고 같이 왔습니다. *...hah • goh gah • chee waht • ssum • nee • dah*
husband/wife	남편/아내 *nahm • pyuhn/ah • neh*

boyfriend/ girlfriend	남자친구/여자친구 *nahm • jah • cheen • goo/ yuh • jah • cheen • goo*
mother/father	어머니/아버지 *uh • muh • nee/ah • buh • jee*
friend/colleague	친구/직장 동료 *cheen • goo/jeek • tzahng dohng • nyo*
When's your birthday?	생일이 언제입니까? *sehng • ee • lee uhn • jeh • eem • nee • kkah*
How old are you?	나이가 어떻게 되십니까? *nah • ee • gah uh • ttuh • keh dweh • seem • nee • kkah*
I'm…	저는… *juh • nun…*
Are you married?	결혼하셨습니까? *gyuh • lohn • hah • syuht • ssum • nee • kkah*
I'm…	저는… *juh • nun…*
single/in a relationship	미혼입니다/사귀는 사람이 있습니다 *mee • hoh • neem • nee • dah/ sah • gwih • nun sah • lah • mee eet • ssum • nee • dah*

engaged/married	약혼했습니다/결혼했습니다 *yahk • khohn • heht • ssum • nee • dah/ gyuh • lohn • heht • ssum • nee • dah*
divorced/ separated	이혼했습니다/별거 중입니다 *ee • hohn • heht • ssum • nee • dah/ byuhl • guh joong • eem • nee • dah*
widowed	사별했습니다 *sah • byuhl • heht • ssum • nee • dah*
Do you have children/ grandchildren?	자녀가/손자가 있으십니까? *jah • nyuh • gah/sohn • jah • gah eet • ssu • seem • nee • kkah*

For Romance, see page 220.

WORK & SCHOOL

What do you do?	무슨 일하십니까? *moo • sun neel • hah • seem • nee • kkah*
What are you studying?	무슨 공부하십니까? *moo • sun gohng • boo • hah • seem • nee • kkah*
I'm studying Korean.	한국어 공부하고 있습니다. *hahn • goo • guh gohng • boo • hah • goh eet • ssum • nee • dah*
I...	저는… *juh • nun...*
work full-time/ part-time	풀타임으로/파트타임으로 일합니다 *pool • tah • ee • mu • loh/ pah • tu • tah • ee • mu • loh eel • hahm • nee • dah*
am unemployed	직업이 없습니다 *jee • guh • bee uhp • ssum • nee • dah*
work at home	재택 근무합니다 *jeh • tehk kkun • moo • hahm • nee • dah*

Who do you work for?	어디에서 근무하십니까? *uh • dee • eh • suh gun • moo • hah • sim • nee • kka*
I work for...	...에서 근무합니다. *...eh • suh gun • moo • hahm • nee • dah*
Here's my business card.	제 명함입니다. *jeh myung • hahm • eem • nee • dah*

For Language Difficulties, see page 37.

WEATHER

What's the forecast?	일기 예보 들었어요? *eel • gee yeh • boh du • luht • ssuh • yo*
What beautiful/ terrible weather!	날씨가 참 좋군요/안 좋군요! *nahl • ssee • gah chahm joh • koon • nyo/ ahn joh • koon • nyo*
Will it be... tomorrow?	내일 날씨…까요? *neh • eel nahl • ssee... kkah • yo*
It's...	…날씨예요. *...nahl • ssee • yeh • yo*
cool/warm	시원한/따뜻한 *see • wuhn • hahn/ttah • ttu • tahn*
cold/hot	추운/더운 *choo • oon/duh • oon*
rainy/sunny	비 오는/화창한 *bee oh • nun/hwah • chahng • hahn*
snowy/icy	눈 내리는/아주 추운 *noon neh • lee • nun/ah • joo choo • oon*
Do I need a jacket/ an umbrella?	잠바가/우산이 필요할까요? *jahm • bah • gah/oo • sah • nee pee • lyo • hahl • kkah • yo*

For Seasons, see page 27.

EXPLORING

GETTING AROUND

NEED TO KNOW

How do I get to town?	시내로 어떻게 갑니까? *see • neh • loh uh • ttuh • keh gahm • nee • kkah*
Where's...?	…어디 있습니까? *...uh • dee eet • ssum • nee • kkah*
the airport	공항 *gohng • hahng*
Where's...?	…어디 있습니까? *...uh • dee eet • ssum • nee • kkah*
the train [railway] station	기차역 *gee • chah • yuhk*
the bus station	버스 정류장 *buh • su juhng • nyoo • jahng*
the subway [underground] station	지하철 역 *jee • hah • chuhl lyuhk*
How far is it?	얼마나 멉니까? *uhl • mah • nah muhm • nee • kkah*

Where do I buy a ticket?	표 어디서 삽니까? *pyo uh • dee • suh sahm • nee • kkah*
A one-way/ round-trip [return] ticket to…	…로 가는 편도표/왕복표. *…loh gah • nun pyuhn • doh • pyo/ wahng • bohk • pyo*
How much?	얼마입니까? *uhl • mah • eem • nee • kkah*
Is there a discount?	할인됩니까? *hah • leen • dwehm • nee • kkah*
Which…?	어떤…? *uh • ttuhn…*
gate	탑승구 *tahp • ssung • goo*
line	노선 *noh • suhn*
platform	승강장 *sung • gahng • jahng*
Where can I get a taxi?	택시 어디서 잡습니까? *tehk • ssee uh • dee • suh jahp • ssum • nee • kkah*
Take me to this address.	이 주소로 가 주십시오. *ee joo • soh • loh gah joo • seep • ssee • oh*
Where's the car hire?	렌터카 어디 있습니까? *len • tuh • kah uh • dee eet • ssum • nee • kkah*
Can I have a map?	지도 하나 주시겠습니까? *jee • doh hah • nah joo • see • geht • ssum • nee • kkah*

TICKETS

When's...to Seoul?	서울로 가는…언제 있습니까? *suh • ool • loh gah • nun...uhn • jeh eet • ssum • nee • kkah*
the (first) bus	(첫) 차 *(chuht) chah*
the (next) flight	(다음) 비행기 *(dah • um) bee • hehng • gee*
the (last) train	(마지막) 기차 *(mah • jee • mahk) gee • chah*
Is there...trip?	…가는 교통편이 있습니까? *...gah • nun gyo • tohng • pyuh • nee eet • ssum • nee • kkah*
an earlier	더 일찍 *duh eel • tzeek*
a later	더 늦게 *duh nut • kkeh*
an overnight	밤새 *bahm • seh*
a cheaper	더 싸게 *duh ssah • geh*
Where do I buy a ticket?	표 어디서 삽니까? *pyo uh • dee • suh sahm • nee • kkah*
One ticket/two tickets, please.	표 한장/두장 주세요. *pyo hahn • jahng/ doo • jahng joo • seh • yo*
For today/tomorrow.	오늘/내일 거요. *oh • nul/neh • eel kkuh • yo*
...ticket.	…표. *...pyo*
A one-way	편도 *pyuhn • doh*

A round-trip [return]	왕복 *wahng • bohk*
A first class	일등석 *eel • ttung • suhk*
A business class	비지니스석 *bee • jee • nee • su • suhk*
An economy class	이코노미석 *ee • koh • noh • mee • suhk*
How much?	얼마입니까? *uhl • mah • eem • nee • kkah*
Is there...discount?	…할인 됩니까? *...hah • leen dwehm • nee • kkah*
a child	어린이 *uh • lee • nee*
a senior citizen	노인 *noh • een*
a student	학생 *hahk • ssehng*
a tourist	관광객 *gwahn • gwahng • gehk*
The express bus/ express train, please.	고속 버스/고속 열차로 부탁합니다. *goh • sohk bus/goh • sohk yeohl • chah • roh boo • tah • kahm • nee • dah*
The local bus/train please.	시내 버스/전철로 부탁합니다. *sih • ne bus/jeon • chul • roh boo • tah • kahm • nee • dah*
I have an e-ticket.	전자티켓이 있습니다. *juhn • jah • tee • keh • see eet • ssum • nee • dah*
Can I buy a ticket on the bus/train?	버스/기차 안에서표 살 수 있습니까? *buh • su/gee • chah ah • neh • suh pyo sahl ssoo eet • ssum • nee • kkah*

Do I have to stamp the ticket before boarding?	승차 전에 티켓 확인이 필요합니까? *seung • chah jeoh • ne ticket hwah • gin • ee pil • yo • hahm • nee • kkah*
How long is this ticket valid?	이 티켓은 언제까지 유효합니까? *ee ticket • eun uhn • jeh • kka • jee yoo • hyo • hahm • nee • kkah*
Can I return on the same ticket?	같은 티켓을 가지고 돌아올 수 있습니까? *gah • tteun ticket • eul gah • jee • goh dohl • ah • oul soo eet • ssum • nee • kkah*
I'd like to…my reservation.	예약을…싶습니다. *yeh • yah • gul… seep • ssum • nee • dah*
cancel	취소하고 *chwih • soh • hah • goh*
change	변경하고 *byuhn • gyuhng • hah • goh*
confirm	확인하고 *hwah • geen • hah • goh*

For Days, see page 25.

AIRPORT TRANSFER

How much is a taxi to the airport?	공항으로 가는 택시 얼마입니까? *gogng • hagng • u • loh gah • nun tehk • ssee uhl • mah • eem • nee • kkah*
To…Airport, please.	…공항으로 가 주십시오. *…gohng • hahng • u • loh gah joo • seep • ssee • oh*
My airline is…	제 항공사는… *jeh hahng • gohng • sah • nun…*
My flight leaves at…	제 비행기는…에 출발합니다. *je bee • hehng • gee • nun…eh chool • bahl • hahm • nee • dah*

I'm in a rush.	급합니다. *gu • pahm • nee • dah*
Can you take an alternate route?	다른 길로 갈 수 있습니까? *dah • lun geel • loh gahl ssoo eet • ssum • nee • kkah*
Can you drive faster/ slower?	더 빨리/천천히 가 주시겠습니까? *duh ppahl • lee/chuhn • chuh • nee gah joo • see • geht • ssum • nee • kkah*

For Time, see page 24.

YOU MAY HEAR...

어느 항공사로 가십니까? *uh • nu hahng • gohng • sah • loh gah • seem • nee • kkah*	What airline are you flying?
국내선입니까, 국제선입니까? *goong • neh • suh • neem • nee • kkah gook • tzeh • suh • neem • nee • kkah*	Domestic or international?
어느 터미널입니까? *uh • nu tuh • mee • nuh • leem • nee • kkah*	What terminal?

CHECKING IN

Where's check-in?	어디서 탑승 수속 합니까? *uh • dee • suh tahp • ssung soo • sohk hahm • nee • kkah*
My name is...	제 이름은…입니다. *jeh ee • lu • mun...eem • nee • dah*
I'm going to...	…갑니다. *...gahm • nee • dah*
I have...	…있습니다. *...eet • ssum • nee • dah*

one suitcase	가방 하나 *gah • bahng hah • nah*
two suitcases	가방 두 개 *gah • bahng doo geh*
one piece of hand luggage	휴대 수하물 하나 *hyoo • deh soo • hah • mool hah • nah*
How much luggage is allowed?	짐은 얼마나 허용됩니까? *jee • mun uhl • mah • nah huh • yong dwehm • nee • kkah*
Is that pounds or kilos?	단위가 파운드입니까 아니면 킬로그램입니까? *dahn • wee • gah pound • eem • nee • kkah ah • nee • myun kilogram • eem • nee • kkah*
Which terminal/ gate?	어느 터미널입니까/탑승구입니까? *uh • nu tuh • mee • nuh • leem • nee • kkah/ tahp • ssung • goo • eem • nee • kkah*
I'd like a window/ an aisle seat.	창문쪽/통로쪽 좌석으로 주십시오. *chahng • moon • tzohk/tohng • noh • tzohk jwah • suh • gu • loh joo • seep • ssee • oh*
When do we leave/ arrive?	우리 언제 출발합니까/도착합니까? *oo • lee uhn • jeh chool • bahl • hahm • nee • kkah/ doh • chah • kahm • nee • kkah*
Is the flight delayed?	비행기가 연착됐습니까? *bee • hehng • gee • gah yuhn • chahk • dweht • ssum • nee • kkah*
How late?	얼마나 늦습니까? *uhl • mah • nah nut • ssum • nee • kkah*

For Numbers, see page 20.

YOU MAY SEE...

도착 *doh • chahk*	arrivals
출발 *chool • bahl*	departures
수하물 찾는 곳 *soo • hah • mool chahn • nun goht*	baggage claim
검색대 *guhm • sehk • tteh*	security
국내선 항공 *goong • neh • suhn hahng • gohng*	domestic flights
국제선 항공 *gook • tzeh • suhn hahng • gohng*	international flights
탑승 수속대 *tahp • ssung soo • sohk • tteh*	check-in
전자티켓 체크인 *juhn • jah • tee • keht cheh • ku • een*	e-ticket check-in
출발 탑승구 *chool • bahl tahp • ssung • goo gates*	departure

YOU MAY HEAR...

다음! *dah • um*	Next!
여권을/비행기표를 보여 주십시오. *yuh • kkwuh • nul/ bee • hehng • gee • pyo • lul boh • yuh joo • seep • ssee • oh*	Your passport/ ticket, please.
부치실 짐이 있습니까? *boo • chee • seel jee • mee eet • ssum • nee • kkah*	Are you checking any luggage?

YOU MAY HEAR...

짐이 너무 많습니다. *jee • mee nuh • moo mahn • ssum • nee • dah*	You have excess luggage.
기내에 휴대하기에는 너무 큽니다. *gee • neh • eh hyoo • deh • hah • gee • eh • nun nuh • moo kum • nee • dah*	That's too large for a carry-on [to carry on board].
이 짐들 직접 싸셨습니까? *ee jeem • dul jeek • tzuhp ssah • syuht • ssum • nee • kkah*	Did you pack these bags yourself?
누군가 물건을 맡긴 적이 있습니까? *noo • goon • gah mool • guh • nul maht • kkeen juh • gee eet • ssum • nee • kkah*	Did anyone give you anything to carry?
신발을 벗어 주십시오. *seen • bah • lul buh • suh joo • seep • ssee • yo*	Take off your shoes.
…탑승해 주십시오. *...tahp • ssung • heh joo • seep • ssee • oh*	Now boarding...

LUGGAGE

Where is/are...?	…어디 있습니까? *...uh • dee eet • ssum • nee • kkah*
the luggage trolleys	카트 *kah • tu*
the luggage lockers	짐 보관함 *jeem boh • gwahn • hahm*
the baggage claim	수하물 찾는 곳 *soo • hah • mool chahn • nun goht*

My luggage has been lost/stolen.	제 짐을 분실했습니다/도난 당했습니다. *jeh jee • mul boon • seel • heht • ssum • nee • dah/ doh • nahn dahng • heht • ssum • nee • dah*
My suitcase is damaged.	제 가방이 손상되었습니다. *jeh gah • bahng • ee sohn • sahng dweh • uht • ssum • nee • dah*

FINDING YOUR WAY

Where is/are...?	…어디 있습니까? *...uh • dee eet • ssum • nee • kkah*
the currency exchange	환전소 *hwahn • juhn • soh*
the car hire	렌터카 *lehn • tuh • kah*
the exit	출구 *chool • goo*
the phones	전화 *juhn • hwah*
the taxis	택시 *tehk • ssee*
Is there...into town?	시내로 가는… 있습니까? *see • neh • loh gah • nun... eet • ssum • nee • kkah*
a bus	버스 *buh • su*
a train	기차 *gee • chah*
a subway [underground]	지하철 *jee • hah • chuhl*

For Asking Directions, see page 68.

TRAIN

Where's the train station?	기차역이 어디 있습니까? *gee • chah • yuh • gee uh • dee eet • ssum • nee • kkah*
How far is it?	얼마나 멉니까? *uhl • mah • nah muhm • nee • kkah*
Where is/are...?	…어디 있습니까? *...uh • dee eet • ssum • nee • kkah*
the ticket office	매표소 *meh • pyo • soh*
the information desk	안내 *ahn • neh*
the luggage lockers	짐 보관함 *jeem boh • gwahn • hahm*
the platforms	승강장 *sung • gahng • jahng*
Can I have a schedule [timetable]?	시간표 하나 주시겠습니까? *see • gahn • pyo hah • nah joo • see • geht • ssum • nee • kkah*
How long is the trip?	얼마나 걸립니까? *uhl • mah • nah guhl • leem • nee • kkah*
Is it a direct train?	직행 기차입니까? *jee • kehng gee • chah • eem • nee • kkah*
Do I have to change trains?	기차를 갈아타야 합니까? *gee • chah • lul gah • lah • tah • yah hahm • nee • kkah*
Is the train on time?	기차가 제시간에 도착합니까? *gee • chah • gah jeh • see • gah • neh doh • chah • kahm • nee • kkah*

For Tickets, see page 48.

YOU MAY SEE...

플랫폼 *pool • leh • pom*	platforms
안내 *ahn • neh*	information
예약 *yeh • yahk*	reservations
대기실 *deh • gi • sil*	waiting room
도착 *doh • chahk*	arrivals
출발 *chool • bahl*	departures

YOU MAY HEAR...

어디 가십니까? *uh • dee gah • seem • nee • kkah*	Where to?
표 몇장요? *pyo myuht • tzahng • yo*	How many tickets?

DEPARTURES

Which track [platform] to...?	어느 승강장이…(으)로 갑니까?* *uh • nu sung • gahng • jahng • ee...(u •) loh gahm • nee • kkah*
Is this the track [platform]/train to...?	여기가…(으)로 가는승강장입니까/기차입니까? *yuh • gee • gah...(u •)loh gah • nun sung • gahng • jahng • eem • nee • kkah/ gee • chah • eem • nee • kkah*
Where is track... [platform] to...?	…(으)로 가는 승강장 어디 있습니까? *(u •)loh gah • nun sung • gahng • jahng uh • dee eet • ssum • nee • kkah*

Where do I change for...?
…가려면 어디서 갈아탑니까?
...gah • lyuh • myuhn uh • dee • suh gah • lah • tahm • nee • kkah

* note above that when the word ends in a consonant, use 으로 *u • loh*; when the word ends in a vowel, use 로 *loh*.

ON BOARD

Can I sit here/ open the window?
여기 앉아도/창문 열어도 됩니까?
yuh • gee ahn • jah • doh/chahng • moon yuh • luh • doh dwehm • nee • kkah

That's my seat.
거기 제 자리입니다.
guh • gee jeh jah • lee • eem • nee • dah

Here's my reservation.
제 예약표 여기 있습니다.
jeh yeh • yahk • pyo yuh • gee eet • ssum • nee • dah

The reliable South Korean train network covers all major cities. Most of the signs, especially at larger stations, are displayed in Korean and English; you may also find ticket windows for foreigners here. The Korean National Tourism Organization, travel agencies and hotel staff will be able to provide information about train reservations and times. Schedules, fares, route maps and additional details can be found in Korean and English on the Korail website (www.korail.com).

YOU MAY HEAR...

탑승해 주세요! *tahp • ssung • heh joo • seh • yo*	All aboard!
표 보여 주세요. *pyo boh • yuh joo • seh • yo*	Tickets, please.
…에서 갈아 타야 합니다. *...eh • suh gah • lah • tah • yah hahm • nee • dah*	You have to change at...
다음 정거장은… *dah • um juhng • guh • jahng • un...*	Next stop is...

BUS

Where's the bus station?	버스 정류장 어디 있습니까? *buh • su juhng • nyoo • jahng uh • dee eet • ssum • nee • kkah*
How far is it?	얼마나 멉니까? *uhl • mah • nah muhm • nee • kkah*
How do I get to...?	…어떻게 갑니까? *...uh • ttuh • keh gahm • nee • kkah*
Is this the bus to...?	…(으)로 가는 버스입니까? *...(u •)loh gah • nun buh • su • eem • nee • kkah*
Can you tell me where to get off?	어디서 내리는지 말씀해 주시겠습니까? *uh • dee • suh neh • lee • nun • jee mahl • ssum • heh joo • see • geht • ssum • nee • kkah*
Do I have to change buses?	버스를 갈아타야 합니까? *buh • su • lul gah • lah • tah • yah hahm • nee • kkah*

How many stops to…?	…까지 몇 정거장입니까? *…kkah • jee myuht juhng • guh • jahng • eem • nee • kkah*
Stop here, please!	여기서 세워 주십시오! *yuh • gee • suh seh • wuh joo • seep • ssee • oh*

For Tickets, see page 48.

South Korea offers two types of bus service: inter-city express and local. Place the fare directly into the fare box next to the bus driver or purchase an electronic card, called T-money, in advance. These cards can be purchased at any convenience store or kiosk that displays the T-money logo. Bus fares are based on the total distance traveled. More information on express bus schedules and fares can be found at the Kobus website (www.kobus.co.kr).

YOU MAY SEE…

버스 정류장 *buh • su juhng • nyoo • jahng*	bus stop
정지 요청 *jeong • jee yo • chung*	request stop
입구/출구 *eep • kkoo/chool • goo*	enter/exit
티켓 확인 ticket *Ticket hwah • gin*	stamp your

SUBWAY

Where's the subway [underground] station?	지하철 역 어디 있습니까? *jee • hah • chuhl lyuhk uh • dee eet • ssum • nee • kkah*
A map, please.	노선도 하나 주세요. *noh • suhn • doh hah • nah joo • seh • yo*
Which line for...?	…은 몇 호선입니까? *...un myuht toh • suh • neem • nee • kkah*
Do I have to transfer [change]?	갈아타야 합니까? *gah • lah • tah • yah hahm • nee • kkah*
Is this the subway [train] to...?	…가는 지하철 맞습니까? *...gah • nun jee • hah • chuhl maht • ssum • nee • kkah*
How many stops to...?	…까지 몇 정거장입니까? *...kkah • jee myuht tzuhng • guh • jahng • eem • nee • kkah*
Where are we?	여기가 어디입니까? *yuh • gee • gah uh • dee • eem • nee • kkah*

For Numbers, see page 20.

> In South Korea, Seoul, Busan, Daegu, Daejeon and Incheon have efficient subways, but they can get very crowded at peak hours. Station signs and route maps—available at subway ticket booths—include English translations. Purchase an electronic card, which can also be used on buses, or buy single-use or multiple-use subway tickets from automatic ticket machines or at ticket booths. Fares vary based on the distance traveled. In North Korea, Pyongyang alone has a subway system.

BOAT & FERRY

When is the ferry to…?	…가는 배가 언제 있습니까? *…gah • nun beh • gah uhn • jeh • eet • ssum • nee • kkah*
Where are the life jackets?	구명 조끼 어디 있습니까? *goo • myuhng joh • kkee uh • dee eet • ssum • nee • kkah*
Can I take my car?	차를 가져갈 수 있습니까? *chah • reul gah • jeoh • gahl soo eet • ssum • nee • kkah*
What time is the next sailing?	다음 배편은 몇 시입니까? *dah • eum beh • pyuhn • eun myuht ssi eem • nee • kkah*
Can I book a seat/ cabin?	자리/선실을 예약할 수 있습니까? *jah • lee/seohn • si • leul yeh • yah • kahl soo eet • ssum • nee • kkah*
How long is the crossing?	횡단하는 데 시간이 얼마나 걸립니까? *hoeng • dahn • hah • nun deh sih • gahn • ee uhl • ma • na guhl • leem • nee • kah*

For Tickets, see page 48.

South Korea is a peninsula, and so there are numerous ferry and boat services allowing for domestic travel as well as travel between Korean harbors and China or Japan. The ferry ride to Jeju-do Island, a UNESCO World Natural Heritage site, promises beautiful ocean scenery and a glimpse of volcanic remains and lava tubes. Visit the Korean Tourism Organization (KTO) or the Visit Korea websites (www.kto.visitkorea.or.kr; www.visitkorea.or.kr).

YOU MAY SEE...

구명 보트 *goo • myuhng boh • tu*	life boat
구명 조끼 *goo • myuhng joh • kkee*	life jacket

TAXI

Where can I get a taxi?	택시 어디서 잡습니까? *tehk • ssee uh • dee • suh jahp • ssum • nee • kkah*
Can you send a taxi?	택시를 보내줄 수 있습니까? *taxi • reul bo • ne • jool soo eet • ssum • nee • kkah*
Do you have the number for a taxi/van taxi?	콜택시/콜밴 전화번호 있습니까? *kohl • tehk • ssee/kohl • behn juhn • hwah • buhn • hoh eet • ssum • nee • kkah*
I'd like a taxi now/in an hour/tomorrow.	지금/1시간 후에/내일 택시를 보내주세요. *jee • keum/Hahn • si • gahn hoo • e/ne • il taxi • reul bo • ne • joo • seh • yo*
Pick me up at...	…(으)로 데리러 와 주세요.* *...(u •)loh deh • lee • luh wah joo • seh • yo*
I'm going to...	…갑니다. *...gahm • nee • dah*
this address	이 주소로 *ee joo • soh • loh*
the airport	공항으로 *gohng • hahng • u • loh*
the train station	기차역으로 *gee • chah • yuh • gu • loh*
I'm late.	늦었습니다. *nu • juht • ssum • nee • dah*

Can you drive faster/ slower?	더 빨리/천천히 갈 수 있습니까? *duh ppahl • lee/chuhn • chuh • nee gahl ssoo eet • ssum • nee • kkah*
Stop/Wait here.	여기서 세워/기다려 주십시오. *yuh • gee • suh seh • wuh/gee • dah • lyuh joo • seep • ssee • oh*
How much?	얼마입니까? *uhl • mah • eem • nee • kkah*
You said it would cost…	…원이라고 하셨지 않습니까 *…wuh • nee • lah • goh hah • syuht • tzee ahn • ssum • nee • kkah*
Can I have a receipt?	영수증 주세요. *yuhng • soo • jung joo • seh • yo*
Keep the change.	거스름돈은 됐습니다. *guh • su • lum • ttoh • nun dweht • ssum • nee • dah*

* Note that when the word ends in a consonant, use 으로 *u • loh*; when the word ends in a vowel, use 로 *loh*.

YOU MAY HEAR…

어디 가십니까? *uh • dee gah • seem • nee • kkah*	Where to?
주소가 어떻게 되십니까? *joo • soh • gah uh • ttuh • keh dweh • seem • nee • kkah*	What's the address?
야간/공항 수수료가 있습니다. *yah • gahn/gohng • hahng soo • soo • lyo • gah eet • ssum • nee • dah*	There's a nighttime/ airport surcharge.

Hail a standard taxi at taxi stands, found in most busy city areas, or on the street. You may reserve a taxi in advance by phone, but the fee may be slightly higher. Nighttime surcharges of about 20% apply. Also available are deluxe taxis, which offer more room per passenger and a higher level of service; look for the black and yellow sign with the words 'Deluxe Taxi' on top of the taxi. For high-tech service, try brand taxis; these offer voice interpretation machines and wireless terminals. Finally, for groups of up to eight, van taxis are available.
In North Korea, taxis can be booked only from tourist hotels.

BICYCLE & MOTORBIKE

I'd like to hire...	…빌리고 싶습니다. *...beel • lee • goh seep • ssum • nee • dah*
a bicycle	자전거 *jah • juhn • guh*
a moped	소형 오토바이 *soh • hyuhng oh • toh • bah • ee*
a motorcycle	오토바이 *oh • toh • bah • ee*
How much per day/ week?	하루에/일주일에 얼마입니까? *hah • loo • eh/eel • tzoo • ee • leh uhl • mah • eem • nee • kkah*
Can I have a helmet/ lock?	헬멧/자물쇠 있습니까? *hehl • meht/jah • mool • ssweh eet • ssum • nee • kkah*

CAR HIRE

Where's the car hire?	렌터카 어디 있습니까? *lehn • tuh • kah uh • dee eet • ssum • nee • kkah*
I'd like…	…이(가) 필요합니다. *…ee(gah) pil • yo • hahm • ni • da*
a cheap/small car	값싼/소형 차 *gahb • ssahn/so • hyung chah*
an automatic	오토매틱 *oh • toh • meh • teek*
a manual	스틱 *su • teek*
air conditioning	에어컨 *eh • uh • keon*
a car seat	카시트 *kah • ssee • tu*
How much…?	…얼마입니까? *…uhl • mah • eem • nee • kkah*
per kilometer	킬로미터당 *kil • lo • mee • tuh • dahng*
per day/week	하루에/일주일에 *hah • loo • eh/eel • tzoo • ee • leh*
for unlimited mileage	무제한 마일리지 *moo • jeh • hahn mah • eel • lee • jee*
with insurance	보험 포함해서 *boh • huhm poh • hahm • heh • suh*
Are there any discounts?	할인됩니까? *hah • leen • dwehm • nee • kkah*

YOU MAY HEAR...

국제 운전 면허증이 있습니까? *gook • je oon • jeon myun • huh • ggeung • ee eet • ssum • nee • kkah*	Do you have an international driver's license?
여권 좀 보여주십시오. *yuh • kkwuhn johm boh • yuh • joo • seep • ssee • oh*	Your passport, please.
보험을 원하십니까? *boh • huh • mul wuhn • hah • seem • nee • kkah*	Do you want insurance?
보증금이 필요합니다. *boh • jung • gu • mee pee • lyo • hahm • nee • dah*	I'll need a deposit.
여기에 사인하십시오. *yuh • gee • eh ssah • een • hah • seep • ssee • yo*	Sign here.

FUEL STATION

Where's the fuel station?	주유소가 어디 있어요? *joo • yoo • soh • gah uh • dee eet • ssuh • yo*
Fill it up.	가득 채워 주세요. *gah • duk cheh • wuh joo • seh • yo*
...Won worth, please.	···원어치 주세요. *...wuh nuh • chee joo • seh • yo*
I'll pay in cash/ by credit card.	현금으로/신용카드로 낼게요. *hyuhn • gu • mu • loh/ see • nyong • kah • du • loh nehl • kkeh • yo*

For Numbers, see page 20.

YOU MAY SEE...

기름 *gee • lum*	gas [petrol]
무연 *moo • yuhn*	unleaded
보통 *boh • tohng*	regular
고급 *goh • gup*	super
디젤 *dee • jehl*	diesel

ASKING DIRECTIONS

Is this the way to...?	이게…(으)로 가는 길입니까?* *ee • geh...(u •)loh gah • nun gee • leem • nee • kkah*
How far is it to...?	…까지 얼마나 멉니까? *...kkah • jee uhl • mah • nah muhm • nee • kkah*
Where's...?	…이(가) 어디입니까? *...ee(gah) uh • dee • eem • nee • kkah*
...Street	…거리 *guh • ree*
this address	이 주소 *ee joo • soh*
the highway [motorway]?	고속도로 *goh • sohk • doh • roh*
Can you show me on the map?	지도에서 보여 주시겠습니까? *jee • doh • eh • suh boh • yuh joo • see • geht • ssum • nee • kkah*
I'm lost.	길을 잃었습니다. *gee • lul ee • luht • ssum • nee • dah*

* Note that when the word ends in a consonant, use 으로 *u • loh*; when the word ends in a vowel, use 로 *loh*.

YOU MAY HEAR...

직진해서 *jeek • tzeen • heh • suh*	straight ahead
왼쪽 *wehn • tzohk*	left
오른쪽 *oh • lun • tzohk*	right
코너에/코너를 돌아서 *koh • nuh • eh/ koh • nuh • lul doh • lah • suh*	on/around the corner
맞은편 *mah • jun • pyuhn*	opposite
뒤에 *dwih • eh*	behind
옆에 *yuh • peh*	next to
지나서 *jee • nah • suh*	after
북쪽/남쪽 *book • tzohk/nahm • tzohk*	north/south
동쪽서쪽 *dohng • tzohk/suh • tzohk*	east/west
신호등에서 *seen • hoh • dung • eh • suh*	at the traffic light
교차로에서 *gyo • chah • loh • eh • suh*	at the intersection

PARKING

Can I park here?	여기에 주차해도 됩니까? *yuh • gee • eh joo • chah • heh • doh dwehm • nee • kkah*

Where's...?	…이(가) 어디 있습니까? *...ee(gah) uh • dee eet • ssum • nee • kkah*
the parking garage	주차장 *joo • chah • jahng*
the parking lot [car park]	주차장 *joo • chah • jahng*
the parking meter	주차 요금 징수기 *joo • chah yo • geum jeeng • soo • gi*
the parking attendant	주차 요원 *joo • chah yoh • wuhn*
the parking meter	주차 미터기 *joo • chah mee • tuh • gee*
How much...?	…얼마입니까? *...uhl • mah • eem • nee • kkah*
per hour	한 시간에 *hahn see • gah • neh*
per day	하루에 *hah • loo • eh*
for overnight	야간에 *yah • gah • neh*

YOU MAY SEE...

정지 *juhng • jee*	stop
천천히 *chuhn • chuh • nee*	slow
양보 *yahng • boh*	yield
진입 금지 *jee • neep kkum • jee*	do not enter
일방통행 *eel • bahng • tohng • hehng*	one way
주정차 금지 *joo • juhng • chah gum • jee*	no parking
입구 *eep • kkoo*	entrance
출구 *chool • goo*	exit
추월 금지 *choo • wuhl gum • jee*	no passing

BREAKDOWN & REPAIR

My car broke down/ won't start.	제 차가 고장났습니다/시동이 안 걸립니다. *jeh chah • gah goh • jahng • naht • ssum • nee • dah/ see • dohng • ee ahn guhl • leem • nee • dah*
Can you fix it (today)?	(오늘) 고칠 수 있습니까? *(oh • nul) goh • cheel ssoo eet • ssum • nee • kkah*
When will it be ready?	언제 다 됩니까? *uhn • jeh dah dwehm • nee • kkah*
How much?	얼마입니까? *uhl • mah • eem • nee • kkah*
I have a puncture/ flat tyre (tire).	타이어에 펑크가 났습니다. *tah • ee • uh • eh puhng • kuh • kah nah • ssum • nee • dah*

ACCIDENTS

There was an accident.	사고가 났습니다. *sah • goh • gah naht • ssum • nee • dah*
Call an ambulance/ the police.	구급차/경찰 불러 주세요. *goo • gup • chah/gyuhng • chahl bool • luh joo • seh • yo*

PLACES TO STAY

NEED TO KNOW

Can you recommend a hotel?	호텔 하나 추천해 주시겠습니까? *hoh • tehl hah • nah choo • chuhn • heh joo • see • geht • ssum • nee • kkah*
I have a reservation.	예약했습니다. *yeh • yah • kheht • ssum • nee • dah*
My name is...	제 이름은…입니다. *jeh ee • lu • mun...eem • nee • dah*
Do you have a room...?	…방이 있습니까? ...bahng•ee *eet • ssum • nee • kkah*
for one/two	일인용/이인용 *ee • leen • nyong/ee • een • nyong*
with a bathroom	화장실 딸린 *hwah • jahng • seel ttahl • leen*
with air conditioning	냉방 되는 *nehng • bahng dweh • nun*
How much for...?	…에 얼마입니까? *...eh uhl • mah • eem • nee • kkah*

tonight	오늘밤 *oh • nul • ppahm*
two nights	이틀 *ee • tul*
one week	일주일 *eel • tzoo • eel*
Is there anything cheaper?	더 싼 방 있습니까? *duh ssan bahng eet • ssum • nee • kkah*
When's check-out?	언제 체크아웃합니까? *uhn • jeh cheh • ku • ah • oot • thahm • nee • kkah*
Can I leave this in the safe?	이걸 금고에 보관해 주시겠습니까? *ee • guhl gum • goh • eh boh • gwahn • heh joo • see • geht • ssum • nee • kkah*
Can I leave my bags?	짐을 맡겨도 됩니까? *jee • mul maht • kkyuh • doh dwehm • nee • kkah*
Can I have my bill/ a receipt?	계산서/영수증 주시겠습니까? *geh • sahn • suh/yuhng • soo • jung joo • see • geht • ssum • nee • kkah*
I'll pay in cash/by credit card.	현금으로/신용카드로 지불하겠습니다. *hyuhn • gu • mu • loh/ see • nyong • kah • du • loh jee • bool • hah • geht • ssum • nee • dah*

If you didn't reserve anywhere to stay before your trip, visit the local 관광 안내소 *gwahn • gwahng ahn • neh • soh* (tourist information office) for recommendations on places to stay.

호텔 *hoh • tehl* (hotels) in South Korea range from luxury to budget. The majority of hotels charge a 10 –15% service fee.

In addition to hotels, you will also find inexpensive 모텔 *moh • tehl* (motels) or 여관 *yuh • gwahn* (inns). Most feature rooms with heated floors and sleeping mats.

아파트 임대 *ah • pah • tu eem • deh* (apartment rentals) are available mainly during off-peak travel times; these usually offer kitchen facilities, pools, exercise rooms and more. Prices vary by location and length of stay.

For travelers looking to stay somewhere cheaper, 게스트 하우스 *geh • su • tu hah • oo • su* (guest houses) and 호스텔 *hoh • su • tehl* (hostels) are popular options.

While in South Korea, you may wish to enjoy a unique cultural experience by reserving 템플 스테이 *tehm • pul su • teh • ee* (a temple stay). Partake in a Buddhist ceremonial service, Zen meditation, tea ceremony and more. For those who would like a glimpse of traditional Korean life, stay at 한옥 *hah • nohk* (a hanok) or 전통 가옥 *juhn • tohng gah • ohk* (traditional home). Here, you will find the surroundings arranged as in traditional times.

SOMEWHERE TO STAY

Can you recommend…?	…추천해 주시겠습니까? *…choo • chuhn • heh joo • see • geht • ssum • nee • kkah*
a hotel	호텔 *hoh • tehl*
a hostel	호스텔 *hoh • su • tehl*
a campsite	캠핑장 *kehm • peeng • jahng*
a bed and breakfast	숙소(B&B) *sook • soh(B&B)*
What is it near?	어디 근처입니까? *uh • dee gun • chuh • eem • nee • kkah*
How do I get there?	거기 어떻게 갑니까? *guh • gee uh • ttuh • keh gahm • nee • kkah*

AT THE HOTEL

I have a reservation.	예약했습니다. *yeh • yah • keht • ssum • nee • dah*
My name is…	제 이름은…입니다. *jeh ee • lu • mun…eem • nee • dah*
Do you have a room…?	…방 있습니까? *…bahng eet • ssum • nee • kkah*
for one/two	일인용/이인용 *ee • leen • nyong/ee • een • nyong*
with a bathroom [toilet]/shower	화장실/샤워 있는 *hwah • jahng • seel/syah • wuh een • nun*
with air conditioning	냉방 되는 *nehng • bahng dweh • nun*

with a single/ double bed	싱글/더블 침대 있는 *sseeng • gul/duh • bul cheem • deh een • nun*
that's smoking/ non-smoking	흡연/금연 *hu • byuhn/gu • myuhn*
How much for...?	…에 얼마입니까? *...eh uhl • mah • eem • nee • kkah*
tonight	오늘밤 *oh • nul • ppahm*
two nights	이틀 *ee • tul*
a week	일주일 *eel • tzoo • eel*
Where can I park?	어디에 주차합니까? *uh • dee • eh joo • chah • hahm • nee • kkah*
Do you have...?	…있습니까? *...eet • ssum • nee • kkah*
a computer	컴퓨터 *kuhm • pyoo • tuh*
an elevator [a lift]	엘리베이터 *ehl • lee • beh • ee • tuh*
(wireless) internet service	(무선) 인터넷 *(moo • suhn) een • tuh • neht*
room service	룸서비스 *loom • ssuh • bee • su*
a TV	텔레비전 *tehl • leh • bee • juhn*
a pool	수영장 *soo • yuhng • jahng*
a gym	헬스클럽 *hehl • ssu • kul • luhp*
I need...	…필요합니다. *...pee • lyo • hahm • nee • dah*

an extra bed	보조 침대 *boh • joh cheem • deh*
a cot	아기용 침대 *ah • gee • yong cheem • deh*
a crib	아기용 침대 *ah • gee • yong cheem • deh*

For Numbers, see page 20.

YOU MAY HEAR...

여권/신용카드 보여주십시오. *yuh • kkwuhn/see • nyong • kah • du boh • yuh • joo • seep • ssee • oh*	Your passport/ credit card, please.
이 용지를 작성해 주십시오. *ee yong • jee • lul jahk • ssuhng • heh joo • seep • ssee • oh*	Fill out this form.
여기 서명해 주십시오. *yuh • gee suh • myuhng • heh joo • seep • ssee • oh*	Sign here.

PRICE

How much per night/ week?	하룻밤에/일주일에 얼마입니까? *hah • loot • ppah • meh/eel • tzoo • ee • leh uhl • mah • eem • nee • kkah*
Does that include breakfast/sales tax [VAT]?	아침식사/ 부가가치세 포함돼 있습니까? *ah • cheem • seek • ssah/boo • gah gah • chee • seh poh • hahm • dweh eet • ssum • nee • kkah*
Are there any discounts?	할인됩니까? *hah • leen • dwehm • nee • kkah*

PREFERENCES

Can I see the room?	방 볼 수 있습니까? *bahng • bohl ssoo eet • ssum • nee • kkah*
I'd like...room.	…방으로 주십시오. *...bahng • u • lo joo • seep • ssee • oh*
a better	더 좋은 *duh joh • un*
a bigger	더 큰 *duh kun*
a cheaper	더 싼 *duh ssahn*
a quieter	더 조용한 *duh joh • yong • hahn*
I'll take it.	이걸로 하겠습니다 *ee • guhl • loh* *hah • geht • ssum • nee • dah*
No, I won't take it.	아니요, 이건 안 하겠습니다. *ah • nee • yo ee • guhn ahn* *hah • geht • ssum • nee • dah*

QUESTIONS

Where's...?	…어디 있습니까? *...uh • dee eet • ssum • nee • kkah*
the bar	바 *bah*
the bathroom [toilet]	화장실 *hwah • jahng • seel*
the elevator [lift]	엘리베이터 *ehl • lee • beh • ee • tuh*
the pool	수영장 *soo • yuhng • jahng*

Can I have...?	…주시겠습니까? *...joo • see • geht • ssum • nee • kkah*
a blanket	담요 *dahm • nyo*
an iron	다리미 *dah • lee • mee*
Can I have...?	…주시겠습니까? *...joo • see • geht • ssum • nee • kkah*
the room key/ key card	방 열쇠/키카드 *bahng yuhl • ssweh/kee • kah • du*
a pillow	베개 *beh • geh*
soap	비누 *bee • noo*
toilet paper	화장실 휴지 *hwah • jahng • seel hyoo • jee*
a towel	수건 *soo • guhn*
Do you have an adapter for this?	이것에 쓸 어댑터가 있습니까? *ee • guh • seh ssul uh • dehp • tuh • gah eet • ssum • nee • kkah*
How do I turn on the lights?	불을 어떻게 켭니까? *boo • lul uh • ttuh • keh kyuhm • nee • kkah*
When does breakfast start/end?	아침 식사 언제 시작합니까/끝납니까? *ah • cheem seek • ssah uhn • jeh see • ja • kahm • nee • kkah/ kkun • nahm • nee • kkah*
Can you wake me at...?	…시에 깨워주시겠습니까? *...see • eh kkeh • wuh joo • see • geht • ssum • nee • kkah*
Can I leave this in the safe?	이걸 금고에 보관해 주시겠습니까? *ee • guhl gum • goh • eh boh • gwahn • heh joo • see • geht • ssum • nee • kkah*

YOU MAY SEE...

미세요/당기세요 *mee • seh • yo/ dahng • gee • seh • yo*	push/pull
화장실 *hwah • jahng • seel*	bathroom [toilet]
샤워실 *syah • wuh • seel*	shower
엘리베이터 *ehl • lee • beh • ee • tuh*	elevator [lift]
계단 *geh • dahn*	stairs
세탁실 *seh • tahk • sseel*	laundry
방해하지 마시오 *bahng • heh • hah • jee mah • see • oh*	do not disturb
방화문 *bahng • hwah • moon*	fire door
(비상) 출구 *(bee • sahng) chool • goo*	(emergency) exit
모닝콜 *moh • neeng • kohl*	wake-up call

Can I have my things from the safe? 금고에서 물건을 찾을 수 있겠습니까? *gum • goh • eh • suh mool • guh • nul chah • jul ssoo eet • kkeh • ssum • nee • kkah*

Is there mail/ a message for me? 저한테 온 우편물이/메시지가 있습니까? *juh • hahn • teh ohn oo • pyuhn • moo • lee/ meh • ssee • jee • gah eet • ssum • nee • kkah*

PROBLEMS

There's a problem. 문제가 있습니다. *moon • jeh • gah eet • ssum • nee • dah*

I lost my key/ key card. 열쇠를/키카드를 잃어 버렸습니다. *yuhl • ssweh • lul/kee • kah • du • lul ee • luh buh • lyuht • ssum • nee • dah*

I'm locked out of the room.	방에서 열쇠를 안 가지고 나왔습니다. *bahng • eh • suh yuhl • ssweh • lul ahn gah • jee • goh nah • waht • ssum • nee • dah*
There's no hot water.	온수가 안 나옵니다. *ohn • soo • gah ahn nah • ohm • nee • dah*
There's no toilet paper.	화장지가 없습니다. *hwah • jahng • jee • gah uhp • ssum • nee • dah*
The room is dirty.	방이 더럽습니다. *bahng • ee duh • luhp • ssum • nee • dah*
There are bugs in the room.	방에 벌레가 있습니다. *bahng • eh buhl • leh • gah eet • ssum • nee • dah*
…doesn't work.	…고장났습니다. *…goh • jahng • naht • ssum • nee • dah*
Can you fix…?	…고쳐 주시겠습니까? *…goh • chyuh joo • see • geht • ssum • nee • kkah*
the air conditioning	에어컨 *eh • uh • kuhn*
the fan	선풍기 *suhn • poong • gee*
the heat [heating]	난방 *nahn • bahng*
the light	전등 *juhn • dung*
the TV	텔레비전 *tehl • leh • bee • juhn*
the toilet	화장실 *hwah • jahng • seel*
I'd like another room.	다른 방으로 바꿔 주십시오. *dah • lun bahng • u • loh bah • kkwuh joo • seep • ssee • oh*

CHECKING OUT

When's check-out?	언제 체크 아웃합니까? *uhn • jeh cheh • ku* *ah • oot • thahm • nee • kkah*
Can I leave my bags here until...?	…까지 여기에 짐을 맡겨도 되겠습니까? *...kkah • jee yuh • gee • eh* *jee • mul maht • kkyuh • doh* *dweh • geht • ssum • nee • kkah*
Can I have an itemized bill/ a receipt?	명세서/영수증 주시겠습니까? *myuhng • seh • suh/yuhng • soo • jung* *joo • see • geht • ssum • nee • kkah*
I think there's a mistake.	착오가 있는 것 같습니다. *chah • goh • gah een • nun guht* *gaht • ssum • nee • dah*
I'll pay in cash/by credit card.	현금으로/신용카드로 지불하겠습니다. *hyuhn • gu • mu • loh/* *see • nyong • kah • du • loh* *jee • bool • hah • geht • ssum • nee • dah*

Tipping is not traditionally done in Korea, but feel free to do so if you've received extraordinary service. In most tourist and luxury hotels, a service charge is added to your bill. Furthermore, in some high-end restaurants and bars, a service charge may be included in your bill.

RENTING

I reserved an apartment/a room.	아파트를/방을 예약했습니다. *ah • pah • tu • lul/bahng • ul* *yeh • yah • keht • ssum • nee • dah*

My name is...	제 이름은…입니다. *jeh ee • lu • mun...eem • nee • dah*
Can I have the key/ key card?	열쇠/키카드 주시겠습니까? *yuhl • ssweh/kee • kah • du joo • see • geht • ssum • nee • kkah*
Are there...?	…있습니까? *...eet • ssum • nee • kkah*
dishes	접시 *juhp • ssee*
pillows	베개 *beh • geh*
sheets	시트 *see • tu*
towels	수건 *soo • guhn*
utensils	식기 *seek • kkee*
When do I put out the bins/recycling?	쓰레기는/재활용은 언제 내놓습니까? *ssu • leh • gee • nun/ jeh • hwah • lyong • un uhn • jeh neh • noht • ssum • nee • kkah*
...is broken.	…고장났습니다. *...goh • jahng • naht • ssum • nee • dah*
How does...work?	…어떻게 씁니까? *...uh • ttuh • keh ssum • nee • kkah*
the air conditioner	에어컨 *eh • uh • kuhn*
the dishwasher	식기 세척기 *seek • kkee seh • chuhk • kkee*
the freezer	냉동고 *nehng • dohng • goh*
the heater	히터 *hee • tuh*
the microwave	전자레인지 *juhn • jah • leh • een • jee*

the refrigerator	냉장고 *nehng • jahng • goh*
the stove	가스레인지 *kkah • su • leh • een • jee*
the washing machine	세탁기 *seh • tahk • kkee*

DOMESTIC ITEMS

I need...	…필요합니다. *...pee • lyo • hahm • nee • dah*
an adapter	어댑터 *uh • dehp • tuh*
aluminum foil	쿠킹 호일 *koo • keeng hoh • eel*
a bottle opener	병따개 *byuhng ttah • geh*
a broom	빗자루 *beet • tzah • loo*
a can opener	통조림 따개 *tohng • joh • leem ttah • geh*
cleaning supplies	세척용품 *seh • chuhng • nyong • poom*
a corkscrew	코르크 마개뽑이 *koh • lu • ku mah • geh • ppoh • bee*
detergent	세제 *seh • jeh*
dishwashing liquid	주방용 세제 *joo • bahng • yong seh • jeh*
bin bags	쓰레기 봉투 *ssu • leh • gee bohng • too*
a light bulb	전구 *juhn • goo*
matches	성냥 *suhng • nyahng*

a mop	대걸레 *deh • guhl • leh*
napkins	냅킨 *nehp • keen*
paper towels	종이 타월 *johng • ee tah • wuhl*
plastic wrap [cling film]	랩 *lehp*
a plunger	변기 뚫는 것 *byuhn • gee ttool • nun • guht*
scissors	가위 *gah • wee*
a vacuum cleaner	진공 청소기 *jeen • gohng chuhng • soh • gee*

For In the Kitchen, see page 188.

AT THE HOSTEL

Is there a bed available?	침대 있습니까? *cheem • deh eet • ssum • nee • kkah*
Can I have...?	…을(를) 주시겠습니까? *...eul(reul)* *joo • see • geht • ssum • nee • kkah*
a single/ double room	싱글/더블 룸 *single/double room*
a blanket	담요 *dahm • nyo*
a pillow	베개 *beh • geh*
sheets	시트 *see • tu*
a towel	수건 *soo • guhn*

Do you have lockers?	락커가 있습니까? *locker • gah eet • ssum • nee • kkah*
When do you lock up?	문 언제 닫습니까? *moon uhn • jeh daht • ssum • nee • kkah*
Do I need a membership card?	멤버십 카드가 필요합니까? *membership card • gah pihl • yo • hahm • nih • kkah*
Here's my International Student Card.	제 국제 학생증 여기 있습니다. *jeh gook • tzeh hahk • ssehng • tzung yuh • gee eet • ssum • nee • dah*

GOING CAMPING

Can I camp here?	여기서 캠핑해도 됩니까? *yuh • gee • suh kehm • peeng • heh • doh dwehm • nee • kkah*
Where's the campsite?	캠핑장 어디 있습니까? *kehm • peeng • jahng uh • dee eet • ssum • nee • kkah*
What is the charge per day/week?	하루에/일주일에 얼마입니까? *hah • loo • eh/eel • tzoo • ee • leh uhl • mah • eem • nee • kkah*
Are there...?	…이(가) 있습니까? *...ee(gah) eet • ssum • nee • kkah*
cooking facilities	주방 시설 *joo • bahng see • suhl*
electric outlets	전기 콘센트 *juhn • gee kohn • sehn • tu*
laundry facilities	세탁 시설 *seh • tahk sih • suhl*
showers	샤워실 *syah • wuh • seel*
tents for hire	텐트 대여 *tehn • tu deh • yuh*

Where can I empty the chemical toilet? 휴대 변기를 어디서 비울 수 있습니까? *hyoo • deh byuhn • gee • lul uh • dee • suh bee • ool ssoo eet • ssum • nee • kkah*

Cabins, cottages, camping grounds and mountain huts can be found at many of South Korea's national parks; these are popular with hikers and nature lovers, so over-crowding can be a concern during the summer and fall months. Facilities available may include kitchenettes, showers and restrooms.
For information and reservations, visit the Korean Tourism Organization (KTO) at www.visitkorea.or.kr. You can also visit the Korea National Park Service website at www.knps.or.kr.

YOU MAY SEE...

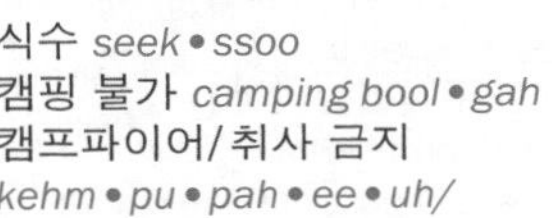

식수 *seek • ssoo* drinking water
캠핑 불가 *camping bool • gah* no camping
캠프파이어/취사 금지 *kehm • pu • pah • ee • uh/ chwih • sah gum • jee* no campfires/ barbecues

COMMUNICATIONS

NEED TO KNOW

Where's an internet cafe?	PC방 어디 있습니까? *pee • ssee • bahng uh • dee eet • ssum • nee • kkah*
Can I access the internet/check e-mail?	인터넷할/이메일 확인할 수 있습니까? *een • tuh • neht • tahl/ee • meh • eel hwah • geen • hahl ssoo eet • ssum • nee • kkah*
How much per hour/ half hour?	한 시간에/삼십 분에 얼마입니까? *hahn see • gah • neh/ sahm • seep ppoo • neh uhl • mah • eem • nee • kkah*
How do I connect / log on?	어떻게 접속/로그온 합니까? *uh • ttuh • keh juhp • ssohk/ loh • gu • ohn hahm • nee • kkah*
A phone card, please.	전화 카드 한 장 주십시오. *juhn • hwah kah • du hahn jahng joo • seep • ssee • oh*
Can I have your phone number?	전화 번호 주시겠습니까? *juhn • hwah buhn • hoh joo • see • geht • ssum • nee • kkah*
Here's my number/ e-mail.	여기 제 전화번호/이메일 주소 있습니다. *yuh • gee jeh juhn • hwah • buhn • hoh/ ee • meh • eel joo • soh eet • ssum • nee • dah*
Call/E-mail me.	전화/이메일 주십시오. *juhn • hwah/ee • meh • eel joo • seep • ssee • oh*

Hello. This is…	여보세요. 저는…입니다. *yuh • boh • seh • yo juh • nun… eem • nee • dah*
Can I speak to…?	…바꿔 주시겠습니까? *…bah • kkwuh joo • see • geht • ssum • nee • kkah*
Can you repeat that?	다시 말씀해 주시겠습니까? *dah • see mahl • ssum • heh joo • see • geht • ssum • nee • kkah*
I'll call back later.	다시 전화 드리겠습니다. *dah • see juhn • hwah du • lee • geht • ssum • nee • dah*
Bye.	안녕히 계세요. *ahn • nyuhng • hee geh • seh • yo*
Where's the post office?	우체국 어디 있습니까? *oo • cheh • gook uh • dee eet • ssum • nee • kkah*
I'd like to send this to…	이걸…(으)로 보내고 싶습니다.* *ee • guhl…(u) • loh boh • neh • goh seep • ssum • nee • dah*

* Note that when the word ends in a consonant, use 으로 *u • loh*; when the word ends in a vowel, use 로 *loh*.

ONLINE

Where's an internet cafe?	PC방 어디 있습니까? *pee • ssee • bahng uh • dee eet • ssum • nee • kkah*

Does it have wireless internet?	무선 인터넷 됩니까? *moo • suhn een • tuh • neht dwehm • nee • kkah*
What is the WiFi password?	WiFi 암호는 무엇입니까? *wifi ahm • hoh • neun mooh • uht • eem • nee • kah*
Is the WiFi free?	WiFi는 무료입니까? *wifi • neun moo • ryo • eem • nee • kah*
How do I turn the computer on/off?	컴퓨터를 어떻게 켭니까/끕니까? *kuhm • pyoo • tuh • lul uh • ttuh • keh kyuhm • nee • kkah/kkum • nee • kkah*
Do you have bluetooth?	블루투스가 됩니까? *bluetooth • gah deum • nee • kah*
Can I…?	…할 수 있습니까? *…hahl ssoo eet • ssum • nee • kkah*
access the internet	인터넷할 *een • tuh • neh • tahl*
burn CDs/DVDs	씨디/디브이디 구울 *ssee • dee/dee • bu • ee • dee goo • ool*
check e-mail	이메일 확인할 *ee • meh • eel hwah • geen • hahl*
print	프린트할 *pu • leen • tu • hahl*
plug in/charge my laptop/iPhone/ iPad/BlackBerry?	랩탑/iPhone/iPad/BlackBerry를 연결/충전할 수 있습니까? *laptop/iphone/ipad/blackberry • reul yeon • gyuhl/choong • jeon • hahl ssoo eet • ssum • nee • kkah*
access Skype?	Skype에 액세스 *skype • eh ehk • ssess*
How much per half hour/hour?	30분/1시간당 얼마입니까? *sahm • si • ppoon/Hahn • si • gahn • dahng uhl • mah • eem • nee • kkah*

use any computer	아무 컴퓨터나 쓸 *ah • moo kuhm • pyoo • tuh • nah ssul*
How do I...?	…어떻게 합니까? *...uh • ttuh • keh hahm • nee • kkah*
connect/ disconnect	접속/접속 끊기 *juhp • ssohk/juhp • ssohk kkun • kee*
log on/off	로그 온/오프 *loh • gu ohn/oh • pu*
type this symbol	이 기호 치는 것 *ee gee • hoh chee • nun guht*
What's your e-mail?	이메일 주소가 어떻게 되십니까? *ee • meh • eel joo • soh • gah uh • ttuh • keh dweh • seem • nee • kkah*
My e-mail is...	제 이메일 주소는…입니다. *jeh ee • meh • eel joo • soh • nun... eem • nee • dah*
Do you have a scanner?	스캐너가 있습니까? *scanner • gah eet • ssum • nee • kkah*

South Korea is a technologically savvy country, and internet services abound. In addition to internet cafes, many public places, such as airports and train and bus stations, offer internet access. Most internet cafes, known as PC방 *pee • ssee • bahng* (PC bangs), are open 24 hours. The Korean National Tourism Organization (KNTO) provides a free PC bang at its location in Joong-gu, Seoul.

SOCIAL MEDIA

Are you on Facebook/Twitter?	Facebook/Twitter를 사용합니까? *facebook/twitter • ruel sah • yong • hahm • nee • kkah*
What's your user name?	이름이 어떻게 됩니까? *ee • ru • mee uh • dduh • keh deum • nee • kah*
I'll add you as a friend.	당신을 친구로 추가하겠습니다. *dahng • si • nul chin • goo • roh choo • gah • hah • geht • ssum • nee • dah*
I'll follow you on Twitter.	Twitter에서 당신을 팔로우하겠습니다. *twitter • eh • suh dang • si • nul pal • lo • woo • hah • geht • ssum • nee • dah*
Are you following...?	…을(를) 팔로잉합니까? *… eul(reul) pal • lo • ing • hahm • nee • kah*
I'll put the pictures on Facebook/Twitter.	Facebook/Twitter에 사진을 올리겠습니다. *facebook/twitter • eh sah • ji • nul ohl • lee • geht • ssum • nee • dah*
I'll tag you in the pictures.	사진에 당신을태깅하겠습니다. *sah • ji • neh dang • si • nul teh • ging • hah • geht • ssum • nee • dah*

PHONE

A phone card/ prepaid phone, please.	전화 카드/선불 휴대폰 주십시오. *juhn • hwah kah • du/suhn • bool hyoo • deh • pohn joo • seep • ssee • oh*
How much?	얼마입니까? *uhl • mah • eem • nee • kkah*
Where's the pay phone?	공중전화 어디 있습니까? *gohng • joong • juhn • hwah uh • dee eet • ssum • nee • kkah*

YOU MAY SEE...

삭제 *sahk • tzeh*	delete
이메일 *ee • meh • eel*	e-mail
종료 *johng • nyo*	exit
도움말 *doh • oom • mahl*	help
메신저 *meh • sseen • juh*	instant messenger
인터넷 *een • tuh • neht*	internet
로그인 *loh • gu • een*	login
새 (메시지) *seh (meh • ssee • jee)*	new (message)
열기 *yuhl • gee*	open
프린트 *pu • leen • tu*	print
저장 *juh • jahng*	save
사용자명/비밀번호 *sah • yong • jah • myuhng/ bee • meel • buhn • hoh*	username/ password
무선 인터넷 *moo • suhn een • tuh • neht*	wireless internet

What's the area/ country code for...? …지역/국가 번호가 무엇입니까? *...jee • yuhk/gook • kkah buhn • hoh • gah moo • uh • seem • nee • kkah*

What's the number for Information?	전화 번호 안내가 몇 번입니까? *juhn • hwah • buhn • hoh ahn • neh • gah myuht ppuh • neem • nee • kkah*
I'd like the number for…	…전화 번호 부탁합니다. *…juhn • hwah • buhn • hoh boo • tah • kahm • nee • dah*
I'd like to call collect [reverse the charges].	수신자 부담으로 걸겠습니다. *soo • seen • jah boo • dah • mu • loh guhl • geht • ssum • nee • dah*
My phone doesn't work here.	여기서는 제 전화가 되지 않습니다. *yuh • gee • suh • nun jeh juhn • hwah • gah dweh • jee ahn • ssum • nee • dah*
What network are you on?	어떤 네트워크를 사용 중입니까? *uh • ddeun network • reul sah • yong joong • eem • nee • kkah*
Is it 3G?	3G입니까? *three • gee • eem • nee • kkah*
I have run out of credit/minutes.	크레딧/사용 시간을 모두 사용했습니다. *credit/sah • yong si • gahn • eul moh • doo sah • yong • heht • ssum • nee • dah*
Can I buy some credit?	크레딧을 구매할 수 있습니까? *credit • eul gooh • meh • hahl soo eet • ssum • nee • kkah*
Do you have a phone charger?	휴대폰 충전기가 있습니까? *hyooh • deh • pohn choong • jeon • gih • gah eet • ssum • nee • kkah*
Can I recharge this phone?	이 전화 요금 충전할 수 있습니까? *ee juhn • hwah yo • gum choong • juhn • hahl ssoo eet • ssum • nee • kkah*
Can I have your number?	전화번호 주시겠습니까? *juhn • hwah • buhn • hoh joo • see • geht • ssum • nee • kkah*

Here's my number.	여기 제 전화번호있습니다. *yuh • gee jeh juhn • hwah • buhn • hoh eet • ssum • nee • dah*
Please call/text me.	전화/문자 주십시오. *juhn • hwah/moon • tzah joo • seep • ssee • oh*
I'll call/text you.	전화/문자 드리겠습니다. *juhn • hwah/moon • tzah du • lee • geht • ssum • nee • dah*

TELEPHONE ETIQUETTE

Hello. This is…	여보세요. 저는…입니다. *yuh • boh • seh • yo juh • nun… eem • nee • dah*
Can I speak to…?	…바꿔 주시겠습니까? *…bah • kkwuh joo • see • geht • ssum • nee • kkah*
Extension…	내선 번호… *neh • suhn buhn • hoh…*
Speak louder/more slowly, please.	더 크게/천천히 말씀해 주십시오. *duh ku • geh/chuhn • chuh • nee mahl • ssum • heh joo • seep • ssee • oh*
Can you repeat that?	다시 말씀해 주시겠습니까? *dah • see mahl • ssum • heh joo • see • geht • ssum • nee • kkah*
I'll call back later.	나중에 다시 전화 드리겠습니다. *nah • joong • eh dah • see juhn • hwah du • lee • geht • ssum • nee • dah*
Bye.	안녕히 계세요. *ahn • nyuhng • hee geh • seh • yo*

YOU MAY HEAR...

누구세요? *noo • goo • seh • yo*	Who's calling?
잠시만요. *jahm • see • mahn • nyo*	Hold on.
그/그녀를 바꿔드리겠습니다. *gu/gu • nyuh • reul bah • kkwuh • du • ree • geht • ssum • nee • dah*	I'll put you through to him/her.
지금 자리에 없습니다. *jee • gum jah • lee • eh uhp • ssum • nee • dah*	He/She is not here.
메시지를 남기시겠습니까? *message • reul nahm • gi • si • geht • ssum • nee • kkah*	Would you like to leave a message?
나중에/10분 후에 다시 전화해 주십시오. *nah • joong • eh/ si • ppoon hoo • eh dah • si jeon • hwah • heh joo • sip • see • oh*	Call back later/ in ten minutes.
다시 전화 드리라고 해도 될까요? *dah • see juhn • hwah du • lee • lah • goh heh • doh dwehl • kkah • yo*	Can he/she call you back?
전화번호가 어떻게 되십니까? *juhn • hwah • buhn • hoh • gah uh • ttuh • keh dweh • seem • nee • kkah*	What's your number?

* Note that when the word ends in a consonant, use 으로 *u • loh*; when the word ends in a vowel, use 로 *loh*.

FAX

Can I send/receive a fax here?	여기서 팩스 보낼/받을 수 있습니까? *yuh • gee • suh pehk • ssu boh • nehl/ bah • dul ssoo eet • ssum • nee • kkah*
What's the fax number?	팩스 번호가 몇 번입니까? *pek • su buhn • hoh • gah myuht ppuh • neem • nee • kkah*
Please fax this to…	이거…(으)로 팩스 보내 주십시오.* *ee • guh…(u •)loh pehk • ssu boh • neh joo • seep • ssee • oh*

POST

Where's the post office/mailbox?	우체국/우체통 어디 있습니까? *oo • cheh • gook/oo • cheh • tohng uh • dee eet • ssum • nee • kkah*
A stamp for this postcard/letter to…	이 엽서를/편지를…(으)로 보낼 우표 주세요. *ee yuhp • ssuh • lul/pyuhn • jee • lul…(u •) loh boh • nehl oo • pyo joo • seh • yo*
How much?	얼마입니까? *uhl • mah • eem • nee • kkah*
Send this package by airmail/express.	이 소포를 항공 우편으로/특급 우편으로 보내주세요. *ee soh • poh • lul hahng • gohng oo • pyuh • nu • loh/ tuk • kkup oo • pyuh • nu • loh boh • neh • joo • seh • yo*
A receipt, please.	영수증 주세요. *yuhng • soo • jung joo • seh • yo*

There are domestic and international mailing services available at 우체국 *oo • cheh • gook* (post offices) throughout North and South Korea. Note that addresses in Korea are written in the reverse of the Western order. The address begins with the postal code, and is followed by country, city, 구 *goo* (urban district), 동 *dohng* (administrative district), street, street number; the name of the recipient is at the end. The post office will deliver your letter even if the address is written in English.
Korea Post has information on locations, hours, services, fees and more on its English-language website.

SIGHTSEEING

NEED TO KNOW

Where's the tourist information office?	관광 안내소가 어디 있습니까? *gwahn • gwahng ahn • neh • soh • gah uh • dee eet • ssum • nee • kkah*
What are the main attractions?	주요 볼 거리가 무엇입니까? *joo • yo bohl kkuh • lee • gah moo • uh • seem • nee • kkah*
Do you have tours in English?	영어 투어 있습니까? *yuhng • uh too • uh eet • ssum • nee • kkah*
Can I have a map/ guide?	지도/안내서 하나 주시겠습니까? *jee • doh/ahn • neh • suh hah • nah joo • see • geht • ssum • nee • kkah*

TOURIST INFORMATION

Do you have information on...?	…에 대한 안내 있습니까? *...eh deh • hahn ahn • neh eet • ssum • nee • kkah*
Can you recommend...?	…추천해 주시겠습니까? *...choo • chuhn • heh joo • see • geht • ssum • nee • kkah*
a boat trip	보트 관광 하나 *boh • tu gwahn • gwahng hah • nah*
an excursion to...	…로 유람 코스 하나 *...loh yoo • lahm koh • su hah • nah*
a sightseeing tour	관광 코스 하나 *gwahn • gwahng koh • su hah • nah*

ON TOUR

I'd like to go on the tour to...	…로 투어 가고 싶습니다. *...loh too • uh gah • goh seep • ssum • nee • dah*
When's the next tour?	다음 투어는 언제입니까? *dah • um too • uh • nun uhn • jeh • eem • nee • kkah*

> 한국 관광 공사 *hahn • gook gwahn • gwahng gohng • sah* (Korean National Tourism Organization, KNTO) provides a wealth of information for travelers online (www.visitkorea.or.kr) and at 관광 안내 전시관 *gwahn • gwahng ahn • neh juhn • see • gwahn* (Tourist Information Centers, TIC). Free internet access is also available at KNTO TICs, as are brochures, maps and other details in print. For 24-hour travel information in English, dial 1330 in Seoul; if calling from a cell phone or from outside of the city, dial the region's area code first.

Are there tours in English?	영어로 하는 투어 있습니까? *yuhng • uh • loh hah • nun too • uh eet • ssum • nee • kkah*
Is there an English guide book/audio guide?	영어 안내책자/음성안내 있습니까? *yuhng • uh ahn • neh • chehk • tzah/ um • suhng • ahn • neh eet • ssum • nee • kkah*
I'd like to see…	…보고 싶습니다. *…boh • goh seep • ssum • nee • dah*
Can we stop here…?	…여기 멈출 수 있습니까? *…yuh • gee muhm • chool ssoo eet • ssum • nee • kkah*
to take photos	사진 찍고 싶은데 *sah • jeen tzeek • kkoh see • pun • deh*
for souvenirs	기념품 사고 싶은데 *gee • nyuhm • poom sah • goh see • pun • deh*
for the restrooms [toilets]	화장실 가고 싶은데 *hwah • jahng • seel gah • goh see • pun • deh*

Can we look around?	둘러봐도 됩니까? *dool • luh • bwah • doh dwehm • nee • kkah*
Is it disabled-accessible?	장애인도 구경할 수 있습니까? *jahng • eh • een • doh goo • gyuhng • hahl ssoo eet • ssum • nee • kkah*

For Tickets, see page 48.

SEEING THE SIGHTS

Where's...?	...이(가) 어디 있습니까? *...ee(gah) uh • dee eet • ssum • nee • kkah*
the battleground	전쟁터 *jeon • jehng • tuh*
the botanical garden	식물원 *seeng • moo • lwuhn*
the castle	성곽 *suhng • gwak*
the downtown area	중심가 *joong • seem • gah*
the fountain	분수 *boon • soo*
the library	도서관 *doh • suh • gwahn*
the market	시장 *see • jahng*
the (war) memorial	(전쟁) 기념관 *(juhn • jehng) gee • nyuhm • gwahn*
the museum	박물관 *bahng • mool • gwahn*
the old town	옛 시가지 *yeht si • gah • jee*
the opera house	오페라하우스 *oh • peh • lah hah • oo • su*

the palace	궁 *goong*
the park	공원 *gohng • wuhn*
the ruins	유적 *yoo • jeok*
the shopping area	상가 *sahng • gah*
the town square	광장 *kwang • jahng*
the theater	극장 *guk • tzahng*
Can you show me on on the map?	지도에서 보여 주시겠습니까? *jee • doh • eh • suh boh • yuh joo • see • geht • ssum • nee • kkah*
It's amazing.	놀랍군요. *nol • lahp • goon • yo*
It's beautiful.	아름다워요. *ah • lum • dahp • wuh • yo*
It's boring.	따분합니다. *ddah • boon • hahm • nee • dah*
It's interesting.	흥미로워요. *hung • mee • loh • wuh • yo*

It's magnificent.	멋집니다. *muht • jeem • nee • dah*
It's romantic.	낭만적이에요. *nahng • mahn • juh • gee • eh • yo*
It's strange.	이상해요. *ee • sahng • heh • yo*
It's terrible.	끔찍해요. *kkum • tzee • keh • yo*
It's ugly.	못생겼어요. *moht • ssehng • gyuht • ssuh • yo*
I (don't) like it.	마음에 (안) 들어요. *mah • u • meh (ahn) du • luh • yo*

For Asking Directions, see page 68.

RELIGIOUS SITES

Where's...?	...이(가) 어디 있습니까? *...ee(gah) uh • dee eet • ssum • nee • kkah*
the cathedral	성당 *suhng • dahng*
the Catholic/ Protestant church	카톨릭/개신교 교회 *kah • tohl • leek/geh • seen • gyo gyo • hweh*
the mosque	회교 사원 *hweh • gyo sah • wuhn*
the shrine	사당 *sah • dahng*
the temple	절 *juhl*
What time is mass/ the service?	미사는/예배는 언제입니까? *mee • sah • nun/yeh • beh • nun uhn • jeh • eem • nee • kkah*

ACTIVITIES

SHOPPING

NEED TO KNOW

Where's the market/ mall [shopping centre]?	시장/상가 어디 있습니까? *see • jahng/ sahng • gah uh • dee eet • ssum • nee • kkah*
I'm just looking.	그냥 둘러보는 중입니다. *gu • nyahng dool • luh • boh • nun joong • eem • nee • dah*
Can you help me?	도와주시겠습니까? *doh • wah • joo • see • geht • ssum • nee • kkah*
I'm being helped.	다른 분이 도와주고 계십니다. *dah • lun boo • nee doh • wah • joo • goh geh • seem • nee • dah*
How much?	얼마입니까? *uhl • mah • eem • nee • kkah*
That one, please.	저거 주세요. *juh • guh joo • seh • yo*
That's all.	다 됐습니다. *dah dweht • ssum • nee • dah*
Where can I pay?	어디서 계산합니까? *uh • dee • suh geh • sahn • hahm • nee • kkah*
I'll pay in cash/by credit card.	현금으로/신용카드로 지불하겠습니다. *hyuhn • gu • mu • loh/ see • nyong • kah • du • loh jee • bool • hah • geht • ssum • nee • dah*
A receipt, please.	영수증 주세요. *yuhng • soo • jung joo • seh • yo*

AT THE SHOPS

Where's...?	…어디 있습니까? *...uh • dee eet • ssum • nee • kkah*
the antiques store	골동품 가게 *gohl • ttohng • poom kkah • geh*
the bakery	제과점 *jeh • gwah • juhm*
the bank	은행 *un • hehng*
the bookstore	서점 *suh • juhm*
Where's...?	…어디 있습니까? *...uh • dee eet • ssum • nee • kkah*
the camera store	카메라 가게 *kah • meh • lah kkah • geh*
the clothing store	옷가게 *oht • kkah • kkeh*
the delicatessen	가공식품점 *gah • gohng • sik • poom • jeom*
the department store	백화점 *beh • kwah • juhm*
the duty-free shop	면세점 *myuhn • seh • juhm*

the florist	꽃집 *kkoht • tzeep*
the gift shop	선물 가게 *suhn • mool kkah • geh*
the hardware store	철물점 *chul • mool • juhm*
the health food store	건강 식품점 *guhn • gahng seek • poom • juhm*
the jeweler	보석상 *boh • suhk • ssahng*
the liquor store [off-licence]	주류 판매점 *joo • lyoo pahn • meh • juhm*
the market	시장 *see • jahng*
the music store	음반 가게 *um • bahn kkah • geh*
the pastry shop	빵집 *bbang • jip*
the pharmacy [chemist]	약국 *yahk • kkook*
the produce [grocery] store	식료품점 *seeng • nyo • poom • juhm*
the shoe store	신발 가게 *seen • bahl kkah • geh*
the shopping mall	상가 *sahng • gah*
the souvenir store	기념품 가게 *gee • nyuhm • poom kkah • geh*
the supermarket	슈퍼마켓 *syoo • puh • mah • keht*
the tobacconist	담배 가게 *dahm • beh kkah • geh*
the toy store	장난감 가게 *jahng • nahn • kkahm kkah • geh*

ASK AN ASSISTANT

When do you open/ close?	언제 문 엽니까/닫습니까? *uhn • jeh moon yuhm • nee • kkah/ daht • ssum • nee • kkah*
Where's...?	…어디 있습니까? *...uh • dee eet • ssum • nee • kkah*
the cashier	계산대 *geh • sahn • deh*
the escalator	에스컬레이터 *eh • su • kuhl • leh • ee • tuh*
the elevator [lift]	엘리베이터 *ehl • lee • beh • ee • tuh*
the fitting room	탈의실 *tah • lee • seel*
the store directory	상가 안내 *sahng • gah ahn • neh*
Can you help me?	도와주시겠습니까? *doh • wah • joo • see • geht • ssum • nee • kkah*
I'm just looking.	그냥 둘러보는 중입니다. *gu • nyahng dool • luh • boh • nun joong • eem • nee • dah*
I'm being helped.	다른 분이 도와주고 계십니다. *dah • lun boo • nee doh • wah • joo • goh gyeh • seem • nee • dah*
Do you have...?	…있습니까? *...eet • ssum • nee • kkah*
Can you show me...?	…보여 주시겠습니까? *...boh • yuh joo • see • geht • ssum • nee • kkah*
Can you ship/ wrap it?	배달해/포장해 주시겠습니까? *beh • dahl • heh/poh • jahng • heh joo • see • geht • ssum • nee • kkah*

How much?	얼마입니까? *uhl • mah • eem • nee • kkah*
That's all.	다 됐습니다. *dah dweht • ssum • nee • dah*

For Clothing, see page 116.

YOU MAY HEAR...

뭘 도와드릴까요? *mwuhl doh • wah • du • leel • kkah • yo*	Can I help you?
무엇을 원하십니까? *moo • uh • sul wuhn • hah • seem • nee • kkah*	What would you like?
더 필요한 거 없으십니까? *duh pee • lyo • hahn guh uhp • ssu • seem • nee • kkah*	Anything else?

PERSONAL PREFERENCES

I'd like something...	…거 주세요. *...guh joo • seh • yo*
cheap/expensive	싼/비싼 *ssahn/bee • ssahn*
larger/smaller	더 큰/더 작은 *duh kun/duh jah • gun*
nicer	더 좋은 *duh joh • un*
from this region	이 지방 *ee jee • bahng*
Around...Won.	…원 정도. *...wuhn juhng • doh*

Can you show me this/ that?	이거/저거 보여 주세요? *ee • guh/juh • guh boh • yuh joo • seh • yo*
That's not quite what I want.	그건 제가 원하는 게 아니에요. *gu • guhn jeh • gah wuhn • hah • nun geh ah • nee • eh • yo*
No, I don't like it.	아니요, 마음에 안 들어요. *ah • nee • yo mah • u • meh ahn du • luh • yo*
It's too expensive.	너무 비싸요. *nuh • moo bee • ssah • yo*
I have to think about it.	생각해 봐야겠어요. *sehng • gah • keh bwah • yah • geht • ssuh • yo*
I'll take it.	이걸로 주세요. *ee • guhl • loh joo • seh • yo*

YOU MAY SEE...

영업 중/영업 끝 *yuhng • uhp tzoong/yuhng • uhp kkut*	open/closed
계산대 *geh • sahn • deh*	cashier
점심 시간 영업 안 함 *jeom • sim si • gahn young • up ahn hahm*	closed for lunch
피팅룸 *pi • ting • room*	fitting room
현금만 받습니다 *hyuhn • gum • mahn baht • ssum • nee • dah*	cash only
신용카드 받습니다 *see • nyong • kah • du baht • ssum • nee • dah*	credit cards accepted
입구/출구 *eep • kkoo/chool • goo*	entrance/exit

Credit and debit cards are accepted at a growing number of stores, restaurants and hotels. However, many vendors still take cash only. Though traveler's checks may be an accepted form of payment at large establishments, it's best to have some cash handy.
A sales tax or value-added tax (VAT) of 10% is charged on most products and services purchased. This tax is included in the retail price.

PAYING & BARGAINING

How much?	얼마예요? *uhl • mah • yeh • yo*
I'll pay...	…낼게요. *...nehl • kkeh • yo*
in cash	현금으로 *hyuhn • gu • mu • loh*
by credit card	신용카드로 *see • nyong • kah • du • loh*
by traveler's check [cheque]	여행자 수표로 *yuh • hehng • jah soo • pyo • loh*
A receipt, please.	영수증 주세요. *yuhng • soo • jung joo • seh • yo*
That's too much.	너무 비싼데요. *nuh • moo bee • ssahn • deh • yo*
I'll give you...	…드릴게요. *...du • leel • kkeh • yo*
I have only... Won.	…원밖에 없습니다. *...won bah • keh uhp • ssum • nee • dah*
Is that your best price?	더 이상 깎아주실 수 없습니까? *duh ee • sahng kka • kka • joo • sil soo uhp • ssum • nee • kkah*

Can you give me a discount? | 깎아 주시겠어요?
kkah • kkah joo • see • geht • ssuh • yo

For Numbers, see page 20.

YOU MAY HEAR...

어떻게 계산하시겠습니까?
uh • ttuh • keh geh • sahn • hah • see • geht • ssum • nee • kkah
How are you paying?

신용카드 결제가 안 됐습니다.
see • nyong • kah • du gyuhl • tzeh • gah ahn dweht • ssum • nee • dah
Your credit card has been declined.

신분증 보여 주십시오.
seen • boon • tzung boh • yuh joo • seep • ssee • oh
ID, please.

현금만 받습니다.
hyuhn • gum • mahn baht • ssum • nee • dah
Cash only, please.

신용카드는 안 받습니다.
sin • yong • card • neun ahn baht • ssum • nee • dah
We don't accept credit cards.

MAKING A COMPLAINT

I'd like... | …주세요.
...joo • seh • yo

to exchange this | 이거 교환해
ee • guh gyo • hwahn • heh

a refund | 환불해
hwahn • bool • heh

to see the manager | 매니저 불러
meh • nee • juh bool • luh

SERVICES

Can you recommend...?	…을(를) 추천해 주시겠습니까? *...eul(reul) choo • chun • heh joo • si • geht • ssum • nee • kkah*
a barber	이발소 *ee • bahl • soh*
a dry cleaner	세탁소 *seh • tahk • ssoh*
a hairstylist	미용실 *mee • yong • seel*
a laundromat [launderette]	빨래방 *ppahl • leh • bahng*
a nail salon	네일숍 *nail • shop*
a spa	사우나 *ssah • oo • nah*
a travel agency	여행사 *yuh • hehng • sah*
Can you...this?	이거…주시겠습니까? *ee • guh... joo • see • geht • ssum • nee • kkah*
alter	수선해 *soo • suhn • heh*
clean	세탁해 *seh • tah • keh*
fix	고쳐 *goh • chuh*
press	다림질해 *dah • leem • jeel • heh*
When will it be ready?	언제 다 됩니까? *uhn • jeh dah dwehm • nee • kkah*

HAIR & BEAUTY

I'd like...	…해 주세요. *...heh joo • seh • yo*
an appointment for today/tomorrow	오늘/내일 예약해 *oh • nul/neh • eel yeh • yah • keh*
some color/ highlights	염색해/브리지해 *yuhm • seh • keh/bu • leet • tzee • heh*
my hair styled/ blow-dried	머리 해/드라이해 *muh • lee heh/du • lah • ee • heh*
a haircut	머리 잘라 *muh • lee jahl • lah*
a trim	다듬어 *dah • du • muh*
Not too short.	너무 짧게 말고요. *nuh • moo tzahl • kkeh mahl • goh • yo*
Shorter here.	여기 더 짧게 해 주세요. *yuh • gee duh tzahl • kkeh heh joo • seh • yo*
I'd like...	…해 주세요. *...heh joo • seh • yo*
an eyebrow/ bikini wax	눈썹/비키니 제모 *noon • ssuhp jeh • moh/bikini je • mo*
a facial	얼굴 마사지 *uhl • gool mah • ssah • jee*
a manicure/ pedicure	매니큐어/페디큐어 *meh • nee • kyoo • uh/ peh • dee • kyoo • uh*
a (sports) massage	(스포츠) 마사지 *(su • poh • chu) mah • ssah • jee*
Do you do acupuncture?	침 놓아요? *cheem noh • ah • yo*

Do you have aromatherapy?	아로마테라피도 합니까? *ah • roh • mah • teh • rah • pee • doh hahm • nee • kkah*
Do you have a sauna?	사우나 있어요? *ssah • oo • nah eet • ssuh • yo*

ANTIQUES

How old is it?	이거 얼마나 됐습니까? *ee • guh uhl • mah • nah dweht • ssum • nee • kkah*
Do you have anything from the … period?	…시대의 물건들도 있습니까? *…si • deh • uh mool • guhn • dul • doh eet • ssum • nee • kkah*
Do I have to fill out any forms?	작성해야 될 서류가 있습니까? *jahk • ssuhng • heh • yah dwehl suh • lyoo • gah eet • ssum • nee • kkah*
Is there a certificate of authenticity?	감정서 있습니까? *gahm • juhng • suh eet • ssum • nee • kkah*
Can you ship/wrap it?	배달/포장해 주시나요? *beh • dahl/poh • jahng • heh joo • si • nah • yo*

CLOTHING

I'd like…	…주세요. *…joo • seh • yo*
Can I try this on?	입어봐도 되요? *ee • buh • bwah • doh dweh • yo*
It doesn't fit.	맞지 않아요. *maht • tzee ah • nah • yo*
It's too…	너무… *nuh • moo…*

big/small	커요/작아요 *kuh • yo/jah • gah • yo*
short/long	짧아요/길어요 *tzal • bah • yo/gee • luh • yo*
tight/loose	껴요/헐렁해요 *kkyuh • yo/huhl • luhng • heh • yo*
Do you have this in size...?	이거…사이즈 있어요? *ee • guh...ssah • ee • ju eet • ssuh • yo*
Do you have this in a bigger/smaller size?	이거 더 큰/작은 사이즈 어요? *ee • guh duh kun/jah • gun ssah • ee • ju eet • ssuh • yo*

For Colors, see page 118.

YOU MAY HEAR...

잘 어울리시네요. *jahl uh • ool • lee • si • neh • yo*	That looks great on you.
잘 맞나요? *jahl man • nah • yo*	How does it fit?
사이즈가 없습니다. *size • gah uhp • ssum • nee • dah*	We don't have your size.

YOU MAY SEE...

신사복 *seen • sah • bohk*	men's
숙녀복 *soong • nyuh • bohk*	women's
아동복 *ah • dohng • bohk*	children's

COLORS

I'd like something…	…색으로 주세요. *…seh • gu • loh joo • seh • yo*
beige	베이지 *beh • ee • jee*
black	검은 *guh • mun*
blue	파란 *pah • lahn*
brown	갈 *gahl*
green	초록 *choh • rohk*
gray	회 *hweh*
orange	오렌지 *oh • lehn • jee*
pink	분홍 *boon • hohng*
purple	보라 *boh • lah*
red	빨간 *ppahl • gahn*
white	흰 *heen*
yellow	노란 *noh • lahn*

CLOTHES & ACCESSORIES

backpack	배낭 *beh • nahng*

belt 벨트
behl • tu

bikini 비키니
bee • kee • nee

blouse 블라우스
bu • lah • oo • su

bra 브래지어
bu • leh • jee • uh

briefs [underpants] 팬티
pehn • tee

coat 코트
koh • tu

dress 드레스
du • leh • su

dress shirt 와이셔츠
wah • ee • syuh • chu

hat 모자
moh • jah

jacket 재킷
jeh • keet

jeans 청바지
chuhng • bah • jee

pajamas [pyjamas] 잠옷
jah • moht

pants [trousers] 바지
bah • jee

pantyhose [tights] 팬티스타킹
pehn • tee • su • tah • keeng

purse [handbag] 핸드백
hehn • du • behk

raincoat 비옷
bee • oht

scarf 스카프
su • kah • pu

shirt	셔츠 *syuh • chu*
shorts	반바지 *bahn • bah • jee*
skirt	치마 *chee • mah*
socks	양말 *yahng • mahl*
suit	양복 *yahng • bohk*
sunglasses	선글라스 *ssuhn • gul • lah • su*
sweater	스웨터 *su • weh • tuh*
sweatshirt	추리닝 *choo • lee • neeng*
swimsuit	수영복 *soo • yuhng • bohk*
T-shirt	티셔츠 *tee • syuh • chu*
tie	넥타이 *nehk • tah • ee*
underwear	속옷 *soh • goht*

FABRIC

I'd like...	…주세요. *...joo • seh • yo*
cotton	면 *myuhn*
denim	데님 *deh • neem*

lace	레이스 *leh • ee • su*
leather	가죽 *gah • jook*
linen	마 *mah*
silk	실크 *sseel • ku*
wool	모 *moh*
Is it machine washable?	세탁기로 빨 수 있나요? *seh • tahk • kkee • loh ppahl ssoo een • nah • yo*

SHOES

I'd like...	…주세요. *...joo • seh • yo*
high-heels/flats	하이힐/낮은 구두 *hah • ee • heel/nah • jun goo • doo*
boots	부츠 *boo • chu*
flip-flops	쪼리 *tzoh • lee*
hiking boots	등산화 *dung • sahn • hwah*
loafers	끈 없는 편한 구두 *kkun uhm • nun pyuhn • hahn goo • doo*
sandals	샌들 *ssehn • dul*
shoes	신발 *seen • bahl*
slippers	슬리퍼 *sul • lee • puh*

sneakers	운동화 *oon • dohng • hwah*
Size...	…사이즈. *...ssah • ee • ju*

For Numbers, see page 20.

SIZES

woman's/man's	여자/남자 *yuh • jah/nahm • jah*
small	소, 55 f / 90 m *soh oh • oh/goo • seep*
medium	중, 66 f / 95 m *joong yoong • nyook/goo • see • boh*
large	대, 77 f / 100 m *deh cheel • cheel/behk*
extra large	특대, 88 f / 105 m *tuk • tteh pahl • pahl/behgoh*
extra extra large	특특대, 110 m *tuk • tuk • tteh behk seep*
petite (cothes size)	작다 *jahk • ddah*

NEWSAGENT & TOBACCONIST

Do you sell English-language newspapers?	영어 신문 파세요? *yuhng • uh seen • moon pah • seh • yo*
I'd like...	…을(를) 주세요. *...eul(reul) joo • seh • yo*
candy [sweets]	사탕 *sah • tahng*

chewing gum	껌 *kkuhm*
a chocolate bar	초콜릿 바 *chocolate bah*
a cigar	담배 *dahm • beh*
a pack/carton of cigarettes	담배 한 갑/보루 *dahm • beh hahn gahp/boh • loo*
a lighter	라이터 *lah • ee • tuh*
a magazine	잡지 *jahp • tzee*
matches	성냥 *suhng • nyahng*
a newspaper	신문 *seen • moon*
a postcard	엽서 *yuhp • ssuh*
a road/town map of...	…도로/시내 지도 *...doh • roh/see • neh jee • doh*
stamps	스탬프 *stamp*

PHOTOGRAPHY

I'd like digital/disposable camera.	디지털/일회용 카메라 주세요. *dee • jee • tuhl/eel • hweh • yong kah • meh • lah joo • seh • yo*
I'd like an automatic camera.	자동 카메라가 필요합니다. *jah • dong kah • meh • rah • gah pil • yo • hahm • nee • dah*
I'd like...	…주세요. *...joo • seh • yo*

a battery	건전지 *guhn • juhn • jee*
digital prints	디지털 프린트 *dee • jee • tuhl pu • leen • tu*
a memory card	메모리카드 *meh • moh • lee • kah • du*
Can I print digital photos here?	여기서 디지털 사진 뽑을 수 있어요? *yuh • gee • suh dee • gee • tuhl sah • jeen ppoh • bul ssoo eet • ssuh • yo*

SOUVENIRS

hanbok (traditional Korean clothing)	한복 *hahn • bohk*
handicrafts	수공예품 *soo • gohng • yeh • poom*
doll	인형 *een • hyuhng*
electronics	전자제품 *juhn • jah • jeh • poom*
embroidery	자수품 *jah • soo • poom*
key ring	열쇠고리 *yuhl • ssweh • goh • lee*
jar of kimchi	김치 한 병 *geem • chee hahn byuhng*
postcard	엽서 *yuhp • ssuh*
pottery	도자기 *doh • jah • gee*
T-shirt	티셔츠 *tee • syuh • chu*

Can I see this/that?	이거/저거 볼 수 있습니까? *ee • guh/juh • guh bohl ssoo eet • ssum • nee • kkah*
It's in the window/ display case.	진열창에/진열장에 있습니다. *jee • nyuhl • chahng • eh/ jee • nyuhl • tzahng • eh eet • ssum • nee • dah*
I'd like...	…주세요. *...joo • seh • yo*
a battery	건전지 *guhn • juhn • jee*
a bracelet	팔찌 *pahl • tzee*
a brooch	브로치 *bu • loh • chee*
a clock	시계 *see • geh*
earrings	귀걸이 *gwih • guh • lee*
a necklace	목걸이 *mohk • kkuh • lee*
a ring	반지 *bahn • jee*
a watch	손목시계 *sohn • mohk • ssee • geh*
I'd like...	…주세요. *...joo • seh • yo*
crystal	수정 *soo • juhng*
cut glass	세공 유리 *seh • gohng yoo • lee*
diamonds	다이아몬드 *dah • ee • ah • mohn • du*

> 인사동 *een • sah • dohng* (Insa-dong) is a favorite outdoor shopping area in Seoul, featuring all kinds of souvenirs, arts and crafts and antiques. Most of the Insa-dong shops sell traditional products, such as pottery, calligraphy, jewelry, books, woodcrafts and papercrafts. Be sure items are labeled 'Made in Korea' if you want to purchase a locally made product. Insa-dong also offers the largest collection of antiques in South Korea. For tourists who would like to bring a taste of Korea home, kimchi and ginseng tea are popular food items that travel well. Shopping malls and department stores are fixtures of most Korean cities. Some malls and large stores feature food courts, playgrounds and other leisure facilities.

white/yellow gold	백금/황금 *behk • kkum/hwahng • gum*
pearls	진주 *jeen • joo*
pewter	백랍 *behng • nahp*
platinum	백금 *behk • kkum*
sterling silver	순은 *soo • nun*
Is this real?	이거 진품입니까? *ee • guh jeen • poo • meem • nee • kkah*
Is there a certificate for it?	보증서가 있습니까? *boh • jung • suh • gah eet • ssum • nee • kkah*
Can you engrave it?	새길 수 있습니까? *seh • geel ssoo eet • ssum • nee • kkah*

SPORT & LEISURE

NEED TO KNOW

When's the game?	경기 언제 합니까? *gyuhng • gee uhn • jeh hahm • nee • kkah*
Where's...?	…어디 있습니까? *...uh • dee eet • ssum • nee • kkah*
the beach	해변 *heh • byuhn*
the park	공원 *kohng • wuhn*
the pool	수영장 *soo • yuhng • jahng*
Is it safe to swim here?	여기 수영하기에 안전합니까? *yuh • gee soo • yuhng • hah • gee • eh ahn • juhn • hahm • nee • kkah*
Can I rent [hire] golf clubs?	골프채 빌릴 수 있습니까? *gohl • pu • cheh beel • leel ssoo eet • ssum • nee • kkah*
How much per hour?	시간당 얼마입니까? *see • gahn • dahng uhl • mah • eem • nee • kkah*
How far is it to...?	…까지 얼마나 멉니까? *...kkah • jee uhl • mah • nah muhm • nee • kkah*
Show me on the map, please.	지도에서 보여 주십시오. *jee • doh • eh • suh boh • yuh joo • seep • ssee • yo*

WATCHING SPORT

When's...game/ match?	…경기 언제 합니까? *...gyuhng • gi uhn • jeh hahm • nee • kkah*
the baseball	야구 *yah • goo*
the basketball	농구 *nohng • goo*
the boxing	권투 *gwuhn • too*
the cricket	크리켓 *cricket*
the golf	골프 *gohl • pu*
the Korean wrestling	씨름 *ssee • lum*
the hockey	하키 *hah • kee*
the soccer [football]	축구 *chook • kkoo*
the tennis	테니스 *teh • nee • su*
the volleyball	배구 *beh • goo*

In addition to the traditional martial arts of 태권도 *teh • kkwuhn • doh* (taekwondo) and 태껸 *teh • kkyuhn* (taekkyeon), practically every classic sport is played in Korea. 씨름 *ssee • lum* (traditional Korean wrestling) can be seen at tournaments held all over the country and is often accompanied by traditional folk music and dance.

Who's playing?	어느 팀이 경기합니까? *uh • nu tee • mee gyuhng • gee hahm • nee • kkah*
Where's the racetrack/stadium?	경마장/경기장 어디 있습니까? *gyuhng • mah • jahng/ gyuhng • gee • jahng uh • dee eet • ssum • nee • kkah*
Where can I place a bet?	어디서 돈을 걸 수 있습니까? *uh • dee • suh doh • nul guhl ssoo eet • ssum • nee • kkah*

For Tickets, see page 48.

PLAYING SPORT

Where is/are...?	…어디 있습니까? *...uh • dee eet • ssum • nee • kkah*
the golf course	골프장 *gohl • pu • jahng*
the gym	헬스클럽 *hehl • ssu • kul • luhp*
the park	공원 *gohng • wuhn*
the tennis courts	테니스장 *teh • nee • su • jahng*

How much per...?	…에 얼마입니까? *...eh uhl • mah eem • nee • kkah*
day	하루 *hah • loo*
hour	시간 *see • gahn*
game	경기 *gyuhng • gee*
round	라운드 *lah • oon • du*
Can I hire...?	…빌릴 수 있습니까? *...beel • leel ssoo eet • ssum • nee • kkah*
clubs	골프채 *gohl • pu • cheh*
equipment	장비 *jahng • bee*
a racket	라켓 *lah • keht*

AT THE BEACH/POOL

Where's the beach/ pool?	해변/수영장 어디 있습니까? *heh • byuhn/soo • yuhng • jahng uh • dee eet • ssum • nee • kkah*
Is there...?	…있습니까? *...eet • ssum • nee • kkah*
a kiddie pool	어린이 수영장 *uh • lee • nee soo • yuhng • jahng*
an indoor/outdoor pool	실내/실외 수영장 *seel • neh/seel • weh soo • yuhng • jahng*
a lifeguard	구조원 *goo • joh • wuhn*
Is it safe...?	…에 안전합니까? *...eh ahn • juhn • hahm • nee • kkah*

to swim	수영하기 *soo • yuhng • hah • gee*
to dive	다이빙하기 *dah • ee • beeng • hah • gee*
for children	아이들 놀기 *ah • ee • dul nohl • gee*
I'd like to hire...	…을(를) 빌리고 싶습니다. *...eul(reul) beel • lee • goh seep • ssum • nee • dah*
a deck chair	접는 의자 *juhm • nun u • jah*
diving equipment	스쿠버다이빙 장비 *su • koo • buh • dah • ee • beeng jahng • bee*
a jet ski	제트스키 *jeh • tu • su • kee*
a motorboat	모터보트 *moh • tuh • boh • tu*
a rowboat	노 젓는 배 *noh juhn • nun beh*
snorkeling equipment	잠수 장비 *jahm • soo jahng • bee*
a surfboard	서핑보드 *surfing • board*
a towel	수건 *soo • guhn*
an umbrella	비치 파라솔 *bee • chee pah • lah • sohl*
water skis	수상스키 *soo • sahng • su • kee*
a windsurfer	윈드서퍼 *windsurfer*
For...hours.	…시간 동안. *...see • gahn ttohng • ahn*

WINTER SPORTS

A lift pass for a day/ five days, please.	하루/5일.리프트 사용권 주세요. *hah • loo/ oh • il lee • pu • tu sah • yong • kkwuhn joo • seh • yo*
I'd like to hire…	…빌리고 싶어요. *…beel • lee • goh see • puh • yo*
boots	부츠 *boo • chu*
a helmet	헬멧 *hehl • meht*
poles	폴대 *pohl • tteh*
skis	스키 *su • kee*
a snowboard	스노우보드 *su • noh • oo • boh • du*
snowshoes	스노슈즈 *su • noh • syoo • ju*
These are too big/ small.	이건 너무 커요/작아요. *ee • guhn nuh • moo kuh • yo/ jah • gah • yo*
Are there lessons?	강습 있어요? *gahng • sup eet • ssuh • yo*

I'm a beginner.	저는 초보입니다. *juh • nun cho • bo • im • nee • dah*
I'm experienced.	저는 상급자입니다. *juh • nun* *sahng • guhp • jjah • im • nee • dah*
A trail map, please.	트레일 지도를 부탁합니다. *trail jee • doh • reul* *boo • tahk • hahm • nee • dah*

YOU MAY SEE...

리프트 *lift*	lifts
드래그 리프트 *drag lift*	drag lift
케이블 카 *cable car*	cable car
체어 리프트 *chair lift*	chair lift
초급 *cho • guhp*	novice
중급 *joong • guhp*	intermediate
상급 *sahng • guhp*	expert
길 막힘 *gil ma • keem*	trail [piste] closed

OUT IN THE COUNTRY

A map of..., please.	…지도 하나 주십시오. *...jee • doh hah • nah joo • seep • ssee • yo*
this region	이 지역 *ee jee • yuhk*
the walking routes	산책로 *sahn • chehng • noh*
A map of..., please.	…지도 하나 주십시오. *...jee • doh hah • nah joo • seep • ssee • yo*
the bike routes	자전거 도로 *jah • juhn • guh doh • loh*

the trails	등산로 *dung • sahn • noh*
Is it easy/difficult?	쉽습니까/어렵습니까? *swihp • ssum • nee • kkah/* *uh • lyuhp • ssum • nee • kkah*
Is it far/steep?	멉니까/가파릅니까? *muhm • nee • kkah/* *gah • pah • lum • nee • kkah*
How far is it to...?	…까지 얼마나 멉니까? *...kkah • jee uhl • mah • nah* *muhm • nee • kkah*
Show me on the map, please.	지도에서 보여주십시오. *jee • doh • eh • suh* *boh • yuh • joo • seep • ssee • yo*
I'm lost.	길을 잃어버렸습니다. *gee • lul* *ee • luh • buh • lyuht • ssum • nee • dah*
Where's...?	…은(는) 어디 있습니까? *...eun(neun) uh • dee* *eet • ssum • nee • kkah*
the bridge	다리 *dah • lee*
the cave	동굴 *dohng • gool*
the farm	농장 *nong • jang*
the field	들판 *deul • pahn*
the forest	숲 *soop*
the hill	언덕 *uhn • duhk*
the lake	호수 *hoh • soo*

the mountain	산 *sahn*
the nature preserve	자연 보호 지역 *jah • yuhn boh • hoh jee • yuhk*
the viewpoint	전망대 *juhn • mahng • deh*
the park	공원 *gohng • wuhn*
the path	산책로 *sahn • chehng • noh*
the peak	산봉우리 *sahn • ppong • oo • ree*
the picnic area	피크닉 구역 *pee • ku • neek kkoo • yuhk*
the pond	연못 *yeon • mot*
the river	강 *gahng*
the sea	바다 *bah • dah*
the spring	샘 *sehm*
the valley	계곡 *gyeh • gok*
the waterfall	폭포 *pohk • poh*

For Asking Directions, see page 68.

TRAVELING WITH CHILDREN

NEED TO KNOW

Is there a discount for kids?	어린이 할인됩니까? *uh • lee • nee hah • leen dwehm • nee • kkah*
Can you recommend a babysitter?	애 봐줄 사람 하나 추천해 주시겠습니까? *eh bwah • jool ssah • lahm hah • nah choo • chuhn • heh joo • see • geht • ssum • nee • kkah*
Do you have a child's seat/highchair?	어린이용/높은 의자 있습니까? *uh • lee • nee • yong/noh • pun u • jah eet • ssum • nee • kkah*
Where can I change the baby?	기저귀 어디서 갈 수 있습니까? *gee • juh • gwih uh • dee • suh gahl ssoo eet • ssum • nee • kkah*

OUT & ABOUT

Can you recommend something for kids?	애들 위한 거 추천해 주시겠습니까? *eh • dul wih • hahn guh choo • chuhn • heh joo • see • geht • ssum • nee • kkah*
Where's...?	…어디 있습니까? *...uh • dee eet • ssum • nee • kkah*
the amusement park	놀이 공원 *noh • lee gohng • wuhn*
the arcade	오락실 *oh • lahk • sseel*
the kiddie pool	어린이 수영장 *uh • lee • nee soo • yuhng • jahng*

the park	공원 *gohng • wuhn*
the playground	놀이터 *noh • lee • tuh*
the zoo	동물원 *dohng • moo • lwuhn*
Are kids allowed?	아이들도 들어갈 수 있습니까? *ah • ee • dul • doh du • luh • gahl ssoo eet • ssum • nee • kkah*
Is it safe for kids?	아이들에게 안전합니까? *ah • ee • dul • eh • geh ahn • juhn • hahm • nee • kkah*
Is it suitable for... year olds?	…살 짜리 아이에게 적절합니까? *...sahl tzah • lee ah • ee • eh • geh juhk • tzuhl • hahm • nee • kkah*

For Child Health & Emergency, see page 157.

YOU MAY HEAR...

귀여워라! *gwih • yuh • wuh • lah*	How cute!
얘 이름이 뭐예요? *yeh ee • lu • mee mwuh • eh • yo*	What's his/her name?
얘 몇 살이에요? *yeh myuht ssah • lee • eh • yo*	How old is he/she?

BABY ESSENTIALS

Do you have ...?	…있습니까? *...eet • ssum • nee • kkah*
a baby bottle	젖병 *juht • ppyuhng*

baby food	이유식 *ee • yoo • seek*
baby wipes	아기용 물휴지 *ah • gee • yong mool • hyoo • jee*
a car seat	카시트 *kah • ssee • tu*
a children's menu	어린이 메뉴 *uh • lee • nee • yong meh • nyoo*
a child's seat/ highchair	어린이용/높은 의자 *uh • lee • nee • yong/noh • pun u • jah*
a crib [child's cot]	아기용 침대 *ah • gee • yong cheem • deh*
diapers [nappies]	기저귀 *gee • juh • gwih*
formula [baby food]	이유식 *ee • yoo • seek*
a pacifier [dummy]	고무 젖꼭지 *goh • moo juht • kkohk • tzee*
a stroller [pushchair]	유모차 *yoo • moh • chah*

Children enjoy a special place in Korean society and are cosseted and fussed over, especially by the older generation. Arriving with a family in tow means you can expect special service in restaurants, hotels, and many other public places. Note that larger babies may not fit Korean-size diapers and that much of the spicy Korean food might not be to Western toddler's tastes, so plan accordingly. If you can persuade your children to learn a few words of Hanguel, expect some bonus points.

Where can I breastfeed/change the baby?	어디서 수유할/기저귀 갈 수 있습니까? *uh • dee • suh soo • yoo • hahl/ gee • juh • gwih gahl ssoo eet • ssum • nee • kkah*

For Dining with Children, see page 171.

BABYSITTING

Can you recommend a babysitter?	애 봐줄 사람 하나 추천해 주시겠습니까? *eh bwah • jool ssah • lahm hah • nah choo • chuhn • heh joo • see • geht • ssum • nee • kkah*
What's the charge?	비용이 어떻게 됩니까? *bee • yong • ee uh • ttuh • keh dwehm • nee • kkah*
I'll be back by...	…까지 돌아오겠습니다. *...kkah • jee doh • lah • oh • geht • ssum • nee • dah*
I can be reached at...	…(으)로 연락 주십시오.* *...(u •)loh yuhl • lahk joo • seep • ssee • oh*

* Note that when the word ends in a consonant, use 으로 *u • loh*; when the word ends in a vowel, use 로 *loh*.

HEALTH & SAFETY

EMERGENCIES

NEED TO KNOW

Help!	도와주세요! *doh • wah • joo • seh • yo*
Go away!	저리 가세요! *juh • lee gah • seh • yo*
Stop, thief!	거기서. 도둑이야! *guh • gee • suh doh • doo • gee • yah*
Get a doctor!	의사 불러 주세요! *u • sah bool • luh joo • seh • yo*
Fire!	불이야! *boo • lee • yah*
I'm lost.	길을 잃어버렸어요. *gee • lul ee • luh • buh • lyuht • ssuh • yo*
Can you help me?	도와주시겠어요? *doh • wah • joo • see • gehtssuh • yo*

YOU MAY HEAR...

이 양식을 작성하십시오. *ee yang • sik • eul* *jahk • ssung • hah • sip • si • oh*	Fill out this form.
신분증 좀 보여 주십시오. *seen • boon • tzung johm boh • yuh* *joo • seep • ssee • oh*	Your identification, please.
언제/어디서 일어난 일입니까? *uhn • jeh/uh • dee • suh ee • luh • nahn* *nee • leem • nee • kkah*	When/Where did it happen?
어떻게 생겼습니까? *uh • ttuh • keh* *sehng • gyuht • ssum • nee • kkah*	What does he/ she look like?

In North Korea, dial **119** for the police, ambulance and fire brigade. In South Korea, dial **112** for the police, and **119** to call an ambulance or fire brigade. For 24-hour non-emergency assistance in English, dial Korea Travel Phone: **1330** in Seoul; if calling from a cell phone or from outside of the city, dial the region's area code first.

POLICE

NEED TO KNOW

Call the police!	경찰 불러주세요! *gyung • chahl bool • luh • joo • seh • yo*
Where's the police station?	경찰서가 어디 있습니까? *gyuhng • chahl • ssuh • gah uh • dee eet • ssum • nee • kkah*
There was an accident.	사고 났습니다. *sah • goh naht • ssum • nee • dah*
There was an attack.	폭행 당했습니다. *poh • kehng dahng • heht • ssum • nee • dah*
My child is missing.	제 아이가 없어졌습니다. *jeh ah • ee • gah uhp • ssuh • juht • ssum • nee • dah*
I need an interpreter.	통역을 불러 주십시오. *tohng • yuh • gul bool • luh joo • seep • ssee • yo*
I need…	…해야겠습니다…. *heh • yah • geht • ssum • nee • dah*

to contact my lawyer	제 변호사에게 연락 *jeh byuhn • hoh • sah • eh • geh yuhl • lahk*
to make a phone call	전화 통화 *juhn • hwah tohng • hwah*
to contact my consulate	영사관에 연락 *yuhng • sah • gwah • neh yuhl • lahk*
I'm innocent.	전 죄가 없습니다. *juhn jweh • gah uhp • ssum • nee • dah*

CRIME & LOST PROPERTY

I want to report...	…신고하고 싶습니다. *...seen • goh • hah • goh seep • ssum • nee • dah*
a mugging	노상강도 *noh • sahng • gahng • doh*
a rape	강간 *gahng • gahn*
I want to report...	…신고하고 싶습니다. *...seen • goh • hah • goh seep • ssum • nee • dah*
a theft	도난 *doh • nahn*
I was mugged/ robbed.	노상강도/도난 당했습니다. *noh • sahng • gahng • doh/doh • nahn dahng • heht • ssum • nee • dahh*
I lost my...	…잃어버렸습니다. … *ee • luh • buh • lyuht • ssum • nee • dah*
My...was/were stolen.	제…도둑 맞았습니다. *je...doh • doong mah • jaht • ssum • nee • dah*

backpack	배낭 *beh • nahng*
bicycle	자전거 *jah • juhn • guh*
camera	카메라 *kah • meh • lah*
(hire) car	(렌터)카 *(lehn • tuh) kah*
computer	컴퓨터 *kuhm • pyoo • tuh*
credit card	신용카드 *see • nyong • kah • du*
jewelry	보석 *boh • suhk*
money	돈 *dohn*
passport	여권 *yuh • kkwuhn*
purse [handbag]	핸드백 *hehn • du • behk*
traveler's checks	여행자 수표 *yuh • hehng • jah soo • pyo*
wallet	지갑 *jee • gahp*
I need a police report.	경찰 조서가 필요합니다. *gyuhng • chahl joh • suh • gah pee • lyo • hahm • nee • dah*
Where is the British/ American/Irish embassy?	영국/미국/아일랜드 대사관은 어디입니까? *young • gook/mee • gook/ ah • il • land • deh sah • kwan • eun uh • dee • eem • nee • kkah*

HEALTH

NEED TO KNOW

I'm sick [ill]. 제가 아픕니다.
jeh • gah ah • pum • nee • dah

I need an English-speaking doctor. 영어 하는 의사가 필요합니다.
yuhng • yuh hah • nun u • sah • gah pee • lyo • hahm • nee • dah

It hurts here. 여기가 아픕니다.
yuh • gee • gah ah • pum • nee • dah

I have a stomachache. 배가 아픕니다.
beh • gah ah • pum • nee • dah

FINDING A DOCTOR

Can you recommend a doctor/dentist? 의사/치과의사 하나 추천해 주시겠습니까?
u • sah/chee • kkwah • u • sah hah • nah choo • chuhn • heh joo • see • geht • ssum • nee • kkah

Can the doctor come here? 의사 선생님이 여기로 오실 수 있습니까?
u • sah suhn • sehng • nee • mee yuh • gee • loh oh • seel ssoo eet • ssum • nee • kkah

I need an English-speaking doctor. 영어 하는 의사가 필요합니다.
yuhng • yuh hah • nun u • sah • gah pee • lyo • hahm • nee • dah

What are the office hours? 진료 시간이 언제입니까?
jeel • lyo see • gah • nee uhn • jeh • eem • nee • kkah

I'd like an appointment for...	…예약하고 싶습니다. *...yeh • yah • kah • goh seep • ssum • nee • dah*
today	오늘 *oh • nul*
tomorrow	내일 *neh • eel*
as soon as possible	가능한 한 빨리 *gah • nung • hahn hahn ppahl • lee*
It's urgent.	급합니다. *gu • pahm • nee • dah*

SYMPTOMS

I'm bleeding.	피가 납니다. *pee • gah nahm • nee • dah*
I'm constipated.	변비 걸렸습니다. *byuhn • bee gyuhl • lyuht • ssum • nee • dah*
I'm dizzy.	어지럽습니다. *uh • jee • ruhp • sum • nee • dah*
I'm nauseous.	토할 거 같습니다. *toh • hahl kkuh gaht • ssum • nee • dah*
I'm vomiting.	자꾸 토합니다. *jah • kkoo toh • hahm • nee • dah*
It hurts here.	여기가 아픕니다. *yuh • gee • gah ah • pum • nee • dah*
I sprained my ankle/ wrist.	발목을/손목을 삐었습니다. *bahl • moh • gul/sohn • moh • gul ppee • uht • ssum • nee • dah*
I have...	…이(가) 있습니다. *...ee(gah) eet • ssum • nee • dah*
an allergic reaction	알레르기 반응 *ahl • leh • lu • gee bah • nung*

chest pain	가슴에 통증 *gah • su • meh tohng • tzung*
congestion	충혈 *choong • hyuhl*
cramps	복통 *bohk • tohng*
diarrhea	설사 *suhl • ssah*
an earache	귀에 통증 *gwih • eh tohng • tzung*
a fever	열 *yuhl*
pain	통증 *tohng • tzung*
a rash	두드러기 *doo • du • luh • gee*
a sprain	염좌 *yuhm • jwah*
some swelling	좀 부어 *johm boo • uh*
a sore throat	목에 통증 *moh • geh tohng • tzung*
a stomachache	복통 *bohk • tohng*
sunstroke	일사병 *eel • ssah • ppyuhng*
I've been sick [ill] for…days.	…일 동안 아팠습니다. *…eel ttohng • ahn ah • paht • ssum • nee • dah*

For Months, see page 26.

CONDITIONS

I'm...	저는…이(가) 있습니다. *juh • nun...ee(gah) eet • ssum • nee • dah*
anemic	빈혈 *been • hyuhl*
asthmatic	천식 *chuhn • seek*
diabetic	당뇨병 *dahng • nyo • ppyuhng*
epileptic	간질 증상 *gahn • jeel juhng • sang*
I'm allergic to antibiotics/penicillin.	항생제에/페니실린에 알레르기가 있습니다. *hahng • sehng • jeh • eh/ peh • nee • seel • lee • neh ahl • leh • lu • gee • gah eet • ssum • nee • dah*
I have...	…이 있습니다. *...ee eet • ssum • nee • dah*
arthritis	관절염 *gwahn • juhl • lyuhm*
a heart condition	심장 질환 *seem • jahng jee • lwahn*
high/low blood pressure	고혈압/저혈압 *goh • hyuh • lahp/juh • hyuh • lahp*
I'm on medication.	약을 복용 중입니다. *yah • gul boh • gyong joong • eem • nee • dah*
I'm on...	…복용 중입니다. *...boh • gyong joong • eem • nee • dah*

YOU MAY HEAR...

어디가 안 좋으세요? *uh • dee • gah ahn joh • u • seh • yo*	What's wrong?
어디가 아프세요? *uh • dee • gah ah • pu • seh • yo*	Where does it hurt?
여기가 아프세요? *yuh • gee • gah ah • pu • seh • yo*	Does it hurt here?
약 드시는 거 있으세요? *yahk du • see • nun guh eet • ssu • seh • yo*	Are you on medication?
알레르기 있으세요? *ahl • leh • lu • gee eet • ssu • seh • yo*	Are you allergic to anything?
입 벌리세요. *eep buhl • lee • seh • yo*	Open your mouth.
숨 깊이 들이쉬세요. *soom gee • pee du • lee • swih • seh • yo*	Breathe deeply.
병원에 가세요. *byuhng • wuh • neh gah • seh • yo*	Go to the hospital.

TREATMENT

Do I need a prescription/ medicine?	처방전/약 필요합니까? *chuh • bahng • juhn/ yahk pee • lyo • hahm • nee • kkah*
Can you prescribe a generic drug [unbranded medication]?	일반 약품을 처방해 주실 수 있습니까? *eel • ban yahk • ppoo • mool chuh • bang • heh joo • sil ssoo eet • ssum • nee • kkah*
Where can I get it?	어디서 구할 수 있습니까? *uh • dee • suh goo • hahl ssoo eet • ssum • nee • kkah*

For What to Take, see page 154.

HOSPITAL

Notify my family, please.	제 가족에게 연락해 주십시오. *jeh gah • joh • geh • geh yuhl • lah • keh joo • seep • ssee • oh*
I'm in pain.	저 지금 아픕니다. *juh jee • gum ah • pum • nee • dah*
I need a doctor/ nurse.	의사/간호사 불러 주십시오. *u • sah/gahn • hoh • sah bool • luh joo • seep • ssee • oh*
When are visiting hours?	방문 시간이 언제입니까? *bahng • moon see • gah • nee uhn • jeh • eem • nee • kkah*
I'm visiting...	…문병왔습니다. *...moon • byuhng • waht • ssum • nee • dah*

DENTIST

I have a broken tooth.	이빨이 부러졌습니다. *ee • ppah • lee boo • luh • jyuht • ssum • nee • dah*
I've lost a filling.	이빨 때운 게 빠졌습니다. *ee • ppahl tteh • oon geh ppah • juht • ssum • nee • dah*
I have a toothache.	이빨이 아픕니다. *ee • ppah • lee ah • pum • nee • dah*
Can you fix this denture?	이 틀니를 고쳐 주시겠습니까? *ee tul • lee • lul goh • chyuh joo • see • geht • ssum • nee • kkah*

GYNECOLOGIST

I have cramps/ a vaginal infection.	복통이/질염이 있습니다. *bok • tohng • ee/jeel • lyuh • mee eet • ssum • nee • dah*

I missed my period.	생리 안 했습니다. *sehng • nee ahn heht • ssum • nee • dah*
I'm on the Pill.	피임약 먹고 있습니다. *pee • eem • nyahk muh • kkoh eet • ssum • nee • dah*
I'm (...months) pregnant.	저는 임신 (…개월)입니다. *juh • nun eem • seen (...geh • wuhl) eem • nee • dah*
I'm not pregnant.	저는 임신하지 않았습니다. *juh • nun eem • seen • hah • jee ah • naht • ssum • nee • dah*
My last period was...	마지막으로…에 생리했습니다. *mah • jee • mah • gu • loh...eh sehng • nee • heht • ssum • nee • dah*

For Numbers, see page 20.

OPTICIAN

I lost...	…잃어버렸습니다. *...ee • luh • buh • ryuht • ssum • nee • dah*
a contact lens	콘택트 렌즈 *kohn • tehk • tu lehn • ju*
my glasses	안경 *ahn • gyuhng*
a lens	안경알 *ahn • gyuhng • ahl*

PAYMENT & INSURANCE

How much?	얼마입니까? *uhl • mah • eem • nee • kkah*
Can I pay by credit card?	신용카드로 계산할 수 있습니까? *see • nyong • kah • du • loh geh • sahn • hahl ssoo eet • ssum • nee • kkah*

I have insurance.	보험이 있습니다. *boh • huh • mee eet • ssum • nee • dah*
I need a receipt for my insurance.	보험용 영수증이 필요합니다. *boh • huhm • nyong yuhng • soo • jung • ee pee • lyo • hahm • nee • dah*

PHARMACY

NEED TO KNOW

Where's the pharmacy?	약국 어디 있습니까? *yahk • kkook uh • dee eet • ssum • nee • kkah*
What time does it open/close?	몇 시에 문 엽니까/닫습니까? *myuh • ssee • eh moon yuhm • nee • kkah/ daht • ssum • nee • kkah*
What would you recommend for...?	…에 좋은 약 있습니까? *...eh joh • un yahk eet • ssum • nee • kkah*
How much do I take?	얼마큼 먹어야 합니까? *uhl • mah • kum muh • guh • yah hahm • nee • kkah*
Can you fill [make up] this prescription?	이 처방대로 약 주시겠습니까? *ee chuh • bahng • deh • loh yahk joo • see • geht • ssum • nee • kkah*
I'm allergic to...	…알레르기가 있습니다. *...ahl • leh • lu • gee • gah eet • ssum • nee • dah*

There are many pharmacies in South Korea, and most Western drugs are available. Some pharmacies sell toiletries and non-prescription medication, as well as traditional remedies. Opening hours are 9:00 a.m. to 9:00 p.m., but this can vary.

WHAT TO TAKE

How much do I take? 얼마큼 먹어야 합니까?
uhl • mah • kum muh • guh • yah hahm • nee • kkah

How often? 얼마 간격으로 먹습니까?
uhl • mah gahn • gyuh • gu • loh muhk • ssum • nee • kkah

Is it safe for children? 어린이가 먹어도 됩니까?
uh • lee • nee • gah muh • guh • doh dwehm • nee • kkah

I'm taking... …복용 중입니다.
...boh • gyong joong • eem • nee • dah

Are there side effects? 부작용 있습니까?
boo • jah • gyong eet • ssum • nee • kkah

I need something for... …약 주세요.
...yahk tzoo • seh • yo

a cold 감기
gahm • gee

a cough 기침
gee • cheem

diarrhea 설사
suhl • ssah

a headache 두통
doo • tong

YOU MAY SEE...

하루 일회/삼회 복용 *hah • loo eel • hweh/sahm • hweh boh • gyong*	once/three times a day
정제 *jeong • jeh*	tablet
방울 *bang • ool*	drop
티스푼 *teaspoon*	teaspoon
식후/식전/식사와 함께 *see • koo/ seek • tzuhn/seek • ssa • wah hahm • kkeh*	after/before/ with meals
공복에 먹을것 *gohng • boh • geh muh • gul • guht*	take on an empty stomach
전부 마실 것 *jeon • boo mah • sil guht*	swallow whole
졸음을 유발할 수 있음 *joh • lu • mul yoo • bahl • hahl ssoo eet • ssum*	may cause drowsiness
복용 금지 *bok • yong geum • jee*	do not ingest

insect bites	벌레 물린데 *buhl • leh mool • leen • deh*
motion sickness	멀미 *muhl • mee*
a sore throat	목 아픈 데 *moh gah • pun deh*
sunburn	일광 화상 *eel • gwahng hwah • sahng*
a toothache	치통 *chi • tong*
an upset stomach	복통 *bohk • tohng*

BASIC SUPPLIES

I'd like...	…을(를) 주세요. *...eul(reul) joo • seh • yo*
acetaminophen [paracetamol]	아세트아미노펜 *ah • seh • tu • ah • mee • noh • pehn*
antiseptic cream	살균 크림 *sahl • gyoon ku • leem*
aspirin	아스피린 *ah • su • pee • leen*
bandages	붕대 *boong • deh*
a comb	빗 *beet*
condoms	콘돔 *kohn • dohm*
contact lens solution	콘텍트 렌즈 용액 *kohn • tehk • tu lehn • ju yong • ehk*
deodorant	탈취제 *tahl • chwee • jeh*
a hairbrush	헤어 브러시 *heh • uh bu • luh • see*
ibuprofen	이부프로펜 *ee • boo • pu • loh • pehn*
insect repellent	제충제 *jeh • choong • jeh*
lotion	로션 *loh • syuhn*
a nail file	손톱줄 *sohn • tohp • tzool*
a (disposable) razor	(일회용) 면도기 *(eel • hweh • yong) myuhn • doh • gee*
razor blades	면도날 *myuhn • doh • nahl*

sanitary napkins [towels]	생리대 *sehng • nee • deh*
shampoo/ conditioner	샴푸/컨디셔너 *syahm • poo/kuhn • dee • syuh • nuh*
soap	비누 *bee • noo*
sunscreen	자외선 차단 크림 *jah • weh • suhn chah • dahn ku • leem*
tampons	탐폰 *tahm • pohn*
tissues	화장지 *hwah • jahng • jee*
toilet paper	화장실 휴지 *hwah • jahng • seel hyoo • jee*
a toothbrush	칫솔 *cheet • ssohl*
toothpaste	치약 *chee • yahk*

For Baby Essentials, see page 137.

CHILD HEALTH & EMERGENCY

Can you recommend a pediatrician?	소아과 의사 하나 추천해 주시겠습니까? *soh • ah • kkwah u • sah* *hah • nah choo • chuhn • heh* *joo • see • geht • ssum • nee • kkah*
My child is allergic to...	제 애는…알레르기가 있습니다. *jeh eh • nun...ahl • leh • lu • gee • gah* *eet • ssum • nee • dah*
My child is missing.	제 아이가 없어졌습니다. *jeh ah • ee • gah* *uhp • ssuh • juht • ssum • nee • dah*

Have you seen a boy/girl?	남자애/여자애 보셨습니까? *nahm • jah • eh/yuh • jah • eh boh • syuht • ssum • nee • kkah*

For Police, see page 143.

DISABLED TRAVELERS

NEED TO KNOW

Is there...?	…있습니까? *...eet • ssum • nee • kkah*
access for the disabled	장애인이 이용할 수 *jahng • eh • ee • nee ee • yong • hahl ssoo*
a wheelchair ramp	휠체어 진입로 *wihl • cheh • uh jee • neem • noh*
a handicapped- [disabled-] accessible toilet	장애인용 화장실 *jahng • eh • een • nyong hwah • jahng • seel*
I need...	…필요합니다. *...pee • lyo • hahm • nee • dah*
assistance	도움이 *doh • oo • mee*
an elevator [a lift]	엘리베이터가 *ehl • lee • beh • ee • tuh • gah*
a ground-floor room	일층방이 *eel • chung • bahng • ee*

ASKING FOR ASSISTANCE

I'm…disabled	저는… *juh • nun…* 장애인입니다 *jahng • eh • ee • neem • nee • dah*
visually impaired	시각 장애인입니다 *see • gahk* *jahng • eh • ee • neem • nee • dah*
deaf	귀가 좋지 않습니다 *gwi • gah jo • chee ahn • ssum • nee • dah*
hearing impaired	청각 장애인입니다 *chuhng • gahk* *jahng • eh • ee • neem • nee • dah*
unable to walk far	멀리 걸을 수 없습니다 *muhl • lee guh • lul ssoo* *uhp • ssum • nee • dah*
unable to use the stairs	계단을 이용할 수 없습니다 *geh • dah • nul ee • yong • hahl ssoo* *uhp • ssum • nee • dah*
Please speak louder.	더 크게 말씀해 주십시오. *duh ku • geh mahl • ssum • heh* *joo • seep • ssee • oh*
Can I bring my wheelchair?	제 휠체어를 가져 와도 됩니까? *jeh wihl • cheh • uh • lul gah • juh* *wah • doh dwehm • nee • kkah*
Are guide dogs permitted?	맹도견이 들어갈 수 있습니까? *mehng • doh • gyuh • nee du • luh • gahl* *ssoo eet • ssum • nee • kkah*
Can you help me?	도와주시겠습니까? *doh • wah • joo • see • geht • ssum • nee • kkah*
Please open/hold the door.	문 좀 열어/잡아 주십시오. *moon johm yuh • luh/jah • bah* *joo • seep • ssee • oh*

in a non-smoking area	금연 구역에 *gu • myuhn goo • yuh • geh*
I'm waiting for someone.	누구 기다리는 중인데요. *noo • goo gee • dah • lee • nun joong • een • deh • yo*
Where's the restroom [toilet]?	화장실 어디 있어요? *hwah • jahng • seel uh • dee eet • ssuh • yo*
A menu, please.	메뉴 좀 주세요. *meh • nyoo johm joo • seh • yo*
What do you recommend?	뭐가 맛있어요? *mwuh • gah mah • seet • ssuh • yo*
I'd like…	…주세요. *…joo • seh • yo*
Some more…, please.	…좀 더 주세요. *…johm duh joo • seh • yo*
Enjoy your meal!	맛있게 드세요! *mah • seet • kkeh du • seh • yo*
The check [bill], please.	계산서 주세요. *geh • sahn • suh joo • seh • yo*
Is service included?	봉사료가 포함돼 있어요? *bohng • sah • lyo • gah poh • hahm • dweh eet • ssuh • yo*
Can I pay by credit card?	신용카드 받으세요? *see • nyong • kah • du bah • du • seh • yo*
Can I have a receipt?	영수증 주시겠어요? *yuhng • soo • jung joo see • geht • ssuh • yo*
Thank you!	감사합니다! *gahm • sah • hahm • nee • dah*

WHERE TO EAT

Can you recommend...?	…을(를) 추천해 주시겠어요? *...eul(reul) choo • chuhn • heh joo • see • geht • ssuh • yo*
a restaurant	음식점 *uhm • seek • tzuhm*
a bar	바 *bah*
a cafe	카페 *kkah • peh*
a fast-food place	패스트푸드 점 *peh • su • tu • poo • du juhm*
a cheap restaurant	저렴한 식당 *juh • ryuhm • hahn sik • ddahng*

Meal times in Korea are similar to those in the U.S. and U.K.
아침 *ah • cheem* (breakfast) is served until 9:00 a.m., 점심 *juhm • seem* (lunch) is served from 12 :00 to 2:00 p.m. and 저녁 *juh • nyuhk* (dinner) is served from 6:00 to 9:00 p.m. Korean food is traditionally spicy and hot, and garlic is a common ingredient. The cuisine is based on meat, poultry and fish, though vegetarian options are increasingly popular. Korean food is not served in courses; instead, dishes are served all at the same time. A Korean meal is typically a combination of 밥 *bahp* (rice), 국 *gook* (soup) and various 반찬 *bahn • chahn* (side dishes).
Note that spoons are used for rice and soup dishes while chopsticks are used for side dishes.

an expensive restaurant	비싼 식당 *bee • ssahn sik • ddahng*
a restaurant with a good view	경치가 좋은 식당 *gyung • chi • gah joh • eun sik • ddahng*
an authentic/ non-touristy restaurant	정통/관광객에 특화되지 않은 식당 *jeong • tong/gwan • gwang • gehk • eh teuk • whah • dweh • jee ah • neun sik • ddang*
a traditional teahouse	전통 찻집 *juhn • tohng chaht • tzeep*

RESERVATIONS & PREFERENCES

I'd like to reserve a table…	…예약하고 싶습니다. *…yeh • yah • kah • goh seep • ssum • nee • dah*
for two	두 명 *doo myuhng*
for this evening	오늘 저녁 *oh • nul tzuh • nyuhk*
for tomorrow at…	내일…시 *neh • eel…see*
A table for two, please.	두 명입니다. *doo • myuhng • eem • nee • dah*
We have a reservation.	예약했습니다. *yeh • yah • keht • ssum • nee • dah*
My name is…	제 이름은…입니다. *jeh ee • lu • mun…eem • nee • dah*
Can we sit…?	…앉아도 됩니까? *…ahn • jah • doh dwehm • nee • kkah*
outside	밖에 *bah • ggeh*
by the window	창가에 *chang • kkah • eh*

here/there	여기/저기 *yuh • gee/juh • gee*
in the shade	그늘진 곳에 *guh • nuhl • jin go • seh*
in the sun	햇빛이 비치는 곳에 *heh • bee • chee bee • chee • nuhn go • seh*
in a non-smoking area	금연 구역에 *gu • myuhn goo • yuh • geh*
outside	밖에 *bah • kkeh*
Where's the restroom [toilet]?	화장실 어디 있습니까? *hwah • jahng • seel uh • dee eet • ssum • nee • kkah*

YOU MAY HEAR...

예약 하셨습니까? *yeh • ya • kahs • yeo • sseum • nee • kkah*	Do you have a reservation?
몇명이십니까? *myeon • myeong • ee • ssim • nee • kkah*	How many?
주문하시겠습니까? *joo • moon • hah • see • geht • ssum • nee • kkah*	Are you ready to order?
어떤 것을 주문하시겠습니까? *eotteon geo • seul ju • mun • hasiged • sseumni • kka*	What would you like?
…추천합니다. *…choo • chuhn • hahm • nee • dah*	I recommend…
맛있게 드십시오. *mah • seet • kkeh du • seep • ssee • yo*	Enjoy your meal.

HOW TO ORDER

Waiter/Waitress!	여기요! *yuh • gee • yo*
We're ready to order.	주문할게요. *joo • moon • hahl • kkeh • yo*
The wine list, please.	포도주 리스트 주세요. *poh • doh • joo lee • su • tu joo • seh • yo*
I'd like a bottle/ glass of...	…한 병/한 잔 주세요. *...hahn byuhng/hahn jahn joo • seh • yo*
I'd like a carafe of...	...을(를) 한 병 주세요. *...eul(reul) hahn byung joo • seh • yo*
The menu, please.	메뉴 좀 주세요. *meh • nyoo johm joo • seh • yo*
Do you have...?	…있어요? *...eet • ssuh • yo*
a menu in English	영어 메뉴 *yuhng • uh meh • nyoo*
a fixed-price menu	세트 메뉴 *sseh • tu meh • nyoo*
a children's menu	어린이 메뉴 *uh • lee • nee meh • nyoo*
What do you recommend?	뭐가 맛있어요? *mwuh • gah mah • seet • ssuh • yo*
What's this?	이건 뭐예요? *ee • guhn mwuh • eh • yo*
What's in it?	뭐 들어 갔어요? *mwuh du • luh • gaht • ssuh • yo*
Is it spicy?	매워요? *meh • wuh • yo*
I'd like...	…주세요. *...joo • seh • yo*
More..., please.	…좀 더 주세요. *...johm duh joo • seh • yo*

With/Without...	...넣어서/ 빼고. *...nuh • uh • suh/ppeh • goh*
I can't have...	...못 먹어요. *...mohn muh • guh • yo*
rare	덜 익힌 *duhl lee • keen*
medium	반 쯤 익힌 *bahn tzum ee • keen*
well-done	완전히 익힌 *wahn • juh • nee ee • keen*
It's to go [take away].	싸 주세요. *ssah joo • seh • yo*

YOU MAY SEE...

테이블 요금 *table yo • guhm*	cover charge
정가 *juhng • kkah*	fixed-price
(오늘의) 특선 메뉴 *(oh • nu • leh) tuk • ssuhn meh • nyoo*	menu (of the day)
서비스료 (불)포함 *ssuh • bee • su • lyo (bool) poh • hahm*	service (not) included
특선 *tuk • ssuhn*	specials

COOKING METHODS

baked	구운 *goo • oon*
boiled	삶은 *sahl • mun*

breaded	빵가루를 입힌 *ppahng • kkah • loo • lul ee • peen*
deep-fried	튀긴 *twih • geen*
diced	잘게 썬 *jahl • geh ssuhn*
grilled	불에 구운 *bu • leh goo • oon*
poached	데친 *deh • cheen*
roasted	구운 *goo • oon*
sautéed	살짝 볶은 *sahl • tzahk boh • kkun*
smoked	훈제한 *hoon • jeh • hahn*
steamed	찐 *tzeen*
stewed	약한 불로 익힌 *yah • kahn bool • loh ee • keen*
stir-fried	볶은 *boh • kkun*
stuffed	속을 채운 *soh • gul cheh • oon*

DIETARY REQUIREMENTS

I'm diabetic/lactose intolerant.	저는 당뇨병/유당 불내증이 있습니다. *juh • nun dahng • nyo • ppyuhng/ yoo • dahng bool • leh • tzng • ee eet • ssum • nee • dah*

I'm a vegetarian/ vegan.	저는 채식주의자입니다/ 채식주의자입니다. *juh • nun cheh • seek • tzoo • ee • jah • eem • nee • dah/cheh • seek • tzoo • ee • jah • eem • nee • dah*
I'm allergic to...	…에 알레르기가 있습니다. *...eh ahl • leh • lu • gee • gah eet • ssum • nee • dah*
I can't eat...	…못 먹습니다. *...mohn muhk • ssum • nee • dah*
dairy	유제품 *yoo • jeh • poom*
gluten	글루텐 *gul • loo • tehn*
nuts	견과류 *gyuhn • gwah • lyoo*
I can't eat...	…못 먹습니다. *...mohn muhk • ssum • nee • dah*
pork	돼지고기 *dweh • jee goh • gee*
shellfish	조개류 *joh • geh • lyoo*
spicy foods	매운 음식 *meh • oon um • seek*
Is it halal/kosher?	할랄/코셔 식품입니까? *halal/kosher sik • poom • eem • nee • kah*
Do you have...?	…이(가) 있습니까? *ee(gah) eet • ssum • nee • kkah*
skimmed milk	탈지유 *tahl • jee • yoo*
whole milk	전지유 *jeon • jee • yoo*
soya milk	두유 *doo • yoo*

DINING WITH CHILDREN

Do you have children's portions?	어린이 메뉴 있어요? *uh • lee • nee meh • nyoo eet • ssuh • yo*
A highchair/child's seat, please.	높은/어린이용 의자 주세요. *noh • pun/uh • lee • nee • yong u • jah joo • seh • yo*
Where can I feed/ change the baby?	어디서 수유 할/기저귀 갈 수 있어요? *uh • dee • suh soo • yoo hahl/ gee • juh • gwih gahl ssoo eet • ssuh • yo*
Can you warm this?	이거 데워 주시겠어요? *ee • guh deh • wuh joo • see • geht • ssuh • yo*

For Traveling with Children, see page 136.

HOW TO COMPLAIN

How much longer will our food be?	음식 얼마나 더 기다려야 합니까? *um • seek uhl • mah • nah duh gee • dah • lyuh • yah hahm • nee • kkah*
We can't wait any longer.	더 이상은 못 기다립니다. *duh ee • sahng • un motht kkee • dah • leem • nee • dah*
We're leaving.	저희 갑니다. *juh • hee gahm • nee • dah*
I didn't order this.	이거 주문한 적 없습니다. *ee • guh joo • moon • hahn juhk uhp • ssum • nee • dah*
I ordered…	저는…시켰습니다. *juh • nun…see • kyuht • ssum • nee • dah*
I can't eat this.	이거 못 먹습니다. *ee • guh mohn muhk • ssum • nee • dah*

This is too…	너무… *nuh • moo*
cold/hot	차갑습니다/뜨겁습니다. *chah • gahp • ssum • nee • dah/ tt • geop • ssum • nee • dah*
salty/spicy	짭니다/맵습니다. *jjahm • nee • dah/mehp • ssum • nee • dah*
This isn't clean/ fresh.	이거 깨끗하지/싱싱하지 않습니다. *ee • guh kkeh • kku • tah • jee/ seeng • seeng • hah • jee ahn • ssum • nee • dah*

PAYING

The check [bill], please.	계산서 주세요. *geh • sahn • suh joo • seh • yo*
Separate checks [bills], please.	따로 계산해 주세요. *ttah • loh geh • sahn • heh joo • seh • yo*
It's all together.	함께 계산해 주세요. *hahm • kkeh geh • sahn • heh joo • seh • yo*
Is service included?	서비스 포함입니까? *service poh • hahm • eem • nee • kkah*
What's this amount for?	이 금액은 뭐지요? *ee gu • meh • gun mwuh • jee • yo*
I didn't have that. I had…	저는 그거 안 먹었는데요. 저는… 먹었어요. *juh • nun gu • guh ahn muh • guhn • nun • deh • yo juh • nun… muh • guht • ssuh • yo*
Can I have a receipt/ an itemized bill?	영수증/명세서 주시겠어요? *yuhng • soo • jung/myuhng • seh • suh joo • see • geht • ssuh • yo*

That was delicious!	맛있었습니다! *mah • seet • sshuht • ssum • nee • dah*
I've already paid.	이미 지불했습니다. *ee • mee* *jee • bool • heht • ssum • nee • dah*

Tipping in restaurants is not customary in North or South Korea. Some high-end restaurants and hotels in South Korea might include a service charge and sales tax, or value-added tax (VAT), in the total price.

MEALS & COOKING

BREAKFAST

bacon	베이컨 *beh • ee • kuhn*
bread	빵 *ppahng*
butter	버터 *buh • tuh*
cereal	시리얼 *ssee • lee • uhl*
cheese	치즈 *chee • ju*
coffee/tea...	…커피/차 *...kuh • pee/chah*
black	블랙 *bul • lehk*

decaf	카페인 없는 *kah • peh • een uhm • nun*
with milk	우유 넣은 *oo • yoo nuh • un*
with sugar	설탕 넣은 *suhl • tahng nuh • un*
with artificial sweetener	인공 감미료 넣은 *een • gohng gahm • mee • lyo nuh • un*
hard-/soft-boiled egg	완숙/반숙 계란 wahn • sook/bahn • sook geh • lahn
jam/jelly	잼/젤리 *tzehm/jehl • lee*
...juice	···주스 *...joo • su*
apple	사과 *sah • gwah*
grapefruit	자몽 *jah • mohng*
orange	오렌지 *oh • lehn • jee*
milk	우유 *oo • yoo*
oatmeal	오트밀 *oh • tu • meel*
omelet	오믈렛 *oh • mool • leht*
roll	롤빵 *lohl • ppahng*
sausage	소시지 *ssoh • seh • jee*
scrambled egg	스크램블 에그 *su • ku • lehm • bul eh • gu*

toast	토스트 *toh • su • tu*
yogurt	요구르트 *yo • goo • lu • tu*

KOREAN BREAKFAST

kimchi (pickled vegetables)	김치 *geem • chee*
poached egg	수란 *soo • lahn*
...pot stew	…찌개 *...tzee • geh*
tofu	두부 *doo • boo*
kimchi	김치 *geem • chee*
soy bean paste	된장 *dwehn • jahng*
porridge	죽 *jook*
rice	밥 *bahp*
roasted seaweed paper	구운 김 *goo • oon geem*
...soup	…국 *...kkook*
bean sprout	콩나물 *kohng • nah • mool*
radish	무 *moo*
seaweed	미역 *mee • yuhk*
soy bean paste	된장 *dwehn • jahng*

Western-style breakfast is popular, and available at most hotels. A typical Korean breakfast often consists of a bowl of rice, soup and some side dishes—similar to a Korean dinner.

spinach	시금치 *see • gum • chee*
seasoned, broiled fish	생선 구이 *sehng • suhn goo • ee*
seasoned vegetable dish with…	…나물 *…nah • mool*
green bean sprouts	숙주 *sook • tzoo*
spinach	시금치 *see • gum • chee*
squash	호박 *hoh • bahk*
steamed egg, Asian style	계란 찜 *gyeh • lahn tzeem*

SIDE DISHES

dumplings	만두 *mahn • doo*
fish cake	오뎅 *oh • dehng*
goldfish cake (pastry filled with	붕어빵 *boong • uh • ppahng*
…kimchi (pickled vegetables)	…김치 *…geem • chee*
Chinese cabbage	배추 *beh • choo*

> Kimchi is a quintessential Korean side dish, and can be made with a variety of pickled vegetables and spiced with chili pepper, ginger, salted seafood or other flavorings. Various types of kimchi are available, based on the region and season.

white Chinese cabbage	백 *behk*
young radish	총각 *chohng • gahk*
Korean sausage	순대 *soon • deh*
mung bean pancake	빈대떡 *been • deh • ttuhk*
pan-fried and breaded…	…전 *…juhn*
fillet of beef	소고기 *soh • goh • gee*
fish fillet	생선 *sehng • suhn*
sliced squash	호박 *hoh • bahk*
rice wrapped in dried seaweed paper	김밥 *geem • ppahp*
rice wrapped in lettuce	상추쌈 *sahng • choo • ssahm*
scallion pancake	파전 *pah • juhn*
seasoned, broiled fish dishes	생선 구이 *sehng • suhn goo • ee*
stir-fried anchovy	멸치 볶음 *myuhl • chee bohk • kkum*

> Throughout South Korea, you'll find many street vendors selling a variety of delicious snacks; these treats are very popular and often nutritious as well. Stop at a 포장마차 *poh • jahng mah • chah* (literally, covered cart bar) to enjoy some local flavors.

stir-fried rice cake with spicy sauce	떡볶이 *ttuhk • ppohk • kkee*
tofu kimchi	두부 김치 *doo • boo geem • chee*

SOUP

beef and bone stew	설렁탕 *suhl • luhng • tahng*
beef rib soup	갈비탕 *gahl • bee • tahng*
ginseng chicken soup	삼계탕 *sahm • geh • tahng*
...soup	…국 *...kkook*
bean sprout	콩나물 *kohng • nah • mool*
dumpling	만두 *mahn • doo*
Korean radish	무 *moo*
rice cake	떡 *ttuhk*
seaweed	미역 *mee • yuhk*

soy bean paste	된장 *dwehn • jahng*
spinach	시금치 *see • gum • chee*

FISH & SEAFOOD

assorted, raw fish	모듬회 *moh • dum • hweh*
clam	조개 *joh • geh*
cod fish soup	대구탕 *deh • goo • tahng*
crab	게 *geh*
grilled eel	장어 구이 *jahng • uh goo • ee*
halibut	넙치 *nuhp • chee*
herring	청어 *chuhng • uh*
lobster	바닷가재 *bah • daht • kkah • jeh*
mackerel	고등어 *goh • dung • uh*
mixed seafood stew	해물 잡탕 *heh • mool jahp • tahng*
monkfish stew	아구탕 *ah • goo • tahng*
mussel	홍합 *hohng • hahp*
octopus	문어 *moo • nuh*

oyster	굴 *gool*
pickled crab in soy sauce	간장 게장 *gahn • jahng geh • jahng*
pollack	명태 *myuhng • teh*
pufferfish	복어 *boh • guh*
salmon	연어 *yuh • nuh*
sea bass	농어 *nohng • uh*
shrimp	새우 *seh • oo*
squid	오징어 *oh • jeeng • uh*
tuna	참치 *chahm • chee*
whitebait	뱅어 *behng • uh*
yellow corvina	조기 *joh • gee*

MEAT & POULTRY

barbecued beef dish	불고기 *bool • goh • gee*
beef	소고기 *soh • goh • gee*
chicken	닭고기 *dahk • kkoh • gee*
duck	오리고기 *oh • lee • goh • gee*

grilled breast of chicken	닭가슴살 구이 *dahk • kkah • sum • sahl goo • ee*
ham	햄 *hehm*
lamb	양고기 *yahng • goh • gee*
leg	다리 *dah • lee*
liver	간 *gahn*
pork	돼지고기 *dweh • jee • goh • gee*
rib of beef	갈비 *gahl • bee*
rib of pork	돼지갈비 *dweh • jee • gahl • bee*
sausage	소시지 *ssoh • seh • jee*
sirloin steak	등심 스테이크 *dung • seem su • teh • ee • ku*
steak	스테이크 *su • teh • ee • ku*
T-bone steak	티본 스테이크 *tee • bohn su • teh • ee • ku*

VEGETABLES & STAPLES

avocado	아보카도 *ah • boh • kah • doh*
bean sprouts	콩나물 *kohng • nah • mool*
bread	빵 *ppahng*

broccoli	브로콜리	*bu • loh • kohl • lee*
buckwheat noodles with eggs, vegetables and red pepper paste	비빔냉면	*bee • beem • nehng • myuhn* *bee • beem • nehng • myuhn*
cabbage	양배추	*yahng • beh • choo*
carrot	당근	*dahng • gun*
Chinese bellflower	도라지	*doh • lah • jee*
Chinese cabbage	배추	*beh • choo*
cold buckwheat noodles in broth with beef, eggs, Korean radish and mustard	물냉면	*mool • lehng • myuhn*
cold noodles with vegetables and red pepper paste	비빔국수	*bee • beem • gook • ssoo*
corn	옥수수	*ohk • ssoo • soo*
cucumber	오이	*oh • ee*
eggplant [aubergine]	가지	*gah • jee*
five-grain rice	오곡밥	*oh • gohk • ppahp*
garlic	마늘	*mah • nul*
green bean	녹두콩	*nohk • doo • kohng*
green pepper	피망	*pee • mahng*
handmade noodles with soup	칼국수	*kahl • gook • ssoo*

kelp	다시마 *dah • see • mah*
Korean radish	무 *moo*
kosari (fern)	고사리 *goh • sah • lee*
lettuce (head/leaf)	양상추/상추 *yahng • sahng • choo/ sahng • choo*
mung bean	녹두 *nohk • ttoo*
mushroom	버섯 *buh • suht*
noodle cassorole	국수 전골 *gook • ssoo juhn • gohl*
olive	올리브 *ohl • lee • bu*
onion	양파 *yahng • pah*
pea	완두콩 *wahn • doo • kohng*
potato	감자 *gahm • jah*
potato cakes	감자전 *gahm • jah • juhn*
red chili pepper	고추 *goh • choo*
rice (uncooked/cooked)	밥/밥 *ssahl/bahp*
rice cooked with bean sprouts	콩나물밥 *kohng • nah • mool • ppahp*
rice with nuts and herbs in a stone pot	영양 돌솥밥 *yuhng • yahng dohl • soht • ppahp*

rice with red beans	팥밥 *paht • ppahp*
rice with vegetables and fried egg, mixed with red pepper sauce	비빔밥 *bee • beem • ppahp*
seaweed	미역 *mee • yuhk*
shiitake (mushroom)	표고(버섯) *pyo • goh (buh • suht)*
spinach	시금치 *see • gum • chee*
spring onion	파 *pah*
squash	호박 *hoh • bahk*
stir-fried noodles with vegetables and meat	잡채 *jahp • cheh*
stir-fried rice with vegetables	볶음밥 *bohk • kkum • bahp*
sweet potato	고구마 *goh • goo • mah*
sweet red pepper	빨간 피망 *ppal • gahn pee • mahng*
tofu kimchi	두부 김치 *doo • boo geem • chee*
tomato	토마토 *toh • mah • toh*
vegetable	채소 *cheh • soh*
wheat noodles with onions, bean curd, red pepper powder and egg	우동 *oo • dohng*

FRUIT

apple	사과 *sah • gwah*
banana	바나나 *bah • nah • nah*
blueberry	블루베리 *bul • loo • beh • lee*
cherry	체리 *cheh • lee*
fruit	과일 *gwah • eel*
grape	포도 *poh • doh*
grapefruit	자몽 *jah • mohng*
Korean melon	참외 *chah • mweh*
Korean pear	배 *beh*
lemon	레몬 *leh • mohn*
lime	라임 *lah • eem*
mandarin	귤 *gyool*
orange	오렌지 *oh • lehn • jee*
peach	복숭아 *bohk • ssoong • ah*
persimmon	감 *gahm*
pineapple	파인애플 *pah • ee • neh • pul*

plum	자두 *jah • doo*
raspberry	산딸기 *sahn • ttahl • gee*
strawberry	딸기 *ttahl • gee*
watermelon	수박 *soo • bahk*

DESSERT

cinnamon punch	수정과 *soo • juhng • gwah*
honey cake	약과 *yahk • kkwah*
ice cream	아이스크림 *ah • ee • su • ku • leem*
sesame cake	깨강정 *kkeh • gahng • johng*
spiced rice with nuts and raisins	약식 *yahk • sseek*
square rice cake with bean flour	인절미 *een • juhl • mee*
steamed rice cake with chestnuts or sesame seeds	송편 *sohng • pyuhn*
sweet, fried rice cake	화전 *hwah • juhn*
sweet rice cake dumpling	경단 *gyuhng • dahn*
sweet rice punch	식혜 *seek • keh*

SAUCES & CONDIMENTS

salt	소금 *soh • guhm*
pepper	후추 *hoo • choo*
mustard	겨자 *gyuh • jah*
ketchup	케첩 *ketchup*

AT THE MARKET

Where are the trolleys/baskets?	카트/바구니 어디 있어요? *kah • tu/bah • goo • nee uh • dee eet • ssuh • yo*
Where is...?	…어디 있어요? *...uh • dee eet • ssuh • yo*
I'd like some of that /this.	저거/이거 주세요. *juh • guh/ee • guh joo • seh • yo*
Can I taste it?	먹어 봐도되요? *muh • guh bwah • doh dweh • yo*
I'd like...	…주세요. *...joo • seh • yo*
a bottle of...	…한 병 *...hahn byuhng*
a kilo/half-kilo of...	…일 킬로/오백 그램 *...eel kee • loh/oh • bek gu • lehm*
a liter of...	…일 리터 *...eel lee • tuh*
more/less	더 많이/더 조금 *duh mah • nee/duh joh • gum*
How much?	얼마예요? *uhl • mah • yeh • yo*

Where do I pay?	어디서 계산해요? *uh • dee • suh geh • sahn • heh • yo*
A bag, please.	봉지 주세요. *bohng • jee joo • seh • yo*
I'm being helped.	다른 분이 도와 주고 계세요. *dah • lun boo • nee doh • wah joo • goh geh • seh • yo*

YOU MAY HEAR...

무엇을 도와드릴까요? *moo • uh • sul doh • wah • du • leel • kkah • yo*	Can I help you?
뭐 드릴까요? *mwuh du • leel • kkah • yo*	What would you like?
더 필요한 거 없으세요? *duh pee • lyo • hahn guh uhp • ssu • seh • yo*	Anything else?
…원이에요. *…wuh • nee • yeh • yo*	That's...Won.

IN THE KITCHEN

bottle opener	병따개 *byuhng • ttah • geh*
bowl	사발 *sah • bahl*
can opener	통조림 따개 *tohng • joh • leem ttah • geh*
chopsticks	젓가락 *juht • kkah • lahk*
corkscrew	코르크 마개뽑이 *koh • lu • ku mah • geh • ppoh • bee*
cup	컵 *kuhp*

fork	포크 *poh • ku*
frying pan	후라이팬 *hoo • lah • ee • pehn*
glass	유리잔 *yoo • lee • jahn*
(steak) knife	(스테이크) 칼 *(su • teh • ee • ku) kahl*
measuring cup/ spoon	계량 컵/스푼 *gyeh • lyahng kuhp/su • poon*
napkin	냅킨 *nehp • keen*
plate	접시 *juhp • ssee*

YOU MAY SEE...

유통 기한…까지 *yoo • tohng gee • hahn...kkah • jee*	best if used by...
칼로리 *kal • loh • lee*	calories
무지방 *moo • jee • bahng*	fat free
냉장 요 *nehng • jahng yo*	keep refrigerated
…을(를) 함유하고 있을 수 있습니다. *eul(reul) hahm • yoo • hah • goh eet • ssul sso eet • ssum • nee • dah*	may contain traces of...
전자레인지 사용 가능 *juhn • jah • leh • een • jee sah • yong gah • nung*	microwaveable
유통 기한…까지 *yoo • tohng gee • hahn...kkah • jee*	sell by...
채식주의자에게 알맞음 *cheh • seek • tzoo • ee • jah • eh • geh ahl • mah • zuhm*	suitable for vegetarians

pot	냄비 *nehm • bee*
rice bowl	밥 그릇 *bahp kku • lut*
rice cooker	밥솥 *bahp • ssoht*
soup bowl	국 그릇 *gook kku • lut*
spoon	숟가락 *soot • kkah • lahk*
steamer	찜통 *tzeem • tohng*

DRINKS

NEED TO KNOW

The wine list/drink menu, please.	와인/주류 메뉴 주세요. *wah • een/joo • lyoo meh • nyoo joo • seh • yo*
What do you recommend?	뭐 추천하세요? *mwuh choo • chuhn • hah • seh • yo*
I'd like a glass/bottle of red/white wine.	적/백 포도주 한 잔/병 주세요. *juhk/behk poh • doh • joo han jahn/ byuhng joo • seh • yo*
The house wine, please.	하우스 와인 주세요. *hah • oo • su wah • een joo • seh • yo*
Another bottle/ glass, please.	한 병/잔 더 주세요. *hahn byuhng/jahn duh joo • seh • yo*

I'd like a local beer.	국산 맥주 주세요. *gook • ssahn mehk • tzoo joo • seh • yo*
Can I buy you a drink?	제가 한 잔 사도 될까요? *jeh • gah hahn jahn sah • doh dwehl • kkah • yo*
Cheers!	건배! *guhn • beh*
A coffee/tea, please.	커피/차 주세요. *kuh • pee/chah joo • seh • yo*
Black.	블랙으로요. *bul • leh • gu • loh • yo*
With...	…넣어서 *...nuh • uh • suh*
milk	우유 *oo • yoo*
sugar	설탕 *suhl • tahng*
artificial sweetener	인공 감미료 *een • gohng gahm • mee • lyo*
..., please.	…주세요. *...joo • seh • yo*
Juice	주스 *joo • su*
Soda	탄산음료 *tahn • sahn • um • nyo*
Sparkling/Spring water	탄산수/생수 *tahn • sahn • soo/sehng • soo*
Is the water safe to drink?	물 마시기에 안전해요? *mool mah • see • gee • eh ahn • juhn • heh • yo*

NON-ALCOHOLIC DRINKS

커피 *kuh • pee*	coffee
콜라 *kohl • lah*	cola
코코아 *koh • koh • ah*	hot chocolate
주스 *joo • su*	juice
레모네이드 *leh • moh • neh • ee • du*	lemonade
우유 *oo • yoo*	milk
식혜 *seek • keh*	rice punch
탄산음료 *tahn • sahn • um • nyo*	soda
두유 *doo • yoo*	soy milk
탄산수/생수 *tahn • sahn • soo/ sehng • soo*	sparkling/spring water
수정과 *soo • juhng • gwah*	sweet cinnamon punch
(아이스) 티 *(ah • ee • su) tee*	(iced) tea
…차 *…chah*	…tea
보리 *boh • lee*	barley
홍 *hohng*	black
옥수수 *ohk • ssoo • soo*	corn

Tea has been an integral part of Korean life for nearly 1,000 years, and the great variety of tea available would please any palate. Visiting a traditional teahouse, participating in a tea ceremony or enjoying a green tea festival are just a few ways one can experience the tasteful tea culture while in South Korea.

생강 *sehng • gahng* — ginger

인삼 *een • sahm* — ginseng

녹 *nohk* — green

오미자 *oh • mee • jah* — 'five-taste' fruit

APERITIFS, COCKTAILS & LIQUEURS

브랜디 *bu • lehn • dee* — brandy

진 *jeen* — gin

인삼주 *een • sahm • joo* — ginseng liquor

막걸리 *mahk • kkuhl • lee* — mild, unrefined rice liquor

럼 *luhm* — rum

스카치 *su • kah • chee* — scotch

소주 *soh • joo* — soju (Korean liquor similar to vodka)

YOU MAY HEAR...

음료수 갖다 드릴까요? *um • nyo • soo gaht • ttah du • leel • kkah • yo*	Can I get you a drink?
우유나 설탕을 넣을까요? *oo • yoo • nah suhl • tahng • eul nuh • eul • kka • yo*	With milk or sugar?
탄산수요, 생수요? *tahn • sahn • soo • yo sehng • soo • yo*	Sparkling or spring water?

테킬라 *teh • kkeel • lah*	tequila
보드카 *boh • du • kah*	vodka
위스키 *wih • su • kee*	whisky

BEER

…맥주 *...mehk • tzoo*	...beer
병/생 *byuhng/sehng*	bottled/draft
흑/순한 *huk/soon • hahn*	dark/light
국산/수입 *gook • ssahn/soo • eep*	local/imported
무알콜 *moo • ahl • kohl*	non-alcoholic

WINE

과실주 *gwah • seel • tzoo*	fruit wine
정종 *juhng • johng*	Korean sake
복분자주 *bohk • ppoon • jah • joo*	raspberry wine
적/백 포도주 *juhk/behk poh • doh • joo*	red/white wine
동동주 *dohng • dohng • joo*	rice wine
법주 *buhp • tzoo*	rice wine of high quality

ON THE MENU

전복 *juhn • bohk*	abalone (seafood)
아몬드 *ah • mohn • du*	almond
멸치 *myuhl • chee*	anchovy
사과 *sah • gwah*	apple
살구 *sahl • goo*	apricot
인공 감미료 *een • gohng gahm • mee • lyo*	artificial sweetener
아보카도 *ah • boh • kah • doh*	avocado
베이컨 *beh • ee • kuhn*	bacon

바나나 *bah • nah • nah*	banana
불고기 *bool • goh • gee*	barbecued beef dish
보리 *boh • lee*	barley
농어 *nohng • uh*	bass
콩나물국 *kohng • nah • mool • kkook*	bean sprout soup
콩나물 *kohng • nah • mool*	bean sprouts
소고기 *soh • goh • gee*	beef
곰국 *gohm • kkook*	beef and bone soup
설렁탕 *suhl • luhng • tahng*	beef and bone stew
갈비탕 *gahl • bee • tahng*	beef rib soup
갈비찜 *gahl • bee • tzeem*	beef rib stew
맥주 *mehk • tzoo*	beer
블루베리 *bul • loo • beh • lee*	blueberry
빵 *ppahng*	bread
닭가슴살 *dahk • kkah • sum • sahl*	breast (of chicken)
육수 *yook • ssoo*	broth
메밀국수 *meh • meel • gook • ssoo*	buckwheat noodles

비빔냉면 *bee • beem • nehng • myuhn*	buckwheat noodles with eggs, vegetables and red pepper paste
버터 *buh • tuh*	butter
양배추 *yahng • beh • choo*	cabbage
케이크 *keh • ee • ku*	cake
사탕 *sah • tahng*	candy [sweets]
캐러멜 *keh • luh • mehl*	caramel
당근 *dahng • gun*	carrot
신선로 *seen • suhl • loh*	casserole of meat, fish, vegetables, nuts and quail eggs
셀러리 *ssehl • luh • lee*	celery
시리얼 *ssee • lee • uhl*	cereal
치즈 *chee • ju*	cheese
체리 *cheh • lee*	cherry
밤 *bahm*	chestnut
닭고기 *dahk • kkoh • gee*	chicken
닭갈비 *dahk • kkahl • bee*	chicken pan-fried with vegetables and hot spices

닭찜 *dahk • tzeem*	chicken stewed with onions, carrots, garlic, black and red pepper, salt or soy sauce
치커리 *chee • kuh • lee*	chicory
고추 *goh • choo*	chili pepper
도라지 *doh • lah • jee*	Chinese bellflower
배추 *beh • choo*	Chinese cabbage
배추김치 *beh • choo • geem • chee*	Chinese cabbage kimchi
초콜릿 *choh • kohl • leet*	chocolate
자른 고기 *jah • lun goh • gee*	chopped [minced] meat
계피 *gyeh • pee*	cinnamon
조개 *joh • geh*	clam
대구 *deh • goo*	cod fish
대구탕 *deh • goo • tahng*	cod fish soup
커피 *kuh • pee*	coffee
물냉면 *mool • lehng • myuhn*	cold buckwheat noodles in broth with beef, eggs, Korean radish and mustard

비빔국수 *bee • beem • gook • ssoo*	cold noodles with vegetables and red pepper paste
쿠키 *koo • kee*	cookie [biscuit]
게 *geh*	crab
게살 *geh • ssahl*	crabmeat
크래커 *ku • leh • kuh*	cracker
크림 *ku • leem*	cream
크림치즈 *ku • leem • chee • ju*	cream cheese
휘핑크림 *hwih • peeng • ku • leem*	cream, whipped
오이 *oh • ee*	cucumber
커스터드 *kuh • su • tuh • du*	custard
깍두기 *kkahk • ttoo • gee*	diced radish kimchi
회덮밥 *hweh • duhp • ppahp*	diced raw fish with mixed vegetables on rice
도넛 *doh • nuht*	doughnut
곶감 *kkoht • kkahm*	dried persimmon

오리고기 *oh • lee • goh • gee*	duck
만두 *mahn • doo*	dumpling
만두국 *mahn • doo • kkook*	dumpling soup
장어 *jahng • uh*	eel
계란 *geh • lahn*	egg
가지 *gah • jee*	eggplant [aubergine]
생선 *sehng • suhn*	fish
오뎅 *oh • dehng*	fish cake
오곡밥 *oh • gohk • ppahp*	five-grain rice
감자튀김 *gahm • jah • twih • geem*	French fries
과일 *gwah • eel*	fruit
마늘 *mah • nul*	garlic
마늘소스 *mah • nul • ssoh • su*	garlic sauce
닭내장 *dahng • neh • jahng*	giblet
진 *jeen*	gin
생강 *sehng • gahng*	ginger
삼계탕 *sahm • geh • tahng*	ginseng chicken soup

붕어빵 *boong • uh • ppahng*	goldfish cake (pastry filled with sweet red bean paste)
자몽 *jah • mohng*	grapefruit
포도 *poh • doh*	grapes
닭가슴살 구이 *dahk • kkah • sum • sahl goo • ee*	grilled breast of chicken
장어 구이 *jahng • uh goo • ee*	grilled eel
넙치 *nuhp • chee*	halibut
햄 *hehm*	ham
햄버거 *hehm • buh • guh*	hamburger
칼국수 *kahl • gook • ssoo*	handmade noodles with soup
헤이즐넛 *heh • ee • jul • nuht*	hazelnut
암탉 *ahm • tahk*	hen
허브 *huh • bu*	herb
청어 *chuhng • uh*	herring
꿀 *kkool*	honey
약과 *yahk • kkwah*	honey cake

매운탕 *meh • oon • tahng*	hot and spicy fish stew
고추장 *goh • choo • jahng*	hot chilli pepper paste
핫도그 *haht • doh • gu*	hot dog
얼음 *uh • lum*	ice (cube)
아이스크림 *ah • ee • su • ku • leem*	ice cream
잼 *tzehm*	jam
젤리 *jehl • lee*	jelly
주스 *joo • su*	juice
대추 *deh • choo*	jujube (fruit)
다시마 *dah • see • mah*	kelp
케첩 *keh • chuhp*	ketchup
김치 *geem • chee*	kimchi (pickled vegetables)
키위 *kee • wih*	kiwi
떡 *ttuhk*	Korean cake (generic)
참외 *chah • mweh*	Korean melon
배 *beh*	Korean pear

무 *moo*	Korean radish
순대 *soon • deh*	Korean sausage
한과 *hahn • gwah*	Korean traditional sweets (generic)
양고기 *yahng • goh • gee*	lamb
다리 *dah • lee*	leg
레몬 *leh • mohn*	lemon
레모네이드 *leh • moh • neh • ee • du*	lemonade
상추 *sahng • choo*	lettuce (leaf)
술 *sool*	liqueur
간 *gahn*	liver
바닷가재 *bah • daht • kkah • jeh*	lobster
마카로니 *mah • kah • loh • nee*	macaroni
고등어 *goh • dung • uh*	mackerel
망고 *mahng • goh*	mango
마요네즈 *mah • yo • neh • ju*	mayonnaise
고기 *goh • gee*	meat
메론 *meh • lohn*	melon

우유 *oo • yoo*	milk
밀크 셰이크 *meel • ku syeh • ee • ku*	milk shake
박하 *bah • kah*	mint
해물 잡탕 *heh • mool jahp • tahng*	mixed seafood stew
아구 *ah • goo*	monkfish
아구탕 *ah • goo • tahng*	monkfish stew
빈대떡 *been • deh • ttuhk*	mung bean pancake
버섯 *buh • suht*	mushroom
홍합 *hohng • hahp*	mussel
겨자 *gyuh • jah*	mustard
국수 *gook • ssoo*	noodle
국수 전골 *gook • ssoo juhn • gohl*	noodle cassorole
견과류 *gyuhn • gwah • lyoo*	nuts
문어 *moo • nuh*	octopus
올리브 *ohl • lee • bu*	olive
올리브유 *ohl • lee • bu • yoo*	olive oil
오물렛 *oh • mool • leht*	omelet

양파 *yahng • pah*	onion
오렌지 *oh • lehn • jee*	orange
내장 *neh • jahng*	organ meat [offal]
소 *soh*	ox
소꼬리 *soh • kkoh • lee*	oxtail
굴 *gool*	oyster
팬케이크 *pehn • keh • ee • ku*	pancake
복숭아 *bohk • ssoong • ah*	peach
땅콩 *ttahng • kohng*	peanut
완두콩 *wahn • doo • kohng*	peas
후추/고추 *hoo • choo/goh • choo*	pepper (seasoning/ vegetable)
깻잎 *kkehn • neep*	perilla (herb)
감 *gahm*	persimmon
피클 *pee • kul*	pickle
간장 게장 *gahn • jahng geh • jahng*	pickled crab in soy sauce
파이 *pah • ee*	pie
파인애플 *pah • ee • neh • pul*	pineapple

피자 *pee • tzah*	pizza
자두 *jah • doo*	plum
수란 *soo • lahn*	poached egg
명태 *myuhng • teh*	pollack
석류 *suhng • nyoo*	pomegranate
돼지고기 *dweh • jee • goh • gee*	pork
죽 *jook*	porridge
찌개 *tzee • geh*	pot stew
감자 *gahm • jah*	potato
감자칩 *gahm • jah • cheep*	potato chips [crisps]
복어 *boh • guh*	pufferfish
복어 매운탕 *boh • guh meh • oon • tahng*	pufferfish and hot pepper stew
늙은 호박 *nul • gun hoh • bahk*	pumpkin
무국 *moo • kkook*	radish soup
건포도 *guhn • poh • doh*	raisin
산딸기 *sahn • ttahl • gee*	raspberry

빨간 양배추 *ppahl • gahn yahng • beh • choo*	red cabbage
갈비 *gahl • bee*	rib of beef
돼지갈비 *dweh • jee • gahl • bee*	rib of pork
밥/밥 *bahp/ssahl*	rice (cooked/ uncooked)
콩나물밥 *kohng • nah • mool • ppahp*	rice with bean sprouts
영양 돌솥밥 *yuhng • yahng dohl • soht • ppahp*	rice with nuts and herbs in a hot hot stone pot
팥밥 *paht • ppahp*	rice with red beans
비빔밥 *bee • beem • ppahp*	rice with vegetables and fried egg, mixed with red pepper sauce
김밥 *geem • ppahp*	rice wrapped in dried seaweed paper
상추쌈 *sahng • choo • ssahm*	rice wrapped in lettuce
구운 김 *goo • oon geem*	roasted seaweed paper
롤빵 *lohl ppahng*	roll
로즈메리 *loh • ju • meh • lee*	rosemary
샐러드 *ssehl • luh • du*	salad

연어 *yuh • nuh*	salmon
훈제 연어 *hoon • jeh yuh • nuh*	salmon, smoked
소금 *soh • gum*	salt
샌드위치 ssehn • du • wih • chee	sandwich
소스 *ssoh • su*	sauce
소시지 *ssoh • seh • jee*	sausage
파 *pah*	scallion [spring onion]
파전 *pah • juhn*	scallion pancake
가리비 *gah • lee • bee*	scallop
스카치 *su • kah • chee*	scotch
해산물 *heh • sahn • mool*	seafood
쌈장 *ssahm • jahng*	seasoned soy bean paste with hot pepper paste
북어찜 *boo • guh • tzeem*	seasoned steamed pollack
생선 구이 *sehng • suhn goo • ee*	seasoned, broiled fish
조미료 *joh • mee • lyo*	seasoning
미역 *mee • yuhk*	seaweed
미역국 *mee • yuhk • kkook*	seaweed soup

깨강정 *kkeh • gahng • johng*	sesame cake
조개류 *joh • geh • lyoo*	shellfish
어깨 살 *uh • kkeh ssahl*	shoulder
새우 *seh • oo*	shrimp
등심 *dung • seem*	sirloin
등심 스테이크 *dung • seem su • teh • ee • ku*	sirloin steak
간식 *gahn • seek*	snack
탄산음료 tahn • sah • num • nyo	soda
서대기 *suh • deh • gee*	sole
국 *gook*	soup
콩 *kohng*	soy bean [soya bean]
된장 *dwehn • jahng*	soy bean paste
된장국 *dwehn • jahng • kkook*	soy bean paste soup
두유 *doo • yoo*	soy milk [soya milk]
간장 *gahn • jahng*	soy sauce
스파게티 *su • pah • geh • tee*	spaghetti
양념 *yahng • nyuhm*	spices

시금치 *see • gum • chee*	spinach
시금치국 *see • gum • chee • kkook*	spinach soup
인절미 *een • juhl • mee*	square rice cake coated with bean flour
호박 *hoh • bahk*	squash
오징어 *oh • jeeng • uh*	squid
스테이크 *su • teh • ee • ku*	steak
계란 찜 *gyeh • lahn tzeem*	steamed egg, Asian style
송편 *sohng • pyuhn*	steamed half-moon rice cake, stuffed with chestnuts or sesame seeds
생선 초밥 *sehng • suhn choh • bahp*	steamed rice balls with raw fish topping
전골 *juhn • gohl*	stew made with tofu and/or vegetables
멸치 볶음 *myuhl • chee bohk • kkum*	stir-fried anchovy
떡볶이 *ttuhk • ppohk • kkee*	stir-fried rice cake with spicy sauce
볶음밥 *bohk • kkum • bahp*	stir-fried rice with vegetables

잡채 *jahp • cheh*	stir-fried vermicelli noodles with vegetables and meat
딸기 *ttahl • gee*	strawberry
설탕 *suhl • tahng*	sugar
수정과 *soo • juhng • gwah*	sweet cinnamon punch
고구마 *goh • goo • mah*	sweet potato
경단 *gyuhng • dahn*	sweet rice cake dumpling
식혜 *seek • keh*	sweet rice punch
화전 *hwah • juhn*	sweet, fried rice cake
약식 *yahk • sseek*	sweet, spiced rice flavored with nuts and raisins
감미료 *gahm • mee • lyo*	sweetener
황새치 *hwahng • seh • chee*	swordfish
시럽 *see • luhp*	syrup
감귤 *gahm • gyool*	tangerine
티본 스테이크 *tee • bohn su • teh • ee • ku*	T-bone steak
차 *chah*	tea

안심 *ahn • seem*	tenderloin
토스트 *toh • su • tu*	toast
두부 *doo • boo*	tofu
두부 김치 *doo • boo geem • chee*	tofu kimchi
토마토 *toh • mah • toh*	tomato
혀 *hyuh*	tongue
탄산수 *tahn • sahn • soo*	tonic water
곱창 전골 *gohp • chahng juhn • gohl*	tripe in a spicy beef broth with noodles and vegetables
송어 *sohng • uh*	trout
참치 *chahm • chee*	tuna
삼겹살 *sahm • gyuhp • ssahl*	unseasoned pork bacon
바닐라 *bah • neel • lah*	vanilla
송아지 고기 *sohng • ah • jee goh • gee*	veal
채소 *cheh • soh*	vegetable
식초 *seek • choh*	vinegar
와플 *wah • pul*	waffle

호두 *hoh • doo*	walnut
물 *mool*	water
수박 *soo • bahk*	watermelon
밀 *meel*	wheat
우동 *oo • dohng*	wheat noodles with onions, fried soybean curd, red pepper powder and egg
위스키 *wee • su • kee*	whisky
백김치 *behk • geem • chee*	white Chinese cabbage kimchi
뱅어 *behng • uh*	whitebait
조기 *joh • gee*	yellow corvina (fish)
요구르트 *yo • goo • ru • tu*	yogurt
총각김치 *chohng • gahk • geem • chee*	young radish kimchi

GOING OUT

GOING OUT

NEED TO KNOW

What's there to do at night?	밤에 할 거 뭐 있습니까? *bah • meh hahl kkuh mwuh eet • ssum • nee • kkah*
Do you have a program of events?	행사 프로그램 있습니까? *hehng • sah pu • loh • gu • lehm eet • ssum • nee • kkah*
What's playing tonight?	오늘 밤에 뭐 있습니까? *oh • nul bah • meh mwuh eet • ssum • nee • kkah*
Where's...?	…어디 있습니까? *...uh • dee eet • ssum • nee • kkah*
the downtown area	시내 *see • neh*
the bar	바 *bah*
the dance club	클럽 *kul • luhp*
Is there a cover charge?	입장료 있습니까? *eep • tzahng • nyo eet • ssum • nee • kkah*

ENTERTAINMENT

Can you recommend...?	…추천해 주시겠습니까? *...choo • chuhn • heh joo • see • geht • ssum • nee • kkah*

a traditional dance event event	전통 춤 *juhn • tohng choom*
a traditional music event	국악 공연 *goo • gahk kkohng • yuhn*
an opera	오페라 *oh • peh • lah*
Can you recommend...?	…추천해 주시겠습니까? *...choo • chuhn • heh joo • see • geht • ssum • nee • kkah*
a play	연극 *yuhn • guk*
When does it start/ end?	언제 시작합니까/끝납니까? *uhn • jeh see • jah • kahm • nee • kkah/ kkun • nahm • nee • kkah*
Where's...?	…어디 있습니까? *...uh • dee eet • ssum • nee • kkah*
the concert hall	연주회장 *yuhn • joo • hweh • jahng*
the opera house	오페라 하우스 *oh • peh • lah hah • oo • su*
the theater	극장 *guk • tzahng*
What's the dress code?	옷은 어떻게 입어야 됩니까 ? *oh • sun uh • ttuh • keh ee • buh • yah dwehm • nee • kkah*
What's playing tonight?	오늘 밤에 뭐 있습니까? *oh • nul bah • meh mwuh eet • ssum • nee • kkah*
I like...	저는 ...을(를) 좋아합니다. *juh • nun...eul(reul) joh • ah • hahm • nee • dah*
classical music	클래식 음악 *classic eu • mahk*

folk music	민속 음악 *min • sohk eu • mahk*
jazz	재즈 *jazz*
pop music	팝 음악 *pop eu • mahk*
rap	랩 *rap*

For Tickets, see page 48.

Information on upcoming events can be found in two English-language newspapers, *The Korea Times* and *The Korea Herald*; your hotel concierge, the local tourist information office and the Korean National Tourism Organization (KNTO) and Korean Broadcasting Commission (KBS) websites can also provide entertainment details (www.visitkorea.or.kr; www.kbs.co.kr).

YOU MAY HEAR...

휴대폰 꺼 주시기 바랍니다. *hyoo • deh • pohn kkuh joo • see • gee bah • lahm • nee • dah*	Turn off your cell [mobile] phones, please.

NIGHTLIFE

What's there to do at night?	밤에 할 거 뭐 있습니까? *bah • meh hahl kkuh mwuh eet • ssum • nee • kkah*
Can you recommend...?	…을(를) 추천해 주시겠습니까? *...eul(reul) choo • chuhn • heh joo • si • geht • ssum • nee • kkah*
a bar	바 *bah*
a casino	카지노 *kah • jee • noh*
a dance club	클럽 *kul • luhp*
a gay club	게이 클럽 *gay • club*
a jazz club	재즈 클럽 *tzeh • ju kul • luhp*
a club with Korean music	한국 음악 나오는 클럽 *hahn • goo gu • mahk nah • oh • nun kul • luhp*
Is there live music?	생음악 있습니까? *sehng • u • mahk eet • ssum • nee • kkah*

How do I get there?	거기 어떻게 갑니까? *guh • gee uh • ttuh • keh gahm • nee • kkah*
Is there a cover charge?	입장료 있습니까? *eep • tzahng • nyo eet • ssum • nee • kkah*
Let's go dancing.	춤추러 갑시다. *choom • choo • luh gahp • ssee • dah*
Is this area safe at night?	이 지역은 밤에 안전합니까? *ee jee • yeok • eun bahm • eh ahn • jeon • hahm • nee • kkah*

ROMANCE

NEED TO KNOW

Would you like to go out for a drink/dinner?	술 한 잔/저녁 같이 하실래요? *sool hahn jahn/juh • nyuhk gah • chee hah • seel • leh • yo*
What are your plans for tonight/tomorrow?	오늘/내일 뭐 하세요? *oh • nul/neh • eel mwuh hah • seh • yo*
Can I have your number?	전화번호 주시겠어요? *juhn • hwah • buhn • hoh joo • see • geht • ssuh • yo*
Can I join you?	같이 앉아도 될까요? *gah • chee ahn • jah • doh dwehl • kkah • yo*
Can I get you a drink?	마실 거 갖다 드릴까요? *mah • seel kkuh gaht • ttah du • leel • kkah • yo*
I like/love you.	좋아해요/사랑해요. *joh • ah • heh • yo/sah • lahng • heh • yo*

THE DATING GAME

Would you like to go out for...?	…같이 하실래요? *...gah • chee hah • seel • leh • yo*
coffee	커피 한 잔 *kuh • pee hahn jahn*
a drink	술 한 잔 *sool hahn jahn*
dinner	저녁 *juh • nyuhk*
What are your plans for...?	…무슨 계획 있으세요? *...moo • sun geh • hwehk eet • ssu • seh • yo*
today	오늘 *oh • nul*
tonight	오늘밤 *oh • nul • ppahm*
tomorrow	내일 *neh • eel*
this weekend	이번 주말 *ee • buhn tzoo • mahl*
Where would you like to go?	어디 가실래요? *uh • dee gah • seel • leh • yo*

I'd like to go to…	…가고 싶어요. *…gah • goh see • puh • yo*
Do you like…?	…좋아하세요? *…joh • ah • hah • seh • yo*
Can I have your number/e-mail?	전화번호/이메일 주소 주시겠어요? *juhn • hwah • buhn • hoh/ee • meh • eel joo • soh joo • see • geht • ssuh • yo*
Are you on Facebook/Twitter?	Facebook/Twitter를 사용합니까? *facebook/twitter • ruel sah • yong • hahm • nee • kkah*
Can I join you?	같이 앉아도 될까요? *gah • chee ahn • jah • doh dwehl • kkah • yo*
You're very attractive.	정말 매력적이세요 *juhng • mahl meh • lyuhk • tzuh • gee • seh • yo*
Let's go somewhere quieter.	더 조용한 곳으로 가요. *duh joh • yong • hahn goh • su • loh gah • yo.*

For Communications, see page 88.

ACCEPTING & REJECTING

I'd love to.	좋아요. *joh • ah • yo*
Where should we meet?	어디서 만날까요? *uh • dee • suh mahn • nahl • kkah • yo*
I'll meet you at the bar/ your hotel.	바에서/호텔에서 뵐게요. *bah • eh • suh/hoh • teh • leh • suh bwehl • kkeh • yo*
I'll come by at…	…시에 들를게요. *…see • eh dul • lul • kkeh • yo*

I'm busy. 저 바빠요.
juh bah • ppah • yo

I'm not interested. 관심 없어요.
gwahn • seem uhp • ssuh • yo

Leave me alone. 혼자 있고 싶어요.
hohn • jah eet • kkoh see • puh • yo

Stop bothering me! 이제 그만하세요!
ee • jeh gu • mahn • hah • seh • yo

GETTING INTIMATE

Can I hug/kiss you? 안아도/키스해도 될까요?
ah • nah • doh/kee • ssu • heh • doh dwehl • kkah • yo

Yes. 네.
neh

No. 아니요.
ah • nee • yo

Stop! 그만해요!
gu • mahn • heh • yo

I like/love you. 좋아해요/사랑해요.
joh • ah • heh • yo/sah • lahng • heh • yo

SEXUAL PREFERENCES

Are you gay? 동성연애자세요?
dohng • suhng • yuh • neh • jah • seh • yo

I'm gay. 저는 동성연애자예요.
juh • nun dohng • suhng • yuh • neh • jah • yeh • yo

Do you like men/women? 남자/여자 좋아하세요?
nahm • jah/yuh • jah joh • ah • hah • seh • yo

48-50
登机口·
47
登机口·

DICTIONARY

ENGLISH–KOREAN

A

access 접근 *juhp • kkun*
accident 사고 *sah • goh*
accidentally 실수로 *seel • ssoo • loh*
accommodations 숙박 시설 *sook • ppahk see • suhl*
accompany 같이 가다 *gah • chee gah • dah*
acetaminophen 아세트아미노펜 *ah • seh • tu • ah • mee • noh • pehn*
acupuncture 침 *cheem*
adapter 어댑터 *uh • dehp • tuh*
address 주소 *joo • soh*
after 지나서 *jee • nah • suh*
aftershave 애프터셰이브 로션 *eh • pu • tuh • syeh • ee • bu loh • syuhn*
afternoon 오후 *oh • hoo*
air conditioning 냉방 *nehng • bahng*
airline 항공사 *hahng • gohng • sah*
airmail 항공우편 *hahng • gohng • oo • pyuhn*
airport 공항 *gohng • hahng*
airsickness 비행기 멀미 *bee • hehng • gee muhl • mee*
aisle 통로 *tohng • noh*
alarm clock 자명종 *jah • myuhng • johng*
allergic 알레르기가 있다 *ahl • leh • lu • gee • gah eet • ttah*
allergy 알레르기 *ahl • leh • lu • gee*
allow 허락하다 *huh • lah • kah • dah*
allowance 허용 한도 *huh • yong hahn • doh*
alone 혼자 *hohn • jah*
already 이미 *ee • mee*
also 또한 *ttoh • hahn*
alter 바꾸다 *bah • kkoo • dah*
alternate 다른 *dah • lun*
aluminum foil 쿠킹 호일 *koo • keeng hoh • eel*
always 항상 *hahng • sahng*
amazing 놀라운 *nohl • lah • oon*
ambassador 대사 *deh • sah*
ambulance 구급차 *goo • gup • chah*
American 미국인 *mee • goo • geen*
amount 금액 *gu • mehk*
amusement park 놀이 공원 *noh • lee gohng • wuhn*
anesthetic 마취제 *mah • chwih • jeh*
and 그리고 *gu • lee • goh*
animal 동물 *dohng • mool*
another 다른 *dah • lun*
antacid 제산제 *jeh • sahn • jeh*
antibiotics 항생제 *hahng • sehng • jeh*
antifreeze 부동액 *boo • dohng • ehk*
antique 골동품 *gohl • ttohng • poom*
antiseptic 소독약 *soh • dohng • nyahk*
any 어떤 *uh • ttuhn*
anyone 누군가 *noo • goon • gah*
anything 무언가 *moo • uhn • gah*

adj adjective
adv adverb
BE British English
n noun
prep preposition
v verb

apartment 아파트 *ah • pah • tu*
apologize 사과하다 *sah • gwah • hah • dah*
appendix 부록 *boo • lohk*
appetite 식욕 *see • gyok*
appointment (meeting) 약속 *yahk • ssohk;* **(doctor, hair, etc.)** 예약 *yeh • yahk*
approve 허락하다 *huh • lah • kah • dah*
area 구역 *goo • yuhk*
area code 지역 번호 *jee • yuhk ppuhn • hoh*
arm 팔 *pahl*
aromatherapy 아로마테라피 *ah • loh • mah • teh • lah • pee*
around (time) 쯤 *tzum*
arrivals 도착 *doh • chahk*
arrive 도착하다 *doh • chah • kah • dah*
art gallery 미술관 *mee • sool • gwahn*
arthritis 관절염 *gwahn • juhl • lyuhm*
ashtray 재떨이 *jeh • ttuh • lee*
ask 묻다 *moot • ttah*
aspirin 아스피린 *ah • su • pee • leen*
assistance 도움 *doh • oom*
asthma 천식 *chuhn • seek*
at 에 *eh*
ATM 현금 인출기 *hyuhn • gum een • chool • gee*
attack 폭행 *poh • kehng*
attractive 매력적인 *meh • lyuhk • tzuh • geen*
audio guide 음성 안내 *um • suhng ahn • meh*
authentic 진짜 *jeen • tzah*
automatic 자동 *jah • dohng*
available 이용할 수 있는 *ee • yong • hahl ssoo een • nun*
away 떨어져 *ttuh • luh • jyuh*

B

baby 아기 *ah • gee*
baby bottle 젖병 *juht • ppyuhng*
baby food 이유식 *ee • yoo • seek*
baby wipe 아기용 물휴지 *ah • gee • yong mool • hyoo • jee*
babysitter 애 봐주는 사람 *eh bwah • joo • nun sah • lahm*
back 등 *dung*
backpack 배낭 *beh • nahng*
bad 나쁜 *nah • ppun*
bag 가방 *gah • bahng*
baggage [BE] 짐 *jeem*
baggage claim 수하물 찾는 곳 *soo • hah • mool chan • nun goht*
bakery 제과점 *jeh • gwah • juhm*
ball 공 *gohng*
ballet 발레 *bahl • leh*
band 악단 *ahk • ttahn*
bandage 붕대 *boong • deh*
bank 은행 *un • hehng*
bar 바 *bah*
barber 이발소 *ee • bahl • soh*
bargain 흥정 *hung • juhng*
baseball 야구 *yah • goo*
basement 지하실 *jee • hah • seel*
basket 바구니 *bah • goo • nee*
basketball 농구 *nohng • goo*
bath 목욕 *moh • gyohk*
bathroom 화장실 *hwah • jahng • seel*
battery 건전지 *guhn • juhn • jee*
battlesite 전적지 *juhn • juhk • tzee*
be 이다 *ee • dah*
beach 해변 *heh • byuhn*
beautiful 아름다운 *ah • lum • dah • oon*
because 때문에 *tteh • moo • neh*
bed 침대 *cheem • deh*
bedding 침구 *cheem • goo*
bedroom 침실 *cheem • seel*
before 전에 *juh • neh*

begin 시작하다 *see • jah • kah • dah*
behind 뒤에 *dwih • eh*
belong 속하다 *soh • kah • dah*
belt 벨트 *bel • tu*
bet 내기 *neh • gee*
between 사이에 *sah • ee • eh*
beware 조심하다 *joh • seem • hah • dah*
bib 턱받이 *tuhk • ppah • jee*
bicycle 자전거 *jah • juhn • guh*
big 큰 *kun*
bike path 자전거 도로 *jah • juhn • guh doh • loh*
bikini 비키니 *bee • kee • nee*
bill 계산서 *geh • sahn • suh*
binoculars 쌍안경 *ssahng • ahn • gyuhng*
bird 새 *seh*
birthday 생일 *sehng • eel*
bite 벌레 물린데 *buhl • leh mool • leen • deh*
bitter 쓴 *ssun*
blanket 담요 *dahm • nyo*
bleach 표백제 *pyo • behk • tzeh*
bleed 피가 나다 *pee•gah nah•dah*
blister 물집 *mool • tzeep*
blood 혈액 *hyuh • lehk*
blood pressure 혈압 *hyuh • lahp*
blouse 블라우스 *bu • lah • oo • su*
board 탑승하다 *tahp • ssung • hah • dah*
boarding card 탑승 카드 *tahp • ssung kah • du*
boat trip 보트 관광 *boh • tu gwahn • gwahng*
bone 뼈 *ppyuh*
book 책 *chehk*
bookstore 서점 *suh • juhm*
boots 부츠 *boo • chu*
boring 따분한 *ttah • boon • hahn*
born 태어난 *teh • uh • nahn*
borrow 빌리다 *beel • lee • dah*
botanical garden 식물원 *seeng • moo • lwuhn*
bother 귀찮게 하다 *gwih • chahn • keh hah • dah*
bottle 병 *byuhng*
bottle opener 병따개 *byuhng • ttah • geh*
bowl 사발 *sah • bahl*
box 상자 *sahng • jah*
boxing 권투 *gwuhn • too*
boy 남자애 *nahm • jah • eh*
boyfriend 애인 *eh • een*
bra 브래지어 *bu • leh • jee • uh*
bracelet 팔찌 *pahl • tzee*
brake 브레이크 *bu • leh • ee • ku*
break 부수다 *boo • soo • dah*
break down 고장 *goh • jang*
breakfast 아침 식사 *ah • cheem seek • ssah*
breast 가슴 *gah • sum*
breastfeed 수유하다 *soo • yoo • hah • dah*
breathe 숨쉬다 *soom • swih • dah*
bridge 다리 *dah • lee*
bring 가져오다 *gah • jyuh • oh • dah*
British 영국인 *yuhng • goo • geen*
brochure 팸플릿 *pahm • pul • leht*
broken 고장난 *goh • jahng • nahn*
broom 빗자루 *beet • tzah • loo*
browse 둘러보다 *dool • luh • boh • dah*
bruise 멍 *muhng*
bucket 양동이 *yahng • dohng • ee*
bug 벌레 *buhl • leh*
building 건물 *guhn • mool*
build 짓다 *jeet • ttah*
burn 화상 *hwah • sahng*
bus 버스 *buh • su*
bus station 버스 터미널 *buh • su tuh • mee • nuhl*
bus stop 버스 정류장 *buh • su juhng • nyoo • jahng*
bus ticket 버스표 *buh • su • pyo*

business 사업 *sah • uhp*
business card 명함 *myuhng • hahm*
business center 비즈니스 센터 *bee • jee • nee • su ssehn • tuh*
business class 비즈니스석 *bee • jee • nee • su • suhk*
business district 상업 지구 *sahng • uhp tzee • goo*
busy 바쁜 *bah • ppun*
but 그러나 *gu • luh • nah*
butane gas 부탄가스 *boo • tahn • kkah • su*
button 단추 *dahn • choo*
buy 사다 *sah • dah*
by (means) 으로 *u • loh;* **(place)** 옆에 *yuh • peh;* **(time)** 까지 *kkah • jee*
bye (to someone leaving) 안녕히 가세요 *ahn • nyuhng • hee gah • seh • yo;* **(to someone staying)** 안녕히 계세요 *ahn • nyuhng • hee geh • seh • yo*

C

cabin 오두막집 *oh • doo • mahk • tzeep*
calendar 달력 *dahl • lyuhk*
call 부르다 *boo • lu • dah*
calorie 칼로리 *kahl • loh • lee*
camera 카메라 *kah • meh • lah*
camp 캠핑하다 *kehm • peeng • hah • dah*
campsite 캠핑장 *kehm • peeng • jahng*
can 깡통 *kkahng • tohng*
can opener 통조림 따개 *tohng • joh • leem ttah • geh*
Canada 캐나다 *keh • nah • dah*
canal 운하 *oon • hah*
cancel 취소하다 *chwih • soh • hah • dah*
cancer 암 *ahm*
candle 양초 *yahng • choh*
candy store 사탕 가게 *sah • tahng kkah • geh*
canoe 카누 *kah • noo*
car 자동차 *jah • dohng • chah*
car hire [BE] 렌터카 *lehn • tuh • kah*
car park [BE] 주차장 *joo • chah • jahng*
car rental 렌터카 *lehn • tuh • kah*
car seat 카시트 *kah • ssee • tu*
card 카드 *kah • du*
carpet 카페트 *kah • peh • tu*
carry-on luggage 기내 휴대 수하물 *gee • neh hyoo • deh soo • hah • mool*
cart 카트 *kah • tu*
carton (cigarettes) 보루 *boh • loo*
cash 현금 *hyuhn • gum*
cash register 계산대 *geh • sahn • deh*
cashier 계산원 *geh • sah • nwuhn*
casino 카지노 *kah • jee • noh*
castle 성 *suhng*
catch 잡다 *jahp • ttah*
caution 조심 *joh • seem*
cave 동굴 *dohng • gool*
CD 시디 *ssee • dee*
CD player 시디플레이어 *ssee • dee • pul • leh • ee • uh*
cell phone 휴대폰 *hyoo • deh • pohn*
cemetery 공동 묘지 *gohng • dohng myo • jee*
ceramics 도자기 *doh • jah • gee*
certificate 보증서 *boh • jung • suh*
chain 사슬 *sah • sul*
change *n* 잔돈 *jahn • dohn; v* 바꾸다 *bah • kkoo • dah*
charge 요금 *yo • gum*
cheap 싼 *ssahn*
check 확인하다 *hwah • geen • hah • dah*

check in 탑승 수속 *tahp • ssung soo • sohk*
check out 체크 아웃 *cheh • ku ah • oot*
cheers 건배 *guhn • beh*
chemical toilet 휴대 변기 *hyoo • deh byuhn • gee*
chemist [BE] 약국 *yahk • kkook*
cheque [BE] 수표 *soo • pyo*
chest 가슴 *gah • sum*
child 어린이 *uh • lee • nee*
child seat 어린이용 의자 *uh • lee • nee • yong u • jah*
children's menu 어린이용 메뉴 *uh • lee • nee • yong meh • nyoo*
children's portion 어린이용 메뉴 *uh • lee • nee • yong meh • nyoo*
choose 고르다 *goh • lu • dah*
chopsticks 젓가락 *juht • kkah • lahk*
church 교회 *gyo • hweh*
cigarette 담배 *dahm • beh*
cigar 시가 *ssee • gah*
cinema [BE] 영화관 *yuhng • hwah • gwahn*
class 등급 *dung • gup*
clean 깨끗한 *kkeh • kku • tahn*
clearance 재고 정리 *jeh • goh juhng • nee*
cliff 절벽 *juhl • byuhk*
cling film [BE] 랩 *lehp*
clinic 병원 *byuhng • wuhn*
clock 시계 *see • geh*
close 닫다 *daht • ttah*
clothes shop [BE] 옷가게 *oht • kkah • geh*
clothing store 옷가게 *oht • kkah • geh*
club (golf) 골프채 *gohl • pu • cheh*
coast 해안 *heh • ahn*
coat 코트 *koh • tu*
coat check 휴대품 보관소 *hyoo • deh • poom boh • gwahn • soh*
code 지역 번호 *jee • yuhk ppuhn • hoh*
coin 동전 *dohng • juhn*
cold *adj* 차가운 *chah • gah • oon*; *n* 감기 *gahm • gee*
collapse 쓰러지다 *ssu • luh • jee • dah*
colleague 동료 *dohng • nyo*
collect 모으다 *moh • u • dah*
collection 수집 *soo • jeep*
color 색 *sehk*
comb 빗 *beet*
come 오다 *oh • dah*
commission 수수료 *soo • soo • lyo*
company 회사 *hweh • sah*
compartment 객실 *gehk • sseel*
computer 컴퓨터 *kuhm • pyoo • tuh*
concert 음악회 *u • mah • kweh*
concert hall 연주회장 *yuhn • joo • hweh • jahng*
concession 양보 *yahng • boh*
concussion 뇌진탕 *nweh • jeen • tahng*
conditioner 컨디셔너 *kuhn • dee • syuh • nuh*
condom 콘돔 *kohn • dohm*
conductor 지휘자 *jee • hwih • jah*
conference 회의 *hweh • ee*
confirm 확인하다 *hwah • geen • hah • dah*
congratulations 축하합니다 *choo • kah • ham • nee • dah*
connect 연결하다 *yuhn • gyuhl • hah • dah*
connection 연결 *yuhn • gyuhl*
conscious 의식하는 *u • see • kah • nun*
conservation area 보호 구역 *boh • hoh goo • yuhk*
constant 일정한 *eel • tzuhng • hahn*

constipation 변비 *byun • bee*
consulate 영사관 *yuhng • sah • gwahn*
consult 상담하다 *sahng • dahm • hah • dah*
contact 연락하다 *yuhl • lah • kah • dah*
contact lens 콘텍트 렌즈 *kohn • tehk • tu lehn • ju*
contact lens solution 콘텍트 렌즈 용액 *kohn • tehk • tu lehn • ju yong • ehk*
contagious 전염성의 *juh • nyuhm • ssuhng • eh*
contain 포함하다 *poh • hahm • hah • dah*
contemporary 현대 *hyuhn • deh*
contest *n* 대회 *deh • hweh*
continuous 끊임없는 *kku • neem • uhm • nun*
contraceptive 피임약 *pee • eem • nyahk*
contribution 기부 *gee • boo*
control *n* 관리 *gwahl • lee*
convention 회의 *hweh • ee*
convention hall 회의장 *hweh • ee • jahng*
cook *v* 요리하다 *yo • lee • hah • dah*
cooking facilities 주방 시설 *joo • bahng see • suhl*
cool 시원한 *see • wuhn • hahn*
copper 구리 *goo • lee*
copy 복사하다 *bohk • ssah • hah • dah*
corkscrew 코르크 마개뽑이 *koh • lu • ku mah • geh • ppoh • bee*
corner 모퉁이 *moh • toong • ee*
correct 맞는 *mahn • nun*
cosmetic 화장품 *hwah • jahng • poom*
cost *n* 비용 *bee • yong*; *v* 들다 *dul • dah*
cot [BE] 아기용 침대 *ah • gee • yong cheem • deh*
cottage 별장 *byuhl • tzang*
cotton 면 *myuhn*
cough *n* 기침 *gee • cheem*; *v* 기침하다 *gee • cheem • hah • dah*
counter 카운터 *kah • oon • tuh*
country 나라 *nah • lah*
country code 국가 번호 *gook • kkah buhn • hoh*
cover charge 입장료 *eep • tzahng • nyo*
cramp 경련 *gyuhng • nyuhn*
credit card 신용카드 *see • nyong • kah • du*
crib 아기용 침대 *ah • gee • yong cheem • deh*
crowd 군중 *goon • joong*
cruise 유람선 여행 *yoo • lahm • suhn yuh • hehng*
crutches 목발 *mohk • ppahl*
crystal 수정 *soo • juhng*
cup 컵 *kuhp*
currency 돈 *dohn*
currency exchange office 환전소 *hwahn • juhn • soh*
curtain 커튼 *kuh • tun*
curve 커브 *kuh • bu*
custom made 맞춤 *maht • choom*
customer service 고객 서비스 *goh • gehk ssuh • bee • su*
customs 세관 *seh • gwahn*
customs declaration form 세관 신고서 *seh • gwahn seen • goh • suh*
cut *n* 절단 *juhl • ttahn*
cute 귀여운 *gwih • yuh • oon*

D

daily 매일 *meh • eel*
dairy 유제품의 *yoo • jeh • poo • meh*
damage 손상 *sohn • sahng*
damp 습한 *su • pahn*

dance 춤추다 *choom • choo • dah*
dance club 클럽 *kul • luhp*
dangerous 위험한 *wih • huhm • hahn*
dark 어두운 *uh • doo • oon*
day 일 *eel*
day trip 당일치기 여행 *dahng • eel • chee • gee yuh • hehng*
dead (battery) 떨어진 *ttuh • luh • jeen*
deaf 귀머거리 *gwih • muh • guh • lee*
deck chair 접는 의자 *juhm • nun u • jah*
declare 신고하다 *seen • goh • hah • dah*
decorative 장식 *jahng • seek*
deep 깊은 *gee • pun*
defrost 녹이다 *noh • gee • dah*
degree 도 *doh*
delay 지연 *jee • yuhn*
delete 삭제하다 *sahk • tzeh • hah • dah*
delicious 맛있는 *mah • seen • nun*
deliver 배달하다 *beh • dahl • hah • dah*
delivery 배달 *beh • dahl*
dental floss 치실 *chee • seel*
dentist 치과 의사 *chee • kkwah u • sah*
denture 틀니 *tul • lee*
deodorant 방취제 *bahng • chwih • jeh*
depart 출발하다 *chool • bahl • hah • dah*
department store 백화점 *beh • kwah • juhm*
departures 출발 *chool • bahl*
deposit 입금 *eep • kkum*
describe 묘사하다 *myo • sah • hah • dah*
destination 목적지 *mohk • juhk • tzee*
detergent 세제 *seh • jeh*
develop 현상하다 *hyuhn • sahng • hah • dah*
diabetes 당뇨병 *dahng • nyo • ppyuhng*
diabetic 당뇨병 환자 *dahng • nyo • ppyuhng hwahn • jah*
dial 전화 걸다 *juhn • hwah guhl • dah*
diamond 다이아몬드 *dah • ee • ah • mohn • du*
diaper 기저귀 *gee • juh • gwih*
diarrhea 설사 *suhl • ssah*
dictionary 사전 *sah • juhn*
diesel 디젤 *dee • jehl*
diet 다이어트 *dah • ee • uh • tu*
difficult 어려운 *uh • lyuh • oon*
digital 디지털 *dee • jee • tuhl*
dine 식사하다 *seek • ssah • hah • dah*
dining car 식당차 *seek • ttahng • chah*
dining room 식당 *seek • ttahng*
dinner 저녁 식사 *juh • nyuhk seek • ssah*
direct *adj* 직행 *jee • kehng*
direction 방향 *bahng • hyahng*
director 이사 *ee • sah*
directory (phone) 전화번호부 *juhn • hwah buhn • hoh • boo*
dirty 더러운 *duh • luh • oon*
disabled 장애인 *jahng • eh • een*
disconnect 접속을 끊다 *juhp • soh • gul kkun • tah*
discount 할인 *hah • leen*
dish (food) 음식 *um • seek;* **(plate)** 접시 *juhp • ssee*
dishwasher 식기 세척기 *seek • kkee seh • chuhk • kkee*

dishwashing liquid 주방용 세제 *joo • bahng • nyong seh • jeh*
dislocate 삐다 *ppee • dah*
display case 진열장 *jee • nyuhl • tzahng*
disposable (camera) 일회용 *(카메라) eel • hweh • yong (kah • meh • lah)*
dissolve 녹이다 *noh • gee • dah*
distance 거리 *guh • lee*
disturb 방해하다 *bahng • heh • hah • dah*
dive 다이빙하다 *dah • ee • beeng • hah • dah*
diving equipment 스쿠버 다이빙 장비 *su • koo • buh dah • ee • beeng jahng • bee*
divorce 이혼 *ee • hohn*
dizzy 어지러운 *uh • jee • luh • oon*
do 하다 *hah • dah*
dock 부두 *boo • doo*
doctor 의사 *u • sah*
dog 개 *geh*
doll 인형 *een • hyuhng*
dollar 달러 *dahl • luh*
domestic 국내 *goong • neh*
donation 기부 *gee • boo*
door 문 *moon*
dosage 복용량 *boh • gyong • nyahng*
double 이인용 *ee • een • nyong*
double room 이인용 방 *ee • een • nyong bahng*
downstairs 아래층 *ah • leh • chung*
downtown 중심가 *joong • seem • gah*
dozen 다스 *dah • su*
dress 드레스 *du • leh • su*
dress code 복장 규정 *bohk • tzang gyoo • juhng*
drink *n* 음료수 *um • nyo • soo;* *n* **(alcoholic)** 술 *sool;* *v* 마시다 *mah • see • dah*
drip 뚝뚝 떨어지다 *ttook • ttook ttuh • luh • jee • dah*
drive 운전하다 *oon • juhn • hah • dah*
driver 운전사 *oon • juhn • sah*
driver's license 운전 면허증 *oon • juhn myuhn • huh • tzung*
drop 떨어뜨리다 *ttuh • luh • ttu • lee • dah*
drown 물에 빠지다 *moo • leh ppah • jee • dah*
drowsy 졸린 *johl • leen*
drowsiness 졸음 *joh • lum*
drugstore 약국 *yahk • kkook*
dry 말리다 *mahl • lee • dah*
dry clean 드라이 클리닝하다 *du • lah • ee kul • lee • neeng • hah • dah*
dry cleaner 세탁소 *seh • tahk • ssoh*
dubbed 더빙된 *duh • beeng • dwehn*
dummy [BE] 고무 젖꼭지 *goh • moo juht • kkohk • tzee*
during 동안 *dohng • ahn*
duty (tax) 세금 *seh • gum*
duty-free 면세 *myuhn • seh*

E

ear 귀 *gwih*
ear drops 귀약 *gwih • yahk*
earache 귀통증 *gwih • tohng • tzung*
early 일찍 *eel • tzeek*
earrings 귀걸이 *gwih • guh • lee*
east 동쪽 *dohng • tzohk*
easy 쉬운 *swih • oon*
eat 먹다 *muhk • ttah*
economy class 이코노미석 *ee • koh • noh • mee • suhk*
electrical outlet 전기 콘센트 *juhn • gee kohn • sehn • tu*

elevator 엘리베이터 *ehl • lee • beh • ee • tuh*
e-mail 이메일 *ee • meh • eel*
e-mail address 이메일 주소 *ee • meh • eel joo • soh*
embassy 대사관 *deh • sah • gwahn*
emerald 에메랄드 *eh • meh • lahl • du*
emergency 비상 *bee • sahng*
emergency brake 비상 브레이크 *bee • sahng bu • leh • ee • ku*
emergency exit 비상구 *bee • sahng • goo*
emergency service 긴급 서비스 *geen • gup ssuh • bee • su*
empty 텅 빈 *tuhng been*
end 끝 *kkut*
engaged 약혼한 *yah • kohn • hahn*
England 영국 *yuhng • gook*
English 영어 *yuhng • uh*
engrave 새기다 *seh • gee • dah*
enjoy 즐기다 *jul • gee • dah*
enlarge 확대하다 *hwahk • tteh • hah • dah*
enough 충분한 *choong • boon • hahn*
entertainment guide 오락 안내 *oh • lah gahn • neh*
entrance 입구 *eep • kkoo*
entrance fee 입장료 *eep • tzang • nyo*
entrance ramp 입구 진입로 *eep • kkoo jee • neem • noh*
entry 입장 *eep • tzahng*
entry visa 입국 비자 *eep • kkook bee • jah*
envelope 편지 봉투 *pyuhn • jee bohng • too*
equipment 장비 *jahng • bee*
error 오류 *oh • lyoo*
escalator 에스컬레이터 *eh • su • kuhl • leh • ee • tuh*
essential 필수적인 *peel • ssoo • juh • geen*
e-ticket 전자티켓 *juhn • jah • tee • keht*
euro 유로 *yoo • loh*
Eurocheque 유로체크 *yoo • loh • cheh • ku*
evening 저녁 *juh • nyuhk*
event 행사 *hehng • sah*
every 모든 *moh • dun*
exact 정확한 *juhng • hwah • kahn*
examination 검사 *guhm • sah*
example 예 *yeh*
except 외에 *weh • eh*
exchange 바꾸다 *bah • kkoo • dah*
exchange rate 환율 *hwahn • nyool*
excursion 짧은 여행 *tzahl • bun yuh • hehng*
exhausted 지친 *jee • cheen*
exit 출구 *chool • goo*
expensive 비싼 *bee • ssahn*
experience 경험 *gyuhng • huhm*
expose 드러내다 *du • luh • neh • dah*
express mail 특급 우편 *tuk • kku boo • pyuhn*
extension (phone) 내선 번호 *neh • suhn buhn • hoh*
extra 여분 *yuh • boon*
extract 뽑아내다 *ppoh • bah • neh • dah*
eye 눈 *noon*
eyebrow 눈썹 *noon • ssuhp*

F

fabric 천 *chuhn*
face 얼굴 *uhl • gool*
facial 얼굴 마사지 *uhl • gool mah • ssah • jee*
facility 시설 *see • suhl*
factor 요인 *yo • een*
faint *v* 기절하다 *gee • juhl • hah • dah*

family 가족 *gah • johk*
famous 유명한 *yoo • myuhng • hahn*
fan 선풍기 *suhn • poong • gee*
far 먼 *muhn*
far-sighted 원시 *wuhn • see*
farm 농장 *nohng • jahng*
fast 빠른 *ppah • lun*
fast food 패스트 푸드 *peh • su • tu poo • du*
faucet 수도꼭지 *soo • doh • kkohk • tzee*
favorite 좋아하는 *joh • ah • hah • nun*
fax 팩스 *pehk • su*
fax machine 팩스기 *pehk • su • gee*
fax number 팩스 번호 *pehk • su buhn • hoh*
feature 특징 *tuk • tzeeng*
feed 먹이다 *muh • gee • dah*
feel 느끼다 *nu • kkee • dah*
female 여자 *yuh • jah*
ferry 보트 *boh • tu*
fever 열 *yuhl*
few 조금 *joh • gum*
field 들판 *dul • pahn*
fight 싸움 *ssah • oom*
fill 채우다 *cheh • oo • dah*
filling 속 *sohk*
film 영화 *yuhng • hwah*
filter 필터 *peel • tuh*
find 찾다 *chaht • ttah*
fine *n* 벌금 *buhl • gum;* ***adj*** 좋은 *joh • un*
finger 손가락 *sohn • kkah • lahk*
fire 불 *bool*
fire alarm 화재 경보 *hwah • jeh gyuhng • boh*
fire door 방화문 *bahng • hwah • moon*
fire escape 화재 비상 계단 *hwah • jeh bee • sahng geh • dahn*
fire exit 화재 비상구 *hwah • jeh bee • sahng • goo*
fire extinguisher 소화기 *soh • hwah • gee*
first 첫 *chuht*
first class 일등석 *eel • ttung • suhk*
fishing 낚시 *nahk • ssee*
fit 맞다 *maht • ttah*
fitting room 탈의실 *tah • lee • seel*
fix 고치다 *goh • chee • dah*
flash 번쩍이다 *buhn • tzuh • gee • dah*
flat 평평한 *pyuhng • pyuhng • hahn*
flavor 맛 *maht*
flea market 벼룩시장 *byuh • look • ssee • jahng*
flight 비행기 *bee • hehng • gee*
flight attendant 승무원 *sung • moo • wuhn*
flight number 항공기 편명 *hahng • gohng • gee pyuhn • myuhng*
floor (level) 층 *chung*
flower 꽃 *kkoht*
flush 물 내리다 *mool neh • lee • dah*
fog 안개 *ahn • geh*
follow 따라가다 *ttah • lah • gah • dah*
food 음식 *um • seek*
food poisoning 식중독 *seek • tzoong • dohk*
foot 발 *bahl*
football [BE] 축구 *chook • kkoo*
for 동안 *dohng • ahn*
for sale 판매용 *pahn • meh • yong*
foreign 외국의 *weh • goo • geh*
forest 숲 *soop*
forget 잊다 *eet • ttah*
fork 포크 *poh • ku*
form 양식 *yahng • seek*
formal dress 정장 *juhng • jahng*
formula (baby) 분유 *boo • nyoo*
fountain 분수 *boon • soo*

fracture 골절상 *gohl • tzuhl • sahng*
free (available) 시간 있는 *see • gahn een • nun*
free of charge 공짜 *gohng • tzah*
freeze 얼리다 *uhl • lee • dah*
freezer 냉동고 *nehng • dohng • goh*
frequent 잦은 *jah • jun*
fresh 신선한 *seen • suhn • hahn*
friend 친구 *cheen • goo*
from 부터 *boo • tuh*
front 앞 *ahp*
frying pan 후라이팬 *hoo • lah • ee • pen*
fuel 연료 *yuhl • lyo*
full 가득 찬 *gah • duk chahn*
fun 재미 *jeh • mee*
funny 웃기는 *oot • kkee • nun*
furniture 가구 *gah • goo*

G

gallery 화랑 *hwah • lahng*
game 경기 *gyuhng • gee*
garage (parking) 차고 *cha • goh;* **(repair)** 정비 공장 *juhng • bee gohng • jahng*
garbage bag 쓰레기 봉투 *ssu • leh • gee bohng • too*
garden 정원 *juhng • wuhn*
gas 기름 *gee • lum*
gas station 주유소 *joo • yoo • soh*
gate (airport) 탑승구 *tahp • ssung • goo*
gauze 거즈 *guh • ju*
gear 기어 *gee • uh*
genuine 진짜 *jeen • tzah*
get (find) 구하다 *goo • hah • dah*
get off (bus) 내리다 *neh • lee • dah*
gift 선물 *suhn • mool*
gift store 선물 가게 *suhn • mool kkah • geh*
girl 여자애 *yuh • jah • eh*
girlfriend 여자 친구 *yuh • jah cheen • goo*
give 주다 *joo • dah*
glass (for drinking) 유리잔 *yoo • lee • jahn*
glasses (optical) 안경 *ahn • gyuhng*
gloves 장갑 *jahng • gahp*
go 가다 *gah • dah*
goggles 물안경 *moo • lahn • gyuhng*
gold 금 *gum*
golf 골프 *gohl • pu*
golf club 골프채 *gohl • pu • cheh*
golf course 골프장 *gohl • pu • jahng*
good 좋은 *joh • un*
goodbye (to someone leaving) 안녕히 가세요 *ahn • nyuhng • hee gah • seh • yo;* **(to someone staying)** 안녕히 계세요 *ahn • nyuhng • hee geh • seh • yo*
gram 그램 *gu • lehm*
grass 잔디 *jahn • dee*
great 근사한 *gun • sah • hahn*
Great Britain 영국 *yuhng • gook*
grocer [BE] 식료품점 *seeng • nyo • poom • juhm*
grocery store 식료품점 *seeng • nyo • poom • juhm*
group 단체 *dahn • cheh*
guarantee 보증 *boh • jung*
guesthouse 숙소 *sook • ssoh*
guide (tour) 안내원 *ahn • neh • wuhn*
guide book 안내 책자 *ahn • neh chehk • tzah*
guide dog 맹도견 *mehng • doh • gyuhn*
guided tour 가이드 투어 *gah • ee • du too • uh*
guitar 기타 *gee • tah*
gym 헬스클럽 *hehl • ssu • kul • luhp*
gynecologist 부인과 *boo • een • kkwah*

H

hair 머리 *muh • lee*
hairbrush 헤어 브러시 *heh • uh bu • luh • see*
hairdresser 미용사 *mee • yong • sah*
halal 이슬람교 식용육 *ee • sul • lahm • gyo see • gyong • nyook*
half 반 *bahn*
hammer 망치 *mahng • chee*
hand 손 *sohn*
hand luggage 손가방 *sohn • kkah • bahng*
handbag [BE] 핸드백 *hehn • du • behk*
handicapped 장애인 *jahng • eh • een*
handicrafts 수공예품 *soo • gohng • yeh • poom*
hanger 옷걸이 *oht • kkuh • lee*
hangover 숙취 *sook • chwih*
happy 행복한 *hehng • boh • kahn*
harbor 항구 *hahng • goo*
hard 딱딱한 *ttahk • ttah • kahn*
hardware store 철물점 *chuhl • mool • juhm*
hat 모자 *moh • jah*
have 갖다 *gaht • ttah*
hay fever 꽃가루 알레르기 *kkoht • kkah • loo ahl • leh • lu • gee*
head 머리 *muh • lee*
headache 두통 *doo • tohng*
headlight 헤드라이트 *heh • du • lah • ee • tu*
health 건강 *guhn • gahng*
health food store 건강 식품점 *guhn • gahng seek • poom • juhm*
health insurance 의료 보험 *u • lyo boh • huhm*
hear 듣다 *dut • ttah*
hearing aid 보청기 *boh • chuhng • gee*
hearing impaired 청각 장애인 *chuhng • gahk jahng • eh • een*
heart 심장 *seem • jahng*
heart attack 심장마비 *seem • jahng • mah • bee*
heart condition 심장 질환 *seem • jahng jeel • hwahn*
heat난방 *nahn • bahng*
heating [BE] 난방 *nahn • bahng*
heavy 무거운 *moo • guh • oon*
heels 하이힐 *hah • ee • heel*
height (person) 키 *kee*
hello 안녕하세요 *ahn • nyuhng • hah • seh • yo*
helmet 헬멧 *hehl • meht*
help *n* 도움 *doh • oom;* *v* 돕다 *dohp • ttah*
here 여기 *yuh • gee*
hi 안녕하세요 *ahn • nyuhng • hah • seh • yo*
high 높은 *noh • pun*
highchair 높은 의자 *noh • pun u • jah*
highway 고속도로 *goh • sohk • ttoh • loh*
hike 하이킹 *hah • ee • keeng*
hill 언덕 *uhn • duhk*
hire 빌리다 *beel • lee • dah*
historical 역사적인 *yuhk • ssah • juh • geen*
hobby 취미 *chwih • mee*
hold 붙들다 *boot • ttul • dah*
hole 구멍 *goo • muhng*
holiday [BE] 휴가 *hyoo • gah*
home 집 *jeep*
homemade 직접 만든 *jeek • tzuhp mahn • dun*
honeymoon 신혼여행 *seen • hohn • yuh • hehng*
horn 뿔 *ppool*
horse 말 *mahl*

horseback riding 승마 *sung • mah*
horse racing 경마 *gyuhng • mah*
horsetrack 경마장 *gyugng • mah • jahng*
hospital 병원 *byuhng • wuhn*
hot 뜨거운 *ttu • guh • oon*
hotel 호텔 *hoh • tehl*
hour 시간 *see • gahn*
house 집 *jeep*
how 어떻게 *uh • ttuh • keh*
how many 몇 개 *myuht kkeh*
how much 얼마나 *ul • mah • nah*
hug 안다 *ahn • ttah*
hunger 배고픔 *beh • goh • pum*
hungry 배고픈 *beh • goh • pun*
hunt 사냥하다 *sah • nyahng • hah • dah*
hurry 서두르다 *suh • doo • lu • dah*
hurt 아프다 *ah • pu • dah*
husband 남편 *nahm • pyuhn*

I

ibuprofen 이부프로펜 *ee • boo • pu • loh • pehn*
ice hockey 아이스 하키 *ah • ee • su hah • kee*
ice skating 아이스 스케이트 *ah • ee • su su • keh • ee • tu*
ice skating rink 아이스 스케이트장 *ah • ee • su su • keh • ee • tuh • jahng*
identification 신분증 *seen • boon • tzung*
ill [BE] 아픈 *ah • pun*
illegal 불법 *bool • ppuhp*
imitation 모조품 *moh • joh • poom*
important 중요한 *joong • yo • hahn*
improve 나아지다 *nah • ah • jee • dah*
in 에 *eh*
include 포함하다 *poh • hahm • hah • dah*
indigestion 소화불량 *soh • hwah • bool • lyahng*
indoor pool 실내 수영장 *seel • leh soo • yuhng • jahng*
inexpensive 저렴한 *juh • lyuhm • hahn*
infect 감염시키다 *gah • myuhm • see • kee • dah*
infection 감염 *gah • myuhm*
inflammation 염증 *yuhm • tzung*
information 안내 *ahn • neh*
information desk 안내 데스크 *ahn • neh deh • su • ku*
injection 주사 *joo • sah*
injure 다치게 하다 *dah • chee • geh hah • dah*
innocent 결백한 *gyuhl • beh • kahn*
insect 벌레 *buhl • leh*
insect bite 벌레 물린 데 *buhl • leh mool • leen deh*
insect repellent 제충제 *jeh • choong • jeh*
insert 삽입하다 *sah • bee • pah • dah*
inside 안에 *ah • neh*
insist 우기다 *oo • gee • dah*
insomnia 불면증 *bool • myuhn • tzung*
instant messenger 메신저 *meh • sseen • juh*
instead 대신에 *deh • see • neh*
instructions 설명서 *suhl • myuhng • suh*
instructor 강사 *gahng • sah*
insulin 인슐린 *een • syool • leen*
insurance 보험 *boh • huhm*
insurance card 보험 카드 *boh • huhm kah • du*
insurance claim 보험금 청구 *boh • huhm • gum chuhng • goo*
interest (hobby) 취미 *chwih • mee*
interference 방해 *bahng • heh*
intermission 막간 *mahk • kkahn*

international 국제 *gook • tzeh*
International Student Card 국제 학생증 *gook • tzeh hahk • ssehng • tzung*
internet 인터넷 *een • tuh • neht*
internet cafe 피시방 *pee • ssee • bahng*
interpreter 통역 *tohng • yuhk*
intersection 교차로 *gyo • chah • loh*
introduce 소개하다 *soh • geh • hah • dah*
invite 초대하다 *choh • deh • hah • dah*
Ireland 아일랜드 *ah • eel • lehn • du*
iron 다리미 *dah • lee • mee*
itch 가려움 *gah • lyuh • oom*
item 품목 *poom • mohk*
itemized 명세 *myuhng • seh*

J

jacket 재킷 *jeh • keet*
jar 병 *byuhng*
jaw 턱 *tuhk*
jeans 청바지 *chuhng • bah • jee*
jet lag 시차 *see • chah*
jeweler 보석상 *boh • suhk • ssahng*
jewelry 보석 *boh • suhk*
job 직업 *jee • guhp*
join 참가하다 *chahm • gah • hah • dh*
joint 관절 *gwahn • juhl*
joke 농담 *nohng • dahm*
journey 여행 *yuh • hehng*

K

keep 보유하다 *boh • yoo • hah • dah*
keep out 들어가지 않다 *du • luh • gah • jee ahn • tah*
key 열쇠 *yuhl • ssweh*
key card 키카드 *kee • kah • du*
key ring 열쇠고리 *yuhl • ssweh • goh • lee*
kiddie pool 어린이 수영장 *uh • lee • nee soo • yuhng • jahng*
kind 친절한 *cheen • juhl • hahn*
kiss 키스하다 *kee • ssu • hah • dah*
kitchen 부엌 *boo • uhk*
knee 무릎 *moo • lup*
knife 칼 *kahl*
knock 두드리다 *doo • du • lee • dah*
know 알다 *ahl • dah*
Korean wrestling 씨름 *ssee • lum*
kosher 유대교 음식 *yoo • deh • gyo um • seek*

L

label 상표 *sahng • pyo*
lace 레이스 *leh • ee • su*
lactose intolerant 유당 불내증 *yoo • dahng bool • leh • tzung*
ladder 사다리 *sah • dah•lee*
lake 호수 *hoh • soo*
lamp 전등 *juhn • dung*
land *n* 땅 *ttahng; v* 착륙하다 *chahng • nyoo • kah • dah*
lane 차선 *chah • suhn*
large 큰 *kun*
last *adj* 마지막 *mah • jee • mahk; v* 지속하다 *jee • soh • kah • dah*
late 늦다 *nut • ttah*
later 나중에 *nah • joong • eh*
launderette [BE] 빨래방 *ppahl • leh • bahng*
laundromat 빨래방 *ppahl • leh • bahng*
laundry service 세탁 서비스 *seh • tahk ssuh • bee • su*
laundry facilities 세탁 시설 *seh • tahk see • suhl*
lawyer 변호사 *byuhn • hoh • sah*
laxative 관장약 *gwahn • jahng • yahk*
lead *n* 납 *nahp; v* 인도하다 *een • doh • hah • dah*

leader (group) 지도자 *jee • doh • jah*
leak *n* 누출 *noo • chool;* *v* 새다 *seh • dah*
learn 배우다 *beh • oo • dah*
leather 가죽 *gah • jook*
leave 떠나다 *ttuh • nah • dah*
left 왼쪽 *wehn • tzohk*
leg 다리 *dah • lee*
legal 합법적 *hahp • ppuhp • tzuhk*
lend 빌려주다 *beel • lyuh • joo • dah*
length 길이 *gee • lee*
lens 렌즈 *lehn • ju*
less 더 적은 *duh juh • gun*
lesson 수업 *soo • uhp*
let 하게 하다 *hah • geh hah • dah*
letter 편지 *pyuhn • jee*
level 단계 *dahn • geh*
library 도서관 *doh • suh • gwahn*
life 생명 *sehng • myuhng*
life boat 구명 보트 *goo • myuhng boh • tu*
life guard 구조원 *goo • joh • wuhn*
life jacket 구명 조끼 *goo • myuhng joh • kkee*
lift [BE] 엘리베이터 *ehl • lee • beh • ee • tuh*
light 전등 *juhn • dung*
lightbulb 전구 *juhn • goo*
lighthouse 등대 *dung • deh*
lighter 라이터 *lah • ee • tuh*
like 좋아하다 *joh • ah • hah • dah*
line 노선 *noh • suhn*
linen 마 *mah*
lip 입술 *eep • ssool*
lipstick 립스틱 *leep • ssu • teek*
liquor store 주류 판매점 *joo • lyoo pahn • meh • juhm*
liter 리터 *lee • tuh*
little 작은 *jah • gun*
live 살다 *sahl • dah*
lobby (theater, hotel) 로비 *loh • bee*
local 지방 *jee • bahng*
lock *n* 자물쇠 *jah • mool • ssweh;* *v* 잠그다 *jahm • gu • dah*
log on 접속하다 *juhp • ssoh • kah • dah*
log off 접속을 끊다 *juhp • ssoh • gul kkun • tah*
long 긴 *geen*
long-distance bus 장거리 버스 *jahng • guh • lee buh • su*
long-sighted [BE] 원시 *wuhn • see*
look 보다 *boh • dah*
loose 헐렁한 *huhl • luhng • hahn*
lose 잃어버리다 *ee • luh • buh • lee • dah*
lost 잃어버린 *ee • luh • buh • leen*
lost-and-found 분실물 센터 *boon • seel • mool ssehn • tuh*
lost property office [BE] 분실물 센터 *boon • seel • mool ssehn • tuh*
lottery 복권 *boh • kkwuhn*
loud 시끄러운 *see • kku • luh • oon*
love *v* 사랑하다 *sah • lahng • hah • dah*
low 낮은 *nah • jun*
luggage 수하물 *soo • hah • mool*
luggage cart 수하물 카트 *soo • hah • mool kah • tu*
luggage trolley [BE] 수하물 카트 *soo • hah • mool kah • tu*
lunch 점심 *juhm • seem*

M

magazine 잡지 *jahp • tzee*
magnificent 웅장한 *oong • jahng • hahn*
mail *n* 편지 *pyuhn • jee;* *v* 편지 보내다 *pyuhn • jee boh • neh • dah*
mailbox 우체통 *oo • cheh • tohng*
main 주요한 *joo • yo • hahn*
make-up 화장 *hwah • jahng*

male 남자 *nahm • jah*
mall 쇼핑센터
syo • peeng • ssehn • tuh
man 남자 *nahm • jah*
manager 매니저 *meh • nee • juh*
mandatory 의무적인
u • moo • juh • geen
manicure 매니큐어
meh • nee • kyoo • uh
many 많이 *mah • nee*
map 지도 *jee • doh*
market 시장 *see • jahng*
marry 결혼하다
gyuhl • hohn • hah • dah
mass 미사 *mee • sah*
massage 마사지 *mah • ssah • jee*
matches 성냥 *suhng • nyahng*
matinée 마티네 *mah • tee • neh*
mattress 매트리스
meh • tu • lee • su
maybe 아마 *ah • mah*
meal 식사 *seek • ssah*
mean *v* 뜻하다 *ttu • tah • dah*
measure 재다 *jeh • dah*
measurement 치수 *chee • soo*
mechanic 자동차 수리공
jah • dohng • chah
soo • lee • gohng
medication 약물 *yahng • mool*
medicine 약 *yahk*
medium 중간 *joong • gahn*
meet 만나다 *mahn • nah • dah*
meeting 회의 *hweh • ee*
meeting room 회의실
hweh • ee • seel
meeting place 회의 장소 *hweh • ee*
jahng • soh
member 회원 *hweh • wuhn*
memorial *n* 기념관
gee • nyuhm • gwahn
memory card 메모리 카드
meh • moh • lee kah • du
mend (clothes) 수선하다
soo • suhn • hah • dah
menstrual cramps 생리통
sehng • nee • tohng
menu 메뉴 *meh • nyoo*
merge 합치다 *hahp • chee • dah*
message 메시지 *meh • ssee • jee*
metal 금속 *gum • sohk*
microwave (oven) 전자레인지
juhn • jah • leh • een • jee
midday [BE] 정오 *juhng • oh*
midnight 자정 *jah • juhng*
migraine 편두통
pyuhn • doo • tohng
mini 소형 *soh • hyuhng*
miniature 축소 모형 *chook • ssoh*
moh • hyuhng
mini-bar 미니바 *mee • nee • bah*
minute 분 *boon*
mirror 거울 *guh • ool*
missing 없어진 *uhp • ssuh • jeen*
mistake 실수 *seel • ssoo*
mobile home 이동식 주택
ee • dohng • seek joo • tehk
mobile phone [BE] 휴대폰
hyoo • deh • pohn
moisturizer (cream) 보습 크림
boh • sup ku • leem
money 돈 *dohn*
money order 우편환
oo • pyuhn • hwahn
month 달 *dahl*
mop 대걸레 *deh • guhl • leh*
more 더 많이 *duh mah • nee*
morning 아침 *ah • cheem*
mosque 회교 사원 *hweh • gyo*
sah • wuhn
motion sickness 멀미 *muhl • mee*
motor 모터 *moh • tuh*
motor boat 모터 보트 *moh • tuh*
boh • tu
motorcycle 오토바이
oh • toh • bah • ee

motorway [BE] 고속도로 *goh • sohk • ttoh • loh*
mountain 산 *sahn*
mouth 입 *eep*
move 옮기다 *ohm • gee • dah*
movie 영화 *yuhng • hwah*
movie theater 영화관 *yuhng • hwah • gwahn*
much 훨씬 *hwuhl • sseen*
mugging 노상 강도 *noh • sahng gahng • doh*
muscle 근육 *gu • nyook*
museum 박물관 *bahng • mool • gwahn*
music 음악 *u • mahk*
must 해야 하다 *heh • yah hah • dah*

N

nail 손톱 *sohn • tohp*
nail salon 미용실 *mee • yong • seel*
name 이름 *ee • lum*
napkin 냅킨 *nehp • keen*
nappy [BE] 기저귀 *gee • juh • gwih*
narrow 좁은 *joh • bun*
national 국가의 *gook • kkah • eh*
nationality 국적 *gook • tzuhk*
native 토박이 *toh • bah • gee*
nature 자연 *jah • yuhn*
nature reserve 자연 보호 지역 *jah • yuhn boh • hoh jee • yuhk*
nature trail 산책로 *sahn • chehng • noh*
nausea 메스꺼움 *meh • su • kkuh • oom*
nauseous 토할 거 같은 *toh • hahl kkuh gah • tun*
near 가까이 *gah • kkah • ee*
nearby 근처에 *gun • chuh • eh*
near-sighted 근시 *gun • see*
necessary 필요한 *pee • lyo • hahn*
neck 목 *mohk*
necklace 목걸이 *mohk • kkuh • lee*
need 필요하다 *pee • lyo • hah • dah*
network 네트워크 *neh • tu • wuh • ku*
never 단 한번도 *dahn hahn • buhn • doh*
new 새로운 *seh • loh • oon*
New Zealand 뉴질랜드 *nyoo • jeel • lehn • du*
news 뉴스 *nyoo • su*
news agent [BE] 신문 가판대 *seen • moon gah • pahn • deh*
newspaper 신문 *seen • moon*
newsstand 신문 가판대 *seen • moon gah • pahn • deh*
next 다음 *dah • um*
nice 좋은 *joh • un*
night 밤 *bahm*
no 아니요 *ah • nee • yo*
noisy 시끄러운 *see • kku • luh • oon*
non-smoking 금연 *gu • myuhn*
non-stop 직행 *jee • kehng*
noon 정오 *juhng • oh*
normal 정상 *juhng • sahng*
north 북쪽 *book • tzohk*
nose 코 *koh*
not 아니다 *ah • nee • dah*
nothing 아무 것도 아님 *ah • moo guht • ttoh ah • neem*
notify 통보하다 *tohng • boh • hah • dah*
now 지금 *jee • gum*
number 번호 *buhn • hoh*
nurse 간호사 *gahn • hoh • sah*

O

office 사무실 *sah • moo • seel*
office hours 영업 시간 *yuhng • uhp ssee • gahn*
off-lisence [BE] 주류 판매점 *joo • lyoo pahn • meh • juhm*
off-peak (ticket) 비수기 *bee • soo • gee*
often 종종 *johng • johng*
oil 기름 *gee • lum*

OK 좋다 *joh • tah*
old (elderly) 늙은 *nul • gun;*
(object)
오래된 *oh • leh • dwehn*
on 에 *eh*
once 한 번 *hahn buhn*
one-way ticket 편도표
pyuhn • doh • pyo
only 오직 *oh • jeek*
open 열다 *yuhl • dah*
opening hours [BE] 영업 시간
yuhng • uhp ssee • gahn
opera 오페라 *oh • peh • lah*
operation 수술 *soo • sool*
opposite 맞은편 *mah • jun • pyuhn*
optician 안경점
ahn • gyuhng • juhm
or 또는 *ttoh • nun*
orchestra 오케스트라
oh • keh • su • tu • lah
order *v* 주문하다
joo • moon • hah • dah
organize 조직하다
joh • jee • kah • dah
original 원조 *wuhn • joh*
out 밖 *bahk*
outdoor 실외 *seel • weh*
outdoor pool 실외 수영장
seel • weh soo • yuhng • jahng
outside 밖에 *bah • kkeh*
oven 오븐 *oh • bun*
over (more than) 이상 *ee • sahng*
overcharged 바가지 쓴
bah • gah • jee ssun
overheat 과열 *gwah • yuhl*
overnight 밤새 *bahm • seh*
owe 빚지다 *beet • tzee • dah*
own *v* 소유하다
soh • yoo • hah • dah
owner 주인 *joo • een*
oxygen 산소 *sahn • soh*

P

pacifier 고무 젖꼭지 *goh • moo*
juht • kkohk • tzee
pack 싸다 *ssah • dah*
package 소포 *soh • poh*
padlock 자물쇠 *jah • mool • ssweh*
pail 양동이 *yahng • dohng • ee*
pain 고통 *goh • tohng*
paint 그리다 *gu • lee • dah*
painting 그림 *gu • leem*
pair 한 쌍 *hahn ssahng*
pajamas 잠옷 *jah • moht*
palace 궁 *goong*
panorama 전경 *juhn • gyuhng*
pants 바지 *bah • jee*
panty hose 팬티스타킹
pehn • tee • su • tah • keeng
paper towel 종이 타월 *johng • ee*
tah • wuhl
parcel [BE] 소포 *soh • poh*
parents 부모님 *boo • moh • neem*
park 공 원 *gohng • wuhn*
parking attendant 주차 요원
joo • chah yo • wuhn
parking garage 주차장
joo • chah • jahng
parking lot 주차장
joo • chah • jahng
parking meter 주차 미터기
joo • chah mee • tuh • gee
parking ticket 주차 위반 딱지
joo • chah wih • bahn ttahk • jee
partner 상대 *sahng • deh*
party 파티 *pah • tee*
pass *v* 지나다 *jee • nah • dah*
passenger 승객 *sung • gehk*
passport 여권 *yuh • kkwuhn*
password 비밀번호
bee • meel • buhn • hoh
patient *n* 환자 *hwahn • jah*
pavement [BE] 보도 *boh • doh*
pay 계산하다 *geh • sahn • hah • dah*

pay phone 공중 전화 *gohng • joong juhn • hwah*
payment 지불 *jee • bool*
pearl 진주 *jeen • joo*
pedestrian *n* 보행자 *boh • hehng • jah*
pedestrian crossing 횡단보도 *hwehng • dahn • boh • doh*
pediatrician 소아과 의사 *soh • ah • kkwah u • sah*
pedicure 페디큐어 *peh • dee • kyoo • uh*
peg 나무 못 *nah • moo moht*
pen 펜 *pehn*
penicillin 페니실린 *peh • nee • seel • leen*
per 에 *eh*
performance 공연 *gohng • yuhn*
perhaps 아마 *ah • mah*
period (historical) 시대 *see • deh;* **(menstrual)** 생리 *sehng • nee*
person 사람 *sah • lahm*
petite 아주 작은 *ah • joo jah • gun;* **(clothing)** 특소 *tuk • ssoh*
petrol [BE] 기름 *gee • lum*
petrol station [BE] 주유소 *joo • yoo • soh*
pharmacy 약국 *yahk • kkook*
phone *n* 전화 *juhn • hwah*
phone call 전화 *juhn • hwah*
phone card 전화 카드 *juhn • hwah kah • du*
phone directory 전화 번호부 *juhn • hwah buhn • hoh • boo*
phone number 전화 번호 *juhn • hwah buhn • hoh*
photocopy *v* 복사하다 *bohk • ssah • hah • dah*
photograph 사진 *sah • jeen*
phrase 구절 *goo • juhl*
phrase book 기본 회화집 *gee • bohn hweh • hwah • jeep*
picnic 피크닉 *pee • ku • neek*
picnic area 피크닉 구역 *pee • ku • neek goo • yuhk*
piece 개 *geh*
pill 알약 *ahl • lyahk*
pillow 베개 *beh • geh*
PIN (personal identification number) 비밀 번호 *bee • meel buhn • hoh*
place 자리 *jah • lee*
plan 계획 *geh • hwehk*
plane 비행기 *bee • hehng • gee*
plaster [BE] 반창고 *bahn • chahng • goh*
plastic 플라스틱 *pul • lah • su • teek*
plastic wrap 랩 *lehp*
plate 접시 *juhp • ssee*
platform 승강장 *sung • gahng • jahng*
platinum 백금 *behk • kkum*
play *n* 연극 *yuhn • guk;* *v* **(sports)** 시합하다 *see • hah • pah • dah;* *v* **(music)** 연주하다 *yuhn • joo • hah • dah*
playground 놀이터 *noh • lee • tuh*
playpen 아기 놀이울 *ah • gee noh • lee • ool*
pleasant 즐거운 *jul • guh • oon*
please 좀 *johm*
plug 플러그 *pul • luh • gu*
plunger 변기 뚫는 것 *byuhn • gee ttool • nun guht*
poison 독 *dohk*
police 경찰 *gyuhng • chahl*
police station 경찰서 *gyuhng • chahl • ssuh*
pollen count 꽃가루 지수 *kkoht • kkah • loo jee • soo*
pond 연못 *yuhn • moht*
pool 수영장 *soo • yuhng • jahng*
popular 인기있는 *een • kkee • een • nun*
porcelain 자기 *jah • gee*
port 항구 *hahng • goo*

porter 짐꾼 *jeem • kkoon*
portion 분량 *bool • lyahng*
post office 우체국 *oo • cheh • gook*
postage 우편 요금 *oo • pyuhn nyo • gum*
postbox [BE] 우체통 *oo • cheh • tohng*
postcard 엽서 *yuhp • ssuh*
pot 냄비 *nehm • bee*
pottery 도자기 *doh • jah • gee*
pound 파운드 *pah • oon • du*
pound sterling 파운드 *pah • oon • du*
power 힘 *heem*
practice *v* 연습하다 *yuhn • su • pah • dah*
pregnant 임신한 *eem • seen • hahn*
prepaid phone card 선불 전화 카드 *suhn • bool juhn • hwah kah • du*
prescription 처방 *chuh • bahng*
present *n* 선물 *suhn • mool*
press 다림질하다 *dah • leem • jeel • hah • dah*
pretty 예쁜 *yeh • ppun*
price 가격 *gah • gyuhk*
print *v* 프린트하다 *pu • leen • tu • hah • dah*
prison 감옥 *gah • mohk*
private 사적인 *sah • tzuh • geen*
profession 직업 *jee • guhp*
problem 문제 *moon • jeh*
prohibited 금지된 *gum • jee • dwehn*
program 프로그램 *pu • loh • gu • lehm*
pronounce 발음하다 *bah • lum • hah • dah*
pub 술집 *sool • tzeep*
public 공공 *gohng • gohng*
pull 당기다 *dahng • gee • dah*
pure 순수한 *soon • soo • hahn*
purpose 목적 *mohk • tzuhk*
purse 핸드백 *hehn • du • behk*
push 밀다 *meel • dah*
push-chair [BE] 유모차 *yoo • moh • chah*
put 넣다 *nuh • tah*

Q

quality 질 *jeel*
quarter 사분의 일 *sah • boo • neh eel*
quick 빠른 *ppah • lun*
quiet 조용한 *joh • yong • hahn*

R

race course [BE] 경마장 *gyuhng • mah • jahng*
racetrack 경마장 *gyuhng • mah • jahng*
racket (tennis) 라켓 *lah • keht*
railway station [BE] 기차역 *gee • chah • yuhk*
rain *n* 비 *bee; v* 비 내리다 *bee neh • lee • dah*
raincoat 비옷 *bee • oht*
rape 강간 *gahng • gahn*
rapids 급류 *gum • nyoo*
rash 두드러기 *doo • du • luh • gee*
razor 면도칼 *myuhn • doh • kahl*
razor blade 면도날 *myuhn • doh • nahl*
reach 연락하다 *yuhl • lah • kah • dah*
reaction 반응 *bah • nung*
read 읽다 *eek • ttah*
ready 준비된 *joon • bee • dwehn*
real (genuine) 진짜 *jeen • tzah*
receipt 영수증 *yuhng • soo • jung*
receive 받다 *baht • ttah*
reception (desk) 접수 *juhp • ssoo*
receptionist 접수원 *juhp • ssoo • wuhn*
recommend 추천하다 *choo • chuhn • hah • dah*

reduce 줄이다 *joo • lee • dah*
reduction 감소 *gahm • soh*
refrigerator 냉장고 *nehng • jahng • goh*
refund 환불 *hwahn • bool*
region 지역 *jee • yuhk*
registered mail 등기 우편 *dung • kkee oo • pyuhn*
registration form 등록 용지 *dung • noh gyong • jee*
regular 보통 *boh • tohng*
relationship 관계 *gwahn • geh*
reliable 믿을 만한 *mee • dul mahn • hahn*
religion 종교 *johng • gyo*
remember 기억하다 *gee • uh • kah • dah*
remove 제거하다 *jeh • guh • hah • dah*
renovation 개조 *geh • joh*
rent *v* 빌리다 *beel • lee • dah*
rental car 렌터카 *lehn • tuh • kah*
repair 수선하다 *soo • suhn • hah • dah*
repeat 되풀이하다 *dweh • poo • lee • hah • dah*
replace 바꾸다 *bah • kkoo • dah*
report *v* 신고하다 *seen • goh • hah • dah*
required 필수 *peel • ssoo*
reservation 예약 *yeh • yahk*
reservation desk 예약 접수처 *yeh • yahk juhp • ssoo • chuh*
reserve 예약하다 *yeh • yah • kah • dah*
reservoir 저수지 *juh • soo • jee*
responsibility 책임 *cheh • geem*
rest 쉬다 *swih • dah*
rest area 휴게소 *hyoo • geh • soh*
restaurant 음식점 *um • seek • tzuhm*
restroom 화장실 *hwah • jahng • seel*
retired 은퇴한 *un • tweh • hahn*
return *v* 돌아가다 *doh • lah • gah • dah*
return ticket [BE] 왕복표 *wahng • bohk • pyo*
rice bowl 밥그릇 *bahp • kku • lut*
rice cooker 밥솥 *bahp • ssoht*
right 오른쪽 *oh • lun • tzohk*
ring 반지 *bahn • jee*
river 강 *gahng*
road 도로 *doh • loh*
rob 빼앗다 *ppeh • aht • ttah*
robbery 강도 *gahng • doh*
rock 록 *lohk*
romantic 낭만적인 *nahng • mahn • juh • geen*
roof 지붕 *jee • boong*
room 방 *bahng*
room service 룸 서비스 *loom ssuh • bee • su*
room temperature 상온 *sahng • ohn*
rope 밧줄 *baht • tzool*
rose 장미 *jahng • mee*
round (of golf) 라운드 *lah • oon • du*
round-trip ticket 왕복표 *wahng • bohk • pyo*
route 길 *geel*
row *n* 노 *noh*
rowboat 노 젓는 배 *noh juhn • nun beh*
rubbish [BE] 쓰레기 *ssu • leh • gee*
rude 무례한 *moo • leh • hahn*
rush 서두르다 *suh • doo • lu • dah*

S

safe *adj* 안전한 *ahn • juhn • hahn; n* 금고 *gum • goh*
safety 안전 *ahn • juhn*
safety pin 안전핀 *ahn • juhn • peen*
sale [BE] 영업 *yuhng • uhp*
sales tax 판매세 *pahn • meh • seh*

same 같은 *gah • tun*
sand 모래 *moh • leh*
sandals 샌들 *sehn • dul*
sanitary napkin 생리대 *sehng • nee • deh*
sanitary pad [BE] 생리대 *sehng • nee • deh*
satin 공단 *gohng • dahn*
saucepan 냄비 *nehm • bee*
sauna 사우나 *ssah • oo • nah*
save 저장하다 *juh • jahng • hah • dah*
savings account 보통 예금 계좌 *boh • tohng yeh • gum geh • jwah*
say 말하다 *mahl • hah • dah*
scarf 스카프 *su • kah • pu*
scale 저울 *juh • ool*
schedule 시간표 *see • gahn • pyo*
scissors 가위 *gah • wih*
Scotland 스코틀랜드 *su • koh • tul • lehn • du*
screwdriver 드라이버 *du • lah • ee • buh*
sea 바다 *bah • dah*
sea level 해발 *heh • bahl*
seasick 뱃멀미 *behn • muhl • mee*
seat (on train, etc.) 좌석 *jwah • suhk*
seat belt 안전벨트 *ahn • juhn • behl • tu*
secondhand 중고 *joong • goh*
sedative 진정제 *jeen • juhng • jeh*
see 보다 *boh • dah*
self-service 셀프서비스 *ssehl • pu • ssuh • bee • su*
sell 팔다 *pahl • dah*
seminar 세미나 *sseh • mee • nah*
send 보내다 *boh • neh • dah*
senior citizen 노인 *noh • een*
separate 따로 *ttah • loh*
separated 별거한 *byuhl • guh • hahn*
serious 심각한 *seem • gah • kahn*
serve 봉사하다 *bohng • sah • hah • dah*
service (religious) 예배 *yeh • beh*
service charge 봉사료 *bohng • sah • lyo*
sew 꿰매다 *kkweh • meh • dah*
sex 성 *suhng*
shadow 그림자 *gu • leem • jah*
shallow 얕은 *yah • tun*
shampoo 샴푸 *syahm • poo*
shape 모양 *moh • yahng*
share *v* 같이 쓰다 *gah • chee ssu • dah*
sharp 날카로운 *nahl • kah • loh • oon*
shave 면도하다 *myuhn • doh • hah • dah*
sheet (bed) 시트 *see • tu*
ship 배 *beh*
shock 충격 *choong • gyuhk*
shoe 신발 *seen • bahl*
shoe repair 신발 수선 *seen • bahl soo • suhn*
shoe store 신발 가게 *seen • bahl kkah • geh*
shop assistant 점원 *juh • mwuhn*
shopping 쇼핑 *syo • peeng*
shopping area 상가 *sahng • gah*
shopping basket 바구니 *bah • goo • nee*
shopping centre [BE] 상가 *sahng • gah*
shopping mall 상가 *sahng • gah*
shopping cart 쇼핑 카트 *syo • peeng kah • tu*
shopping trolley [BE] 쇼핑 카트 *syo • peeng kah • tu*
short 짧은 *tzahl • bun*
short-sighted [BE] 근시 *gun • see*
shorts 반바지 *bahn • bah • jee*
shoulder 어깨 *uh • kkeh*
shovel 삽 *sahp*
show 보여주다 *boh • yuh • joo • dah*

shower 샤워 *syah • wuh*
shut *adj* 닫힌 *dah • cheen;* **n** 닫다 *daht • ttah*
sick 아픈 *ah • pun*
side effect 부작용 *boo • jah • gyong*
sidewalk 보도 *boh • doh*
sight (attraction) 구경거리 *goo • gyuhng • kkuh • lee*
sightseeing tour 관광 코스 *gwahn • gwahng koh • su*
sign *n* 표지 *pyo • jee;* *v* 서명하다 *suh • myuhng • hah • dah*
silk 실크 *seel • ku*
silver 은 *un*
single (individual) 일인용 *ee • leen • yong;* **(marital status)** 미혼 *mee • hohn*
single room 일인용 방 *ee • leen • yong bahng*
sink 세면대 *seh • myuhn • deh*
sit 앉다 *ahn • ttah*
site 장소 *jahng • soh*
size 사이즈 *ssah • ee • ju*
ski slope 스키장 *su • kee • jahng*
skin 피부 *pee • boo*
skirt 치마 *chee • mah*
sleep 자다 *jah • dah*
sleeper car (train) 침대차 *cheem • deh • chah*
sleeping bag 침낭 *cheem • nahng*
sleeping pill 수면제 *soo • myuhn • jeh*
sleeve 소매 *soh • meh*
slice 조각 *joh • gahk*
slippers 슬리퍼 *sul • lee • puh*
slow 느린 *nu • leen*
small 작은 *jah • gun*
smell 냄새 맡다 *nehm • seh maht • ttah*
smoke 담배를 피우다 *dahm • beh • lul pee • oo • dah*
smoking area 흡연석 *hu • byuhn • suhk*
snack 간식 *gahn • seek*
snack bar 간이 식당 *gah • nee seek • ttahng*
sneakers 운동화 *oon • dohng • hwah*
snorkle 잠수용 튜브 *jahm • soo • yong tyoo • bu*
snow 눈 *noon*
soap 비누 *bee • noo*
soccer 축구 *chook • kkoo*
socket 소켓 *soh • keht*
socks 양말 *yahng • mahl*
sold out 매진 *meh • jeen*
some 다소 *dah • soh*
someone 누군가 *noo • goon • gah*
something 무언가 *moo • uhn • gah*
sometimes 가끔 *gah • kkum*
somewhere 어딘가 *uh • deen • gah*
soon 곧 *goht*
soother [BE] 고무 젖꼭지 *goh • moo juht • kkohk • jee*
sore 쑤시는 *ssoo • see • nun*
sore throat 목 아픈 데 *moh gah • pun deh*
sorry 미안하다 *mee • ahn • hah • dah*
sour 시큼한 *see • kum • hahn*
south 남쪽 *nahm • tzohk*
souvenir 기념품 *gee • nyuhm • poom*
souvenir guide 기념품 안내 *gee • nyuhm • poom ahn • neh*
souvenir store 기념품 가게 *gee • nyuhm • poom kkah • geh*
spa 스파 *su • pah*
space 자리 *jah • lee*
spare 여분 *yuh • boon*
speak 얘기하다 *yeh • gee • hah • dah*
special 특별한 *tuk • ppyuhl • hahn*
specialist 전문의 *juhn • moo • nee*
specimen 표본 *pyo • bohn*

speed *n* 속도 *sohk • ttoh;* *v* 과속하다 *gwah • soh • kah • dah*
speed limit 제한 속도 *jeh • hahn sohk • ttoh*
spell 철자하다 *chuhl • tzah • hah • dah*
spend 쓰다 *ssu • dah*
sponge 스폰지 *su • pohn • jee*
spoon 숟가락 *soot • kkah • lahk*
sport 운동 *oon • dohng*
sporting goods store 스포츠 용품점 *su • poh • chu yong • poom • juhm*
sports club 스포츠 클럽 *su • poh • chu kul • luhp*
spot (place, site) 장소 *jahng • soh*
spouse 배우자 *beh • oo • jah*
sprain 삐다 *ppee • dah*
square 광장 *gwahng • jahng*
stadium 경기장 *gyuhng • gee • jahng*
staff 직원 *jee • gwuhn*
stainless steel 스테인레스 *su • teh • een • leh • su*
stairs 계단 *geh • dahn*
stamp 우표 *oo • pyo*
stand *n* 정류장 *juhng • nyoo • jahng;* *v* 일어서다 *ee • luh • suh • dah*
standard 표준 *pyo • joon*
standby ticket 대기표 *deh • gee • pyo*
start (begin) 시작하다 *see • jah • kah • dah*
stationery 문구류 *moon • goo • lyoo*
statue 동상 *dohng • sahng*
stay 묵다 *mook • ttah*
steal 훔치다 *hoom • chee • dah*
steel 철 *chuhl*
steep 가파른 *gah • pah • lun*
sterilizing solution 소독액 *soh • doh • gehk*
sterling silver 순은 *soo • nun*
stolen 도난 당한 *doh • nahn dahng • hahn*
stomach 위 *wih*
stomachache 복통 *bohk • tohng*
stop *n* 정거장 *juhng • guh • jahng;* *v* 세우다 *seh • oo • dah*
store 가게 *gah • geh*
store directory 상가 안내 *sahng • gah ahn • neh*
stove 가스 레인지 *gah • su leh • een • jee*
straight 똑바른 *ttohk • bah • lun*
stream 개울 *geh • ool*
street 길 *geel*
stroller 유모차 *yoo • moh • chah*
strong 강한 *gahng • hahn*
student 학생 *hahk • ssehng*
study 공부하다 *gohng • boo • hah • dah*
style 스타일 *su • tah • eel*
subtitled 자막 나오는 *jah • mahng nah • oh • nun*
suburb 교외 *gyo • weh*
subway 지하철 *jee • hah • chuhl*
subway map 지하철 노선도 *jee • hah • chuhl noh • suhn • doh*
subway station 지하철역 *jee • hah • chuhl • lyuhk*
suggest 제안하다 *jeh • ahn • hah • dah*
suit 양복 *yahng • bohk*
suitable 적당한 *juhk • ttahng • hahn*
suitcase 여행 가방 *yuh • hehng kkah • bahng*
sun 해 *heh*
sunbathe 일광욕하다 *eel • gwahng • nyo • kah • dah*
sunburn 일광 화상 *eel • gwahng hwah • sahng*
sunglasses 선글라스 *ssuhn • gul • lah • su*

sunscreen 자외선 차단 크림 *jah • weh • suhn chah • dahn ku • leem*
sunstroke 일사병 *eel • ssah • ppyuhng*
suntan lotion 선탠 크림 *ssuhn • tehn ku • leem*
superb 최고 *chweh • goh*
supermarket 슈퍼마켓 *syoo • puh • mah • keht*
supervision 감독 *gahm • dohk*
supplement 추가 *choo • gah*
suppository 좌약 *jwah • yahk*
sure 확실한 *hwahk • sseel • hahn*
surfboard 서핑보드 *ssuh • peeng • boh • du*
swallow 삼키다 *sahm • kee • dah*
sweater 스웨터 *su • weh • tuh*
sweep 쓸다 *ssul • dah*
sweet (taste) 달콤한 *dahl • kohm • hahn*
swelling 부은 데 *boo • un deh*
swim 수영하다 *soo • yuhng • hah • dah*
swimsuit 수영복 *soo • yuhng • bohk*
swimming pool 수영장 *soo • yuhng • jahng*
swimming trunks 수영복 *soo • yuhng • bohk*
swollen 부은 *boo • un*
symbol 기호 *gee • hoh*
symptom 증상 *jung • sahng*
synagogue 유대교 회당 *yoo • deh • gyo hweh • dahng*
synthetic 합성 *hahp • ssuhng*

T

T-shirt 티셔츠 *tee • syuh • chu*
table 테이블 *teh • ee • bul*
tablet 알약 *ahl • lyahk*
take (things) 가지다 *gah • jee • dah*
taken 임자 있는 *eem • jah een • nun*
take away [BE] 싸가다 *ssah • gah • dah*
take off (clothing) 벗다 *buht • ttah;* **(plane)** 이륙하다 *ee • lyoo • kah • dah*
talk 얘기하다 *yeh • gee • hah • dah*
tall 키 큰 *kee kun*
tampon 탐폰 *tahm • pohn*
tan 태우다 *teh • oo • dah*
tap [BE] 수도꼭지 *soo • doh • kkohk • jee*
taste 맛보다 *maht • ppoh • dah*
taxi 택시 *tehk • ssee*
taxi stand 택시 승차장 *tehk • ssee sung • chah • jahng*
teaspoon 티스푼 *tee • su • poon*
team 팀 *teem*
tear 찢다 *tzeet • ttah*
telephone 전화 *juhn • hwah*
telephone number 전화 번호 *juhn • hwah buhn • hoh*
television 텔레비전 *tehl • leh • bee • juhn*
tell 말하다 *mahl • hah • dah*
temperature 온도 *ohn • doh*
tennis 테니스 *teh • nee • su*
tennis court 테니스 코트 *teh•nee • su koh • tu*
tent 텐트 *tehn • tu*
terminal 터미널 *tuh • mee • nuhl*
terrible 끔찍한 *kkum • tzee • kahn*
terrific 굉장한 *gwehng • jahng • hahn*
text 문자 *moon • tzah*
thank 감사하다 *gahm • sah • hah • dah*
that 그것 *gu • guht*
theater 극장 *guk • tzahng*
theft 도난 *doh • nahn*
then (time) 그때 *gu • tteh*
there 거기 *guh • gee*
thermometer 온도계 *ohn • doh • geh*

thick 두꺼운 *doo • kkuh • oon*
thief 도둑 *doh • dook*
thigh 넓적다리 *nuhp • tzuhk • ttah • lee*
thin 가는 *gah • nun*
thing 물건 *mool • guhn*
think 생각하다 *sehng • gah • kah • dah*
thirsty 목마르다 *mohng • mah • lu • dah*
throat 목구멍 *mohk • kkoo • muhng*
through 통해서 *tohng • heh • suh*
thumb 엄지손가락 *uhm • jee • sohn • kkah • lahk*
ticket 표 *pyo*
ticket inspector 검표원 *guhm • pyo • wuhn*
ticket office 매표소 *meh • pyo • soh*
tie 넥타이 *nehk • tah • ee*
tight 끼는 *kkee • nun*
tile 타일 *tah • eel*
time 시간 *see • gahn*
timetable [BE] 시간표 *see • gahn • pyo*
tin opener [BE] 통조림 따개 *tohng • joh • leem ttah • geh*
tint 빛깔 *beet • kkahl*
tip 팁 *teep*
tire 타이어 *tah • ee • uh*
tired 피곤한 *pee • gohn • hahn*
tissue 화장지 *hwah • jahng • jee*
to (place) 으로 *u • loh*
tobacco 담배 *dahm • beh*
tobacconist 담배 가게 *dahm • beh kkah • geh*
today 오늘 *oh • nul*
toe 발가락 *bahl • kkah • lahk*
toilet [BE] 화장실 *hwah • jahng • seel*
toilet paper 화장실 휴지 *hwah • jahng • seel hyoo • jee*
tomorrow 내일 *neh • eel*
tongue 혀 *hyuh*
tonight 오늘밤 *oh • nul • ppahm*
too 너무 *nuh • moo*
tooth 이빨 *ee • ppahl*
toothache 치통 *chee • tohng*
toothbrush 칫솔 *cheet • ssohl*
toothpaste 치약 *chee • yahk*
top 위 *wih*
torn 찢어진 *tzee • juh • jeen*
tough 질긴 *jeel • geen*
tour 여행 *yuh • hehng*
tour guide 여행 가이드 *yuh • hehng gah • ee • du*
tourist 관광객 *gwahn • gwahng • gehk*
tourist office 여행 안내소 *yuh • hehng ahn • neh • soh*
tournament 대회 *deh • hweh*
tow truck 견인차 *gyuh • neen • chah*
towel 수건 *soo • guhn*
tower 탑 *tahp*
town 시내 *see • neh*
town map 시내 지도 *see • neh jee • doh*
toy 장난감 *jahng • nahn • kkahm*
toy store 장난감 가게 *jahng • nahn • kkahm gah • geh*
traditional 전통 *juhn • tohng*
traditional dance 전통춤 *juhn • tohng • choom*
traditional music 국악 *goo • gahk*
traffic 교통 *gyo • tohng*
trail 등산로 *dung • sahn • noh*
trailer 트레일러 *tu • leh • eel • luh*
train 기차 *gee • chah*
train station 기차역 *gee • chah • yuhk*
tram 전차 *juhn • chah*
transfer 갈아타다 *gah • lah • tah • dah*
transport 수송 *soo • sohng*

translate 번역하다 *buh • nyuh • kah • dah*
translation 번역 *buh • nyuhk*
translator 번역사 *buh • nyuhk • ssah*
trash 쓰레기 *ssu • leh • gee*
trash can 쓰레기통 *ssu • leh • gee • tohng*
travel *n* 여행 *yuh • hehng*
travel agency 여행사 *yuh • hehng • sah*
travel sickness 멀미 *muhl • mee*
traveler's check 여행자 수표 *yuh • hehng • jah soo • pyo*
traveler's cheque [BE] 여행자 수표 *yuh • hehng • jah soo • pyo*
tray 쟁반 *jehng • bahn*
treatment 치료 *chee • lyo*
tree 나무 *nah • moo*
trim 다듬다 *dah • dum • ttah*
trip 여행 *yuh • hehng*
trolley 카트 *kah • tu*
trousers [BE] 바지 *bah • jee*
truck 트럭 *tu • luhk*
true 사실 *sah • seel*
try on (clothes) 입어 보다 *ee • buh boh • dah;* **(shoes)** 신어 보다 *see • nuh boh • dah*
tumor 종양 *johng • yahng*
tunnel 터널 *tuh • nuhl*
turn 돌다 *dohl • dah*
tweezers 족집게 *johk • tzeep • geh*
twist 비틀다 *bee • tul • dah*
type 종류 *johng • nyoo*
typical 전형적인 *juhn • hyuhng • juh • geen*

U

ugly 못생긴 *moht • ssehng • geen*
umbrella 우산 *oo • sahn*
unconscious 의식을 잃은 *u • see • gul ee • lun*
under 아래 *ah • leh*
underground [BE] 지하철 *jee • hah • chuhl*
underground station [BE] 지하철 역 *jee • hah • chuhl lyuhk*
understand 알다 *ahl • dah*
unemployed 실업자 *see • luhp • tzah*
United Kingdom 영국 *yuhng • gook*
United States 미국 *mee • gook*
until 까지 *kkah • jee*
upstairs 위층 *wih • chung*
urgent 급한 *gu • pahn*
use 사용하다 *sah • yong • hah • dah*
username 사용자명 *sah • yong • jah • myuhng*

V

vacant 빈 *been*
vacation 휴가 *hyoo • gah*
vacuum cleaner 진공 청소기 *jeen • gohng chuhng • soh • gee*
vagina 질 *jeel*
valet service 주차 서비스 *joo • chah ssuh • bee • su*
valid 유효한 *yoo • hyo • hahn*
validate 확인하다 *hwah • geen • hah • dah*
valuable 귀중한 *gwih • joong • hahn*
value 가격 *gah • gyuhk*
valve 밸브 *behl • bu*
van taxi 콜 밴 *kohl • behn*
VAT [BE] 부가가치세 *boo • gah • gah • chee • seh*
vegetarian 채식주의자 *cheh • seek • jtzoo • ee • jah*
vehicle 자동차 *jah • dohng • chah*
vein 정맥 *juhng • mehk*
version 버전 *buh • juhn*
very 매우 *meh • oo*
view 전망 *juhn • mahng*
viewpoint 전망대 *juhn • mahng • deh*
village 마을 *mah • ul*

vineyard 포도밭 *poh • doh • baht*
visa 비자 *bee • jah*
visit *n* 방문 *bahng • moon;*
v 방문하다
bahng • moon • hah • dah
visiting hours 방문 시간
bahng • moon see • gahn
visually impaired 시각 장애인
see • gahk jahng • eh • een
volleyball 배구 *beh • goo*
vomit 토하다 *toh • hah • dah*

W

wait 기다리다 *gee • dah • lee • dah*
waiter 남자 종업원 *nahm • jah*
johng • uh • bwuhn
waiting room 대기실
deh • gee • seel
waitress 여자 종업원 *yuh • jah*
johng • uh • bwuhn
wake 깨우다 *kkeh • oo • dah*
wake-up call 모닝콜
moh • neeng • kohl
walk 걷다 *guht • ttah*
wall 벽 *byuhk*
wallet 지갑 *jee • gahp*
ward (hospital) 병동
byuhng • dohng
warm 따뜻한 *ttah • ttu • tahn*
war memorial 전쟁 기념관
juhn • jehng gee • nyuhm • gwahn
warning 경고 *gyuhng • goh*
washing machine 세탁기
seh • tahk • kkee
watch 시계 *see • geh*
water 물 *mool*
water skis 수상 스키 *soo • sahng*
su • kee
waterfall 폭포 *pohk • poh*
waterproof 방수 *bahng • soo*
wave 파도 *pah • doh*
way 길 *geel*
wear 입다 *eep • ttah*
weather 날씨 *nahl • ssee*
weather forecast 일기 예보
eel • gee yeh • boh
wedding 결혼식 *gyuhl • hohn • seek*
week 주일 *joo • eel*
weekday 평일 *pyuhng • eel*
weekend 주말 *joo • mahl*
weekend rate 주말 요금 *joo • mahl*
lyo • gum
weekly 매주 *meh • joo*
weigh 무게를 달다 *moo • geh • lul*
dahl • dah
weight 무게 *moo • geh*
welcome 환영 *hwah • nyuhng*
west 서쪽 *suh • tzohk*
wetsuit 잠수복 *jahm • soo • bohk*
what 무엇 *moo • uht*
wheelchair 휠체어 *wihl • cheh • uh*
wheelchair ramp 휠체어 진입로
wihl • cheh • uh jee • neem • noh
when 언제 *uhn • jeh*
where 어디 *uh • dee*
who 누구 *noo • goo*
why 왜 *weh*
wide 넓은 *nuhl • bun*
wife 아내 *ah • neh*
wildlife 야생 *yah • sehng*
wind 바람 *bah • lahm*
windbreaker 윈드브레이커
wihn • du • bu • leh • ee • kuh
windscreen 차 앞유리 *chah*
ahm • nyoo • lee
windsurfing 윈드서핑
wihn • du • ssuh • peeng
window 창문 *chahng • moon*
window seat 창문석
chahng • moon • suhk
wipe 닦다 *dahk • ttah*
wireless 무선 *moo • suhn*
wish 바라다 *bah • lah • dah*
with 하고 같이 *hah • goh gah • chee*
withdraw 출금하다
chool • gum • hah • dah

withdrawal 출금 *chool•gum*
within 안에 *ah•neh*
without 없이 *uhp•ssee*
witness 목격자 *mohk•kkyuhk•tzah*
Won (Korean currency) 원 *wuhn*
wool 양모 *yahng•moh*
work *n* 일 *eel; v* 일하다 *eel•hah•dah*
wrap *n* 랩 *leph; v* 싸다 *ssah•dah*
write 쓰다 *ssu•dah*
writing paper 필기 용지 *peel•gee yong•jee*
wrong 잘못된 *jahl•moht•ttwehn*

X

x-ray 엑스레이 *ehk•ssu•leh•ee*

Y

yacht 요트 *yo•tu*
year 년 *nyuhn*
yes 네 *neh*
yesterday 어제 *uh•jeh*
yield 양보하다 *yahng•boh•hah•dah*
young 젊은 *juhl•mun*
youth 젊음 *juhl•mum*
youth hostel 유스호스텔 *yoo•su•hoh•su•tehl*

Z

zipper 지퍼 *jee•puh*
zoo 동물원 *dohng•moo•lwuhn*

KOREAN–ENGLISH

ㄱ

가게 *gah•geh* **store**
가격 *gah•gyuhk* **price, value**
가구 *gah•goo* **furniture**
가까이 *gah•kkah•ee* **near**
가끔 *gah•kkum* **sometimes**
가는 *gah•nun* **thin**
가다 *gah•dah* **go, take (road)**
가득 찬 *gah•duk chahn* **full**
가득 채우다 *gah•duk cheh•oo•dah* **fill up**
가려움 *gah•lyuh•oom* **itch**
가로질러 *gah•loh•jeel•luh* **across**
가방 *gah•bahng* **bag**
가스 레인지 *kkah•su leh•een•jee* **stove**
가슴 *gah•sum* **breast, chest**
가위 *gah•wih* **scissors**
가이드 투어 *gah•ee•du too•uh* **guided tour**
가져오다 *gah•jyuh•oh•dah* **bring**
가족 *gah•johk* **family**
가죽 *gah•jook* **leather**
가지다 *gah•jee•dah* **take**
가파른 *gah•pah•lun* **steep**
간식 *gahn•seek* **snack**
간이 식당 *gah•nee seek•ttahng* **snack bar**
간호사 *gahn•hoh•sah* **nurse**
갈아타다 *gah•lah•tah•dah* **transfer**
감기 *gahm•gee n* **cold**
감독 *gahm•dohk* **supervision**
감사하다 *gahm•sah•hah•dah* **thank**
감소 *gahm•soh* **reduction**
감염 *gah•myuhm* **infection**
감염시키다 *gah•myuhm•see•kee•dah* **infect**
감옥 *gah•mohk* **prison**
강 *gahng* **river**
강간 *gahng•gahn* **rape**

강도 *gahng•doh* **robbery**
강사 *gahng•sah* **instructor**
강한 *gahng•hahn* **strong**
갖다 *gaht•ttah* **have**
같은 *gah•tun* **same**
같이 가다 *gah•chee gah•dah* **accompany**
같이 쓰다 *gah•chee ssu•dah v* **share**
개 *geh* **dog; piece**
개울 *geh•ool* **stream**
개조 *geh•joh* **renovation**
객실 *gehk•sseel* **compartment**
거기 *guh•gee* **there**
거리 *guh•lee* **distance**
거실 *guh•seel* **living room**
거울 *guh•ool* **mirror**
거즈 *guh•ju* **gauze**
건강 *guhn•gahng* **health**
건강 식품점 *guhn•gahng seek•poom•juhm* **health food store**
건물 *guhn•mool* **building**
건배 *guhn•beh* **cheers (toast)**
건전지 *guhn•juhn•jee* **battery**
걷다 *guht•ttah* **walk**
검사 *guhm•sah* **examination**
검표원 *guhm•pyo•wuhn* **ticket inspector**
견인차 *gyuh•neen•chah* **tow truck**
결백한 *gyuhl•beh•kahn* **innocent**
결혼식 *gyuhl•hohn•seek* **wedding**
결혼하다 *gyuhl•hohn•hah•dah* **marry**
경고 *gyuhng•goh* **warning**
경기 *gyuhng•gee* **game**
경기장 *gyuhng•gee•jahng* **stadium**
경련 *gyuhng•nyuhn* **cramp**
경마 *gyuhng•mah* **horse racing**
경마장 *gyugng•mah•jahng* **horsetrack [race course BE]**
경사 *gyuhng•sah n* **incline**
경찰 *gyuhng•chahl* **police**
경찰서 *gyuhng•chahl•ssuh* **police station**
경찰 조서 *gyuhng•chahl joh•suh* **police report**
경험 *gyuhng•huhm* **experience**
계단 *geh•dahn* **stairs**
계량스푼 *geh•lyahng•su•poon* **measuring spoon**
계량컵 *geh•lyahng•kuhp* **measuring cup**
계산대 *geh•sahn•deh* **cash register**
계산서 *geh•sahn•suh* **bill**
계산원 *geh•sah•nwuhn* **cashier**
계산하다 *geh•sahn•hah•dah* **pay**
계획 *geh•hwehk* **plan**
고객 서비스 *goh•gehk ssuh•bee•su* **customer service**
고르다 *goh•lu•dah* **choose**
고무 젖꼭지 *goh•moo juht•kkohk•tzee* **pacifier [soother BE]**
고속도로 *goh•sohk•ttoh•loh* **highway [motorway BE]**
고장난 *goh•jahng•nahn* **break down, broken**
고전적인 *goh•juhn•juh•geen* **classical**
고치다 *goh•chee•dah* **fix, repair**
고통 *goh•tohng* **pain**
곧 *goht* **soon**
골동품 *gohl•ttohng•poom* **antique**
골절상 *gohl•tzuhl•sahng* **fracture**
골프 *gohl•pu* **golf**
골프장 *gohl•pu•jahng* **golf course**
골프채 *gohl•pu•cheh* **golf club**
공 *gohng* **ball, zero**
공공 *gohng•gohng* **public**
공단 *gohng•dahn* **satin**
공동묘지 *gohng•dohng•myo•jee* **cemetery**
공부하다 *gohng•boo•hah•dah* **study**

공연 *gohng•yuhn* **performance**
공예점 *gohng•yeh•juhm* **craft shop**
공원 *gohng•wuhn* **park**
공중전화 *gohng•joong•juhn•hwah* **pay phone**
공짜 *gohng•tzah* **free of charge**
공항 *gohng•hahng* **airport**
과속하다 *gwah•soh•khah•dah v* **speed**
과열 *gwah•yuhl* **overheat**
관계 *gwahn•geh* **relationship**
관광 코스 *gwahn•gwahng koh•su* **sightseeing tour**
관광객 *gwahn•gwahng•gehk* **tourist**
관리 *gwahl•lee n* **control**
관장약 *gwahn•jahng•yahk* **laxative**
관절 *gwahn•juhl* **joint**
관절염 *gwahn•juhl•lyuhm* **arthritis**
광장 *gwahng•jahng* **square**
굉장한 *gwehng•jahng•hahn* **terrific**
교외 *gyo•weh* **suburb**
교차로 *gyo•chah•loh* **intersection**
교통 *gyo•tohng* **traffic**
교통 정체 *gyo•tohng juhng•cheh* **traffic jam**
교회 *gyo•hweh* **church**
구경거리 *goo•gyuhng•kkuh•lee* **sight (attraction)**
구급차 *goo•gup•chah* **ambulance**
구리 *goo•lee* **copper**
구멍 *goo•muhng* **hole**
구명 보트 *goo•myuhng boh•tu* **life boat**
구명 조끼 *goo•myuhng joh•kkee* **life jacket**
구역 *goo•yuhk* **area**
구절 *goo•juhl* **phrase**
구조원 *goo•joh•wuhn* **life guard**
구하다 *goo•hah•dah* **get (find)**
국가 번호 *gook•kkah buhn•hoh* **country code**
국가의 *gook•kkah•eh* **national**
국내 *goong•neh* **domestic**
국악 *goo•gahk* **traditional music**
국적 *gook•tzuhk* **nationality**
국제 *gook•tzeh* **international**
국제 학생증 *gook•tzeh hahk•ssehng•tzung* **International Student Card**
군중 *goon•joong* **crowd**
궁 *goong* **palace**
권투 *gwuhn•too* **boxing**
귀 *gwih* **ear**
귀걸이 *gwih•guh•lee* **earrings**
귀머거리 *gwih•muh•guh•lee* **deaf**
귀약 *gwih•yahk* **ear drops**
귀여운 *gwih•yuh•oon* **cute**
귀중한 *gwih•joong•hahn* **valuable**
귀찮게 하다 *gwih•chahn•keh hah•dah* **bother**
귀통증 *gwih•tohng•tzung* **earache**
그것 *gu•guht* **that**
그것들 *gu•guht•ttul* **those**
그때 *gu•tteh* **then (time)**
그램 *gu•lehm* **gram**
그러나 *gu•luh•nah* **but**
그리고 *gu•lee•goh* **and**
그리다 *gu•lee•dah* **paint**
그림 *gu•leem* **painting**
그림자 *gu•leem•jah* **shadow**
극장 *guk•tzahng* **theater**
근사한 *gun•sah•hahn* **great**
근시 *gun•see* **near-sighted [short-sighted BE]**
근육 *gu•nyook* **muscle**
근처에 *gun•chuh•eh* **nearby**
글루텐 *gul•loo•tehn* **gluten**
금 *gum* **gold**
금고 *gum•goh n* **safe**
금속 *gum•sohk* **metal**
금액 *gu•mehk* **amount**
금연 *gu•myuhn* **non-smoking**
금지된 *gum•jee•dwehn* **prohibited**
급류 *gum•nyoo* **rapids**
급한 *gu•pahn* **urgent**

기내 휴대 수하물 *gee•neh hyoo•deh soo•hah•mool* **carry-on luggage**
기념관 *gee•nyuhm•gwahn n* **memorial**
기념품 *gee•nyuhm•poom* **souvenir**
기념품 가게 *gee•nyuhm•poom kkah•geh* **souvenir store**
기념품 안내 *gee•nyuhm•poom ahn•neh* **souvenir guide**
기다리다 *gee•dah•lee•dah* **wait**
기름 *gee•lum* **gas [petrol BE], oil**
기름통 *gee•lum•tohng* **gas tank**
기본회화집 *gee•bohn hweh•hwah•jeep* **phrase book**
기부 *gee•boo* **contribution, donation**
기어 *gee•uh* **gear**
기억하다 *gee•uh•kah•dah* **remember**
기저귀 *gee•juh•gwih* **diaper [nappy BE]**
기절하다 *gee•juhl•hah•dah v* **faint**
기차 *gee•chah* **train**
기차역 *gee•chah•yuhk* **train [railway BE] station**
기침 *gee•cheem n* **cough**
기침하다 *gee•cheem•hah•dah v* **cough**
기타 *gee•tah* **guitar**
기호 *gee•hoh* **symbol**
긴 *geen* **long**
긴급 서비스 *geen•gup ssuh•bee•su* **emergency service**
길 *geel* **route, street, way**
길이 *gee•lee* **length**
깊은 *gee•pun* **deep**
까지 *kkah•jee* **until**
깔개 *kkahl•geh* **groundcloth [groundsheet BE]**
깡통 *kkahng•tohng n* **can**
깨우다 *kkeh•oo•dah* **wake**
꽃 *kkoht* **flower**
꽃가루 알레르기 *kkoht•kkah•loo ahl•leh•lu•gee* **hay fever**
꽃가루 지수 *kkoht•kkah•loo jee•soo* **pollen count**
꿰매다 *kkweh•meh•dah* **sew**
끄다 *kku•dah* **turn off**
끊임없는 *kku•neem•uhm•nun* **continuous**
끔찍한 *kkum•tzee•kahn* **terrible, awful**
끝 *kkut* **end**
끼는 *kkee•nun* **tight**

ㄴ

나라 *nah•lah* **country**
나무 *nah•moo* **tree**
나무 못 *nah•moo moht* **peg**
나쁜 *nah•ppun* **bad**
나아지다 *nah•ah•jee•dah* **improve**
나중에 *nah•joong•eh* **later**
낚시 *nahk•ssee* **fishing**
난방 *nahn•bahng* **heat [heating BE]**
날씨 *nahl•ssee* **weather**
날카로운 *nahl•kah•loh•oon* **sharp**
남자 *nahm•jah* **male, man**
남자애 *nahm•jah•eh* **boy**
남자 종업원 *nahm•jah johng•uh•bwuhn* **waiter**
남자 친구 *nahm•jah cheen•goo* **boyfriend**
남자 형제 *nahm•jah hyuhng•jeh* **brother**
남쪽 *nahm•tzohk* **south**
남편 *nahm•pyuhn* **husband**
납 *nahp n* **lead**
낭만적인 *nahng•mahn•juh•geen* **romantic**
낮은 *nah•jun* **low**
낮추다 *naht•choo•dah* **turn down**
내기 *neh•gee* **bet**
내리다 *neh•lee•dah* **get off (bus)**

내선 번호 *neh•suhn buhn•hoh* **extension (phone)**
내일 *neh•eel* **tomorrow**
냄비 *nehm•bee* **pot, saucepan**
냄새 맡다 *nehm•seh maht•ttah* **smell**
냅킨 *nehp•keen* **napkin**
냉방 *nehng•bahng* **air conditioning**
냉동고 *nehng•dohng•goh* **freezer**
냉장고 *nehng•jahng•goh* **refrigerator**
너무 *nuh•moo* **too**
넓은 *nuhl•bun* **wide**
넓적다리 *nuhp•tzuhk•ttah•lee* **thigh**
넣다 *nuh•tah* **put**
네 *neh* **yes**
네트워크 *neh•tu•wuh•ku* **network**
넥타이 *nehk•tah•ee* **tie**
년 *nyuhn* **year**
노 *noh* *n* **row**
노상 강도 *noh•sahng gahng•doh* **mugging**
노선 *noh•suhn* **line**
노인 *noh•een* **senior citizen**
노 젓는 배 *noh juhn•nun beh* **rowboat**
녹이다 *noh•gee•dah* **dissolve, defrost**
놀라운 *nohl•lah•oon* **amazing**
놀이 공원 *noh•lee gohng•wuhn* **amusement park**
놀이터 *noh•lee•tuh* **playground**
농구 *nohng•goo* **basketball**
농담 *nohng•dahm* **joke**
농장 *nohng•jahng* **farm**
높은 *noh•pun* **high**
높은 의자 *noh•pun u•jah* **highchair**
높이다 *noh•pee•dah* **turn up**
뇌진탕 *nweh•jeen•tahng* **concussion**
누구 *noo•goo* **who**
누구의 *noo•goo•eh* **whose**
누군가 *noo•goon•gah* **anyone, someone**
누출 *noo•chool* *n* **leak**
눈 *noon* **eye, snow**
눈썹 *noon•ssuhp* **eyebrow**
뉴스 *nyoo•su* **news**
뉴질랜드 *nyoo•jeel•lehn•du* **New Zealand**
느끼다 *nu•kkee•dah* **feel**
느린 *nu•leen* **slow**
늙은 *nul•gun* **old (person)**
늦다 *nut•ttah* **late**

ㄷ

다듬다 *dah•dum•ttah* **trim**
다른 *dah•lun* **another, alternate**
다리 *dah•lee* **leg, bridge**
다리미 *dah•lee•mee* **iron**
다림질하다 *dah•leem•jeel•hah•dah* **press**
다소 *dah•soh* **some**
다스 *dah•su* **dozen**
다음 *dah•um* **next**
다이빙하다 *dah•ee•beeng•hah•dah* **dive**
다이아몬드 *dah•ee•ah•mohn•du* **diamond**
다이어트 *dah•ee•uh•tu* **diet**
다치게 하다 *dah•chee•geh hah•dah* **injure**
닦다 *dahk•ttah* **wipe**
단 한번도 *dahn hahn•buhn•doh* **never**
단계 *dahn•geh* **level**
단체 *dahn•cheh* **group**
단추 *dahn•choo* **button**
닫다 *daht•ttah* **close, shut**
닫힌 *dah•cheen* *adj* **shut**
달 *dahl* **month**
달러 *dahl•luh* **dollar**
달력 *dahl•lyuhk* **calendar**
달콤한 *dahl•kohm•hahn* **sweet (taste)**

담배 *dahm•beh* **cigarette, tobacco**
담배 가게 *dahm•beh kkah•geh* **tobacconist**
담배를 피우다 *dahm•beh•lul pee•oo•dah* **smoke**
담요 *dahm•nyo* **blanket**
당기다 *dahng•gee•dah* **pull**
당뇨병 *dahng•nyo•ppyuhng* **diabetes**
당뇨병 환자 *dahng•nyo•ppyuhng hwahn•jah* **diabetic**
당일치기 여행 *dahng•eel•chee•gee yuh•hehng* **day trip**
대걸레 *deh•guhl•leh* **mop**
대기실 *deh•gee•seel* **waiting room**
대기표 *deh•gee•pyo* **standby ticket**
대사 *deh•sah* **ambassador**
대사관 *deh•sah•gwahn* **embassy**
대신에 *deh•see•neh* **instead**
대회 *deh•hweh* **contest, tournament**
더 많이 *duh mah•nee* **more**
더 적은 *duh juh•gun* **less**
더러운 *duh•luh•oon* **dirty**
더빙된 *duh•beeng•dwehn* **dubbed**
데님 *deh•neem* **denim**
도 *doh* **degree**
도난 *doh•nahn* **theft**
도난 당한 *doh•nahn dahng•hahn* **stolen**
도둑 *doh•dook* **thief**
도로 *doh•loh* **road**
도서관 *doh•suh•gwahn* **library**
도움 *doh•oom* **help, assistance**
도자기 *doh•jah•gee* **pottery, ceramics**
도착 *doh•chahk* **arrivals**
도착하다 *doh•chah•kah•dah* **arrive,** *v* **land**
독 *dohk* **poison**
독감 *dohk•kkahm* **flu**
돈 *dohn* **money, currency**
돌다 *dohl•dah* **turn**
돌아가다 *doh•lah•gah•dah v* **return**
돕다 *dohp•ttah v* **help**
동굴 *dohng•gool* **cave**
동료 *dohng•nyo* **colleague**
동물 *dohng•mool* **animal**
동물원 *dohng•moo•lwuhn* **zoo**
동상 *dohng•sahng* **statue**
동안 *dohng•ahn* **while, during**
동전 *dohng•juhn* **coin**
동쪽 *dohng•tzohk* **east**
되풀이하다 *dweh•poo•lee•hah•dah* **repeat**
두꺼운 *doo•kkuh•oon* **thick**
두드러기 *doo•du•luh•gee* **rash**
두드리다 *doo•du•lee•dah* **knock**
두통 *doo•tohng* **headache**
둘러보다 *dool•luh•boh•dah* **browse**
뒤에 *dwih•eh* **behind**
드라이 *du•lah•ee* **blow dry**
드라이버 *du•lah•ee•buh* **screw-driver**
드라이 클리닝하다 *du•lah•ee kul•lee•neeng•hah•dah* **dry clean**
드러내다 *du•luh•neh•dah* **expose**
드레스 *du•leh•su* **dress**
듣다 *dut•ttah* **hear**
들다 *dul•dah v* **cost**
들어가지 않다 *du•luh•gah•jee ahn•tah* **keep out**
들판 *dul•pahn* **field**
등 *dung* **back**
등급 *dung•gup* **class**
등기 우편 *dung•gee oo•pyuhn* **registered mail**
등대 *dung•deh* **lighthouse**
등록 용지 *dung•noh gyong•jee* **registration form**
등산로 *dung•sahn•noh* **trail**
디젤 *dee•jehl* **diesel**
디지털 *dee•jee•tuhl* **digital**
따뜻한 *ttah•ttu•tahn* **warm**
따라가다 *ttah•lah•gah•dah* **follow**
따로 *ttah•loh* **separate**

따분한 *ttah•boon•hahn* **boring**
딱딱한 *ttahk•ttah•kahn* **hard**
땅 *ttahng n* **land**
때문에 *tteh•moo•neh* **because**
떠나다 *ttuh•nah•dah* **leave**
떨어뜨리다 *ttuh•luh•ttu•lee•dah* **drop**
떨어져 *ttuh•luh•jyuh* **away**
떨어진 *ttuh•luh•jeen* **dead (battery)**
떼어내다 *tteh•uh•neh•dah* **tear off**
또는 *ttoh•nun* **or**
또한 *ttoh•hahn* **also**
똑바른 *ttohk•bah•lun* **straight**
뚝뚝 떨어지다 *ttook•ttook ttuh•luh•jee•dah* **drip**
뜨거운 *ttu•guh•oon* **hot**
뜻하다 *ttu•tah•dah v* **mean**

ㄹ

라운드 *lah•oon•du* **round (of golf)**
라이터 *lah•ee•tuh* **lighter**
라켓 *lah•keht* **racket (tennis)**
랩 *lehp* **plastic wrap [cling film BE]**
러시 아워 *luh•ssee•ah•wuh* **rush hour**
레이스 *leh•ee•su* **lace**
렌즈 *lehn•ju* **lens**
렌터카 *lehn•tuh•kah* **car rental [car hire BE]**
로비 *loh•bee* **lobby**
록 *lohk* **rock**
룸 서비스 *loom ssuh•bee•su* **room service**
리터 *lee•tuh* **liter**
립스틱 *leep•ssu•teek* **lipstick**

ㅁ

마 *mah* **linen**
마사지 *mah•ssah•jee* **massage**
마시다 *mah•see•dah v* **drink**
마을 *mah•ul* **village**
마지막 *mah•jee•mahk adj* **last**
마취제 *mah•chwih•jeh* **anesthetic**
마티네 *mah•tee•neh* **matinee**
막간 *mahk•kkahn* **intermission**
만나다 *mahn•nah•dah* **meet**
많이 *mah•nee* **many**
말 *mahl* **horse**
말도 안 돼 *mahl•doh ahn dweh* **no way**
말리다 *mahl•lee•dah* **dry**
말하다 *mahl•hah•dah* **say, tell**
맛 *maht* **flavor**
맛보다 *maht•ppoh•dah* **taste**
맛있는 *mah•seen•nun* **delicious**
망치 *mahng•chee* **hammer**
맞는 *mahn•nun* **correct**
맞다 *maht•ttah* **fit**
맞은편 *mah•jun•pyuhn* **opposite**
맞춤 *maht•choom* **custom made**
매니저 *meh•nee•juh* **manager**
매니큐어 *meh•nee•kyoo•uh* **manicure**
매력적인 *meh•lyuhk•tzuh•geen* **attractive**
매우 *meh•oo* **very**
매일 *meh•eel* **daily**
매주 *meh•joo* **weekly**
매진 *meh•jeen* **sold out**
매트리스 *meh•tu•lee•su* **mattress**
매표소 *meh•pyo•soh* **ticket office**
맹도견 *mehng•doh•gyuhn* **guide dog**
머리 *muh•lee* **hair, head**
먹다 *muhk•ttah* **eat**
먹이다 *muh•gee•dah* **feed**
먼 *muhn* **far**
멀미 *muhl•mee* **motion sickness**
멋진 *muht•tzeen* **stunning**
멍 *muhng* **bruise**
메뉴 *meh•nyoo* **menu**
메모리 카드 *meh•moh•lee kah•du* **memory card**
메스꺼움 *meh•su•kkuh•oom* **nausea**
메시지 *meh•ssee•jee* **message**

메신저 *meh•sseen•juh* **instant messenger**
면 *myuhn* **cotton**
면도 크림 *myuhn•doh ku•leem* **shaving cream**
면도날 *myuhn•doh•nahl* **razor blade**
면도칼 *myuhn•doh•kahl* **razor**
면도하다 *myuhn•doh•hah•dah* **shave**
면세 *myuhn•seh* **duty-free**
명세 *myuhng•seh* **itemized**
명함 *myuhng•hahm* **business card**
몇 개 *myuht kkeh* **how many**
모기 물린 데 *moh•gee mool•leen deh* **mosquito bite**
모닝콜 *moh•neeng•kohl* **wake-up call**
모두 *moh•doo* **all**
모든 *moh•dun* **every**
모래 *moh•leh* **sand**
모양 *moh•yahng* **shape**
모으다 *moh•u•dah* **collect**
모자 *moh•jah* **hat**
모조품 *moh•joh•poom* **imitation**
모터 *moh•tuh* **motor**
모터 보트 *moh•tuh boh•tu* **motor boat**
모퉁이 *moh•toong•ee* **corner**
목 *mohk* **neck**
목걸이 *mohk•kkuh•lee* **necklace**
목격자 *mohk•kkyuhk•tzah* **witness**
목구멍 *mohk•kkoo•muhng* **throat**
목마르다 *mohng•mah•lu•dah* **thirsty**
목발 *mohk•ppahl* **crutches**
목 아픈 데 *moh gah•pun deh* **sore throat**
목욕 *moh•gyok* **bath**
목적 *mohk•tzuhk* **purpose**
목적지 *mohk•tzuhk•tzee* **destination**
못생긴 *moht•ssehng•geen* **ugly**
묘사하다 *myo•sah•hah•dah* **describe**
무거운 *moo•guh•oon* **heavy**
무게 *moo•geh* **weight**
무게를 달다 *moo•geh•lul dahl•dah* **weigh**
무례한 *moo•leh•hahn* **rude**
무릎 *moo•lup* **knee**
무선 *moo•suhn* **wireless**
무언가 *moo•uhn•gah* **anything, something**
무엇 *moo•uht* **what**
묵다 *mook•ttah* **stay**
문 *moon* **door**
문구류 *moon•goo•lyoo* **stationery**
문자 *moon•tzah* **text**
문제 *moon•jeh* **problem**
묻다 *moot•ttah* **ask**
물 *mool* **water**
물건 *mool•guhn* **thing**
물 내리다 *mool neh•lee•dah* **flush**
물안경 *moo•lahn•gyuhng* **goggles**
물에 빠지다 *moo•leh ppah•jee•dah* **drown**
물집 *mool•tzeep* **blister**
미국 *mee•gook* **United States**
미국인 *mee•goo•geen* **American**
미니바 *mee•nee•bah* **mini-bar**
미사 *mee•sah* **mass**
미술관 *mee•sool•gwahn* **art gallery**
미안하다 *mee•ahn•hah•dah* **sorry**
미용사 *mee•yong•sah* **hairdresser**
미용실 *mee•yong•seel* **nail salon**
미혼 *mee•hohn* **single (marital status)**
믿을 만한 *mee•dul mahn•hahn* **reliable**
밀다 *meel•dah* **push**

ㅂ

바 *bah* **bar**
바가지 쓴 *bah•gah•jee ssun* **overcharged**

바구니 *bah•goo•nee* **basket**
바꾸다 *bah•kkoo•dah* **alter, change, exchange, replace**
바다 *bah•dah* **sea**
바라다 *bah•lah•dah* **wish**
바람 *bah•lahm* **wind**
바람이 부는 *bah•lah•mee boo•nun* **windy**
바쁜 *bah•ppun* **busy**
바지 *bah•jee* **pants [trousers BE]**
박물관 *bahng•mool•gwahn* **museum**
밖 *bahk* **out**
밖에 *bah•kkeh* **outside**
반 *bahn* **half**
반바지 *bahn•bah•jee* **shorts**
반응 *bah•nung* **reaction**
반지 *bahn•jee* **ring**
반창고 *bahn•chahng•goh* **plaster**
받다 *baht•ttah* **accept, receive**
발 *bahl* **foot**
발가락 *bahl•kkah•lahk* **toe**
발레 *bahl•leh* **ballet**
발음하다 *bah•lum•hah•dah* **pronounce**
밤 *bahm* **night**
밤새 *bahm•seh* **overnight**
밧줄 *baht•tzool* **rope**
방 *bahng* **room**
방광 *bahng•gwahng* **bladder**
방문 *bahng•moon* ***n*** **visit**
방문 시간 *bahng•moon see•gahn* **visiting hours**
방문하다 *bahng•moon•hah•dah* ***v*** **visit**
방수 *bahng•soo* **waterproof**
방해 *bahng•heh* **interference**
방해하다 *bahng•heh•hah•dah* **disturb**
방향 *bahng•hyahng* **direction**
방화문 *bahng•hwah•moon* **fire door**
배 *beh* **ship**
배고픈 *beh•goh•pun* **hungry**
배고픔 *beh•goh•pum* **hunger**
배구 *beh•goo* **volleyball**
배낭 *beh•nahng* **backpack**
배달 *beh•dahl* **delivery**
배달하다 *beh•dahl•hah•dah* **deliver**
배우다 *beh•oo•dah* **learn**
배우자 *beh•oo•jah* **spouse**
백금 *behk•kkum* **platinum**
백랍 *behng•nahp* **pewter**
백화점 *beh•kwah•juhm* **department store**
밸브 *behl•bu* **valve**
뱃멀미 *behn•muhl•mee* **seasick**
버스 *buh•su* **bus**
버스 정류장 *buh•su juhng•nyoo•jahng* **bus stop**
버스 터미널 *buh•su tuh•mee•nuhl* **bus station**
버스표 *buh•su•pyo* **bus ticket**
버전 *buh•juhn* **version**
번역 *buh•nyuhk* **translation**
번역사 *buh•nyuhk•ssah* **translator**
번역하다 *buh•nyuh•kah•dah* **translate**
번쩍이다 *buhn•tzuh•gee•dah* **flash**
번호 *buhn•hoh* **number**
벌금 *buhl•gum* ***n*** **fine**
벌레 *buhl•leh* **bug, insect**
벌레 물린 데 *buhl•leh mool•leen deh* **insect bite**
법원 *buh•bwuhn* **courthouse**
벗다 *buht•ttah* **take off (clothing)**
베개 *beh•geh* **pillow**
벨트 *bel•tu* **belt**
벼룩시장 *byuh•look•ssee•jahng* **flea market**
벽 *byuhk* **wall**
변기 뚫는 것 *byun•gee ttool•nun guht* **plunger**
변비 *byun•bee* **constipation**
변호사 *byuhn•hoh•sah* **lawyer**
별거한 *byuhl•guh•hahn* **separated**
별장 *byuhl•tzang* **cottage**

병 *byuhng* **bottle, jar**
병동 *byuhng•dohng* **ward (hospital)**
병따개 *byuhng•ttah•geh* **bottle opener**
병원 *byuhng•wuhn* **clinic, hospital**
보내다 *boh•neh•dah* **send**
보다 *boh•dah* **look, see**
보도 *boh•doh* **sidewalk [pavement BE]**
보루 *boh•loo* **carton (cigarettes)**
보석 *boh•suhk* **jewelry**
보석상 *boh•suhk•ssahng* **jeweler**
보습 크림 *boh•sup ku•leem* **moisturizer (cream)**
보여주다 *boh•yuh•joo•dah* **show**
보유하다 *boh•yoo•hah•dah* **keep**
보증 *boh•jung* **guarantee**
보증서 *boh•jung•suh* **certificate**
보청기 *boh•chuhng•gee* **hearing aid**
보통 *boh•tohng* **regular**
보통 예금 계좌 *boh•tohng yeh•gum geh•jwah* **savings account**
보트 *boh•tu* **ferry**
보트 관광 *boh•tu gwahn•gwahng* **boat trip**
보행자 *boh•hehng•jah n* **pedestrian**
보행자 전용 구역 *boh•hehng•jah juh•nyong goo•yuhk* **pedestrian zone [precinct BE]**
보험 *boh•huhm* **insurance**
보험 카드 *boh•huhm kah•du* **insurance card**
보험금 청구 *boh•huhm•gum chuhng•goo* **insurance claim**
보호 구역 *boh•hoh goo•yuhk* **conservation area**
복권 *boh•kkwuhn* **lottery**
복사하다 *bohk•ssah•hah•dah* **copy, photocopy**
복용량 *boh•gyong•nyahng* **dosage**
복장 규정 *bohk•tzang gyoo•juhng* **dress code**
복통 *bohk•tohng* **stomachache**
볼링장 *bohl•leeng•jahng* **bowling alley**
봉사료 *bohng•sah•lyo* **service charge**
봉사하다 *bohng•sah•hah•dah* **serve**
부가가치세 *boo•gah•gah•chee•sseh* **sales tax [VAT BE]**
부동액 *boo•dohng•ehk* **antifreeze**
부두 *boo•doo* **dock**
부록 *boo•lohk* **appendix**
부르다 *boo•lu•dah* **call**
부모님 *boo•moh•neem* **parents**
부수다 *boo•soo•dah* **break**
부엌 *boo•uhk* **kitchen**
부은 *boo•un* **swollen**
부은 데 *boo•un deh* **swelling**
부인과 *boo•een•kkwah* **gynecologist**
부작용 *boo•jah•gyong* **side effect**
부츠 *boo•chu* **boots**
부탄가스 *boo•tahn•kkah•su* **butane gas**
부터 *boo•tuh* **from**
북쪽 *book•tzohk* **north**
분 *boon* **minute**
분량 *bool•lyahng* **portion**
분수 *boon•soo* **fountain**
분실물 센터 *boon•seel•mool sehn•tuh* **lost-and-found [lost property office BE]**
분유 *boo•nyoo* **formula (baby)**
불 *bool* **fire**
불면증 *bool•myuhn•tzung* **insomnia**
불법 *bool•ppuhp* **illegal**
붕대 *boong•deh* **bandage**
붙들다 *boot•ttul•dah* **hold**
브래지어 *bu•leh•jee•uh* **bra**
브레이크 *bu•leh•ee•ku* **brake**
브로치 *bu•loh•chee* **brooch**

블라우스 *bul•lah•oo•su* **blouse**
비 *bee* *n* **rain**
비 내리다 *bee neh•lee•dah* *v* **rain**
비누 *bee•noo* **soap**
비디오 게임 *bee•dee•oh geh•eem* **video game**
비밀번호 *bee•meel•buhn•hoh* **password, PIN**
비상 *bee•sahng* **emergency**
비상 브레이크 *bee•sahng bu•leh•ee•ku* **emergency brake**
비상구 *bee•sahng•goo* **emergency exit**
비수기 *bee•soo•gee* **off-peak (ticket)**
비싼 *bee•ssahn* **expensive**
비옷 *bee•oht* **raincoat**
비용 *bee•yong* *n* **cost**
비자 *bee•jah* **visa**
비즈니스 센터 *bee•jee•nee•su ssehn•tuh* **business center**
비즈니스석 *bee•jee•nee•su•suhk* **business class**
비키니 *bee•kee•nee* **bikini**
비틀다 *bee•tul•dah* **twist**
비행기 *bee•hehng•gee* **plane, flight**
비행기 멀미 *bee•hehng•gee muhl•mee* **airsickness**
빈 *been* **vacant**
빌려주다 *beel•lyuh•joo•dah* **lend**
빌리다 *beel•lee•dah* **borrow, rent**
빗 *beet* **comb**
빗자루 *beet•tzah•loo* **broom**
빚지다 *beet•tzee•dah* **owe**
빛깔 *beet•kkahl* **tint**
빠른 *ppah•lun* **fast, quick**
빨래방 *ppahl•leh•bahng* **laundromat [launderette BE]**
빼앗다 *ppeh•aht•ttah* **rob**
뻣뻣한 *ppuh•ppuh•tahn* **stiff**
뼈 *ppyuh* **bone**
뽑아내다 *ppoh•bah•neh•dah* **extract**
뿔 *ppool* **horn**
삐다 *ppee•dah* **dislocate, sprain**

ㅅ

사고 *sah•goh* **accident**
사과하다 *sah•gwah•hah•dah* **apologize**
사냥하다 *sah•nyahng•hah•dah* **hunt**
사다 *sah•dah* **buy**
사다리 *sah•dah•lee* **ladder**
사람 *sah•lahm* **person**
사랑하다 *sah•lahng•hah•dah* *v* **love**
사무실 *sah•moo•seel* **office**
사발 *sah•bahl* **bowl**
사분의 일 *sah•boo•neh eel* **quarter**
사슬 *sah•sul* **chain**
사실 *sah•seel* **true**
사업 *sah•uhp* **business**
사용자명 *sah•yong•jah•myuhng* **username**
사용하다 *sah•yong•hah•dah* **use**
사우나 *ssah•oo•nah* **sauna**
사이에 *sah•ee•eh* **between**
사이즈 *ssah•ee•ju* **size**
사적인 *sah•tzuh•geen* **private**
사전 *sah•juhn* **dictionary**
사진 *sah•jeen* **photograph**
사탕 가게 *sah•tahng kkah•geh* **candy store**
삭제하다 *sahk•tzeh•hah•dah* **delete**
산 *sahn* **mountain**
산소 *sahn•soh* **oxygen**
산책로 *sahn•chehng•noh* **nature trail**
살다 *sahl•dah* **live**
삼키다 *sahm•kee•dah* **swallow**
삽 *sahp* **shovel**
삽입하다 *sah•bee•pah•dah* **insert**
상가 *sahng•gah* **shopping area, shopping mall [centre BE]**

상가 안내 *sahng•gah ahn•neh* **store directory**
상급자 *sahng•gup•tzah* **expert**
상담하다 *sahng•dahm•hah•dah* **consult**
상대 *sahng•deh* **partner**
상업 지구 *sahng•uhp tzee•goo* **business district**
상온 *sahng•ohn* **room temperature**
상자 *sahng•jah* **box**
상표 *sahng•pyo* **label**
새 *seh* **bird**
새기다 *seh•gee•dah* **engrave**
새다 *seh•dah v* **leak**
새로운 *seh•loh•oon* **new**
색 *sehk* **color**
샌들 *ssehn•dul* **sandals**
생각하다 *sehng•gah•kah•dah* **think**
생년월일 *sehng•nyuh•nwuh•leel* **date of birth**
생리 *sehng•nee* **period (menstrual)**
생리대 *sehng•nee•deh* **sanitary napkin [pad BE]**
생리통 *sehng•nee•tohng* **menstrual cramps**
생명 *sehng•myuhng* **life**
생일 *sehng•eel* **birthday**
샤워 *syah•wuh* **shower**
샴푸 *syahm•poo* **shampoo**
서두르다 *suh•doo•lu•dah* **hurry, rush**
서명하다 *suh•myuhng•hah•dah v* **sign**
서점 *suh•juhm* **bookstore**
서쪽 *suh•tzohk* **west**
서핑보드 *ssuh•peeng•boh•du* **surfboard**
선글라스 *ssuhn•gul•lah•su* **sunglasses**
선물 *suhn•mool* **gift, present**
선물 가게 *suhn•mool kkah•geh* **gift store**
선불 전화 카드 *suhn•bool juhn•hwah kah•du* **prepaid phone card**
선탠 크림 *ssuhn•tehn ku•leem* **suntan lotion**
선풍기 *suhn•poong•gee* **fan**
설명서 *suhl•myuhng•suh* **instructions**
설사 *suhl•ssah* **diarrhea**
성 *suhng* **sex**
성냥 *suhng•nyahng* **matches**
성당 *suhng•dahng* **cathedral**
세관 *seh•gwahn* **customs**
세관 신고서 *seh•gwahn seen•goh•suh* **customs declaration form**
세금 *seh•gum* **duty (tax)**
세면대 *seh•myuhn•deh* **sink**
세미나 *sseh•mee•nah* **seminar**
세우다 *seh•oo•dah v* **stop**
세제 *seh•jeh* **detergent**
세탁 가능 *seh•tahk kkah•nung* **washable**
세탁기 *seh•tahk•kkee* **washing machine**
세탁기로 빨 수 있는 *seh•tahk•kkee•loh ppahl ssoo een•nun* **machine washable**
세탁 서비스 *seh•tahk ssuh•bee•su* **laundry service**
세탁 시설 *seh•tahk see•suhl* **laundry facilities**
세탁소 *seh•tahk•ssoh* **dry cleaner**
세탁하다 *seh•tah•kah•dah* **clean**
셀프서비스 *ssehl•pu•ssuh•bee•su* **self-service**
셔츠 *syuh•chu* **shirt**
소개하다 *soh•geh•hah•dah* **introduce**
소독액 *soh•doh•gehk* **sterilizing solution**
소독약 *soh•dohng•nyahk* **antiseptic**

소매 *soh•meh* **sleeve**
소방서 *soh•bahng•suh* **fire department [fire brigade BE]**
소아과 의사 *soh•ah•kkwah u•sah* **pediatrician**
소유하다 *soh•yoo•hah•dah v* **own**
소켓 *soh•keht* **socket**
소포 *soh•poh* **package [parcel BE]**
소형 *soh•hyuhng* **mini**
소화기 *soh•hwah•gee* **fire extinguisher**
소화불량 *soh•hwah•bool•lyahng* **indigestion**
속 *sohk* **filling**
속도 *sohk•ttoh n* **speed**
속하다 *soh•kah•dah* **belong**
손 *sohn* **hand**
손가락 *sohn•kkah•lahk* **finger**
손가방 *sohn•kkah•bahng* **hand luggage**
손상 *sohn•sahng* **damage**
손톱 *sohn•tohp* **nail**
손톱줄 *sohn•tohp•tzool* **nail file**
쇼핑 *syo•peeng* **shopping**
쇼핑센터 *syo•peeng•ssehn•tuh* **mall**
쇼핑 카트 *syo•peeng kah•tu* **shopping cart [trolley BE]**
수건 *soo•guhn* **towel**
수공예품 *soo•gohng•yeh•poom* **handicrafts**
수도꼭지 *soo•doh•kkohk•tzee* **faucet [tap BE]**
수돗물 *soo•dohn•mool* **tap water**
수면제 *soo•myuhn•jeh* **sleeping pill**
수상스키 *soo•sahng•su•kee* **water skis**
수선하다 *soo•suhn•hah•dah* **mend (clothes)**
수송 *soo•sohng* **transport**
수수료 *soo•sso•lyo* **commission**
수술 *soo•sool* **operation**
수업 *soo•uhp* **lesson**
수영복 *soo•yuhng•bohk* **swimsuit, swimming trunks**
수영장 *soo•yuhng•jahng* **pool**
수영하다 *soo•yuhng•hah•dah* **swim**
수유하다 *soo•yoo•hah•dah* **breastfeed**
수정 *soo•juhng* **crystal**
수집 *soo•jeep* **collection**
수표 *soo•pyo* **check [cheque BE]**
수하물 *soo•hah•mool* **luggage**
수하물 찾는 곳 *soo•hah•mool chan•nun goht* **baggage claim**
수하물 카트 *soo•hah•mool kah•tu* **luggage cart [trolley BE]**
숙박 시설 *sook•ppahk see•suhl* **accommodations**
숙소 *sook•ssoh* **guesthouse**
숙취 *sook•chwih* **hangover**
순수한 *soon•soo•hahn* **pure**
순은 *soo•nun* **sterling silver**
숟가락 *soot•kkah•lahk* **spoon**
술 *sool* **drink (alcoholic)**
술집 *sool•tzeep* **pub**
숨막히는 *soom•mah•kee•nun* **breathtaking**
숨쉬다 *soom•swih•dah* **breathe**
숲 *soop* **forest**
쉬다 *swih•dah* **rest**
쉬운 *swih•oon* **easy**
슈퍼마켓 *syoo•puh•mah•keht* **supermarket**
스웨터 *su•weh•tuh* **sweater**
스카프 *su•kah•pu* **scarf**
스코틀랜드 *su•koh•tul•lehn•du* **Scotland**
스쿠버 다이빙 장비 *su•koo•buh dah•ee•beeng jahng•bee* **diving equipment**
스키장 *su•kee•jahng* **ski slope**
스타일 *su•tah•eel* **style**
스테인레스 *su•teh•een•leh•su* **stainless steel**
스파 *su•pah* **spa**

스포츠 용품점 *su•poh•chu yong•poom•juhm* **sporting goods store**
스포츠 클럽 *su•poh•chu kul•luhp* **sports club**
스폰지 *su•pohn•jee* **sponge**
슬리퍼 *sul•lee•puh* **slippers**
습한 *su•pahn* **damp**
승강장 *sung•gahng•jahng* **platform**
승객 *sung•gehk* **passenger**
승마 *sung•mah* **horseback riding**
승무원 *sung•moo•wuhn* **flight attendant**
시 *see* **o'clock**
시가 *ssee•gah* **cigar**
시각 장애인 *see•gahk jahng•eh•een* **visually impaired**
시간 *see•gahn* **hour, time**
시간 있는 *see•gah neen•nun* **available, free**
시간표 *see•gahn•pyo* **schedule [timetable BE]**
시계 *see•geh* **clock, watch**
시끄러운 *see•kku•luh•oon* **loud, noisy**
시내 *see•neh* **town**
시대 *see•deh* **period (historical)**
시디 *ssee•dee* **CD**
시디플레이어 *ssee•dee•pul•leh•ee•uh* **CD player**
시설 *see•suhl* **facility**
시원한 *see•wuhn•hahn* **cool**
시작하다 *see•jah•kah•dah* **begin, start**
시장 *see•jahng* **market**
시차 *see•chah* **jet lag**
시큼한 *see•kum•hahn* **sour**
시트 *see•tu* **sheet (bed)**
시합하다 *see•hahp•hah•dah* **play (sports)**
식기 세척기 *seek•kkee seh•chuhk•kkee* **dishwasher**
식당 *seek•ttahng* **dining room**
식당차 *seek•ttahng•chah* **dining car**
식료품점 *seeng•nyo•poom•juhm* **grocery store [grocer BE]**
식물원 *seeng•moo•lwuhn* **botanical garden**
식사 *seek•ssah* **meal**
식사하다 *seek•ssah•hah•dah* **dine**
식욕 *see•gyok* **appetite**
식중독 *seek•tzoong•dohk* **food poisoning**
신고하다 *seen•goh•hah•dah* **declare, report**
신문 *seen•moon* **newspaper**
신문 가판대 *seen•moon gah•pahn•deh* **newsstand [news agent BE]**
신발 *seen•bahl* **shoe**
신발 가게 *seen•bahl kkah•geh* **shoe store**
신발 수선 *seen•bahl soo•suhn* **shoe repair**
신분증 *seen•boon•tzung* **identification**
신사 *seen•sah* **gentleman**
신선한 *seen•suhn•hahn* **fresh**
신어 보다 *seen•uh boh•dah* **try on (shoes)**
신용카드 *see•nyong•kah•du* **credit card**
신장 *seen•jahng* **kidney**
신호등 *seen•hoh•dung* **traffic light**
신혼여행 *seen•hohn•yuh•hehng* **honeymoon**
실내 수영장 *seel•leh soo•yuhng•jahng* **indoor pool**
실수 *seel•ssoo* **mistake**
실수로 *seel•ssoo•loh* **accidentally**
실업자 *see•luhp•tzah* **unemployed**
실외 *seel•weh* **outdoor**
실외 수영장 *seel•weh soo•yuhng•jahng* **outdoor pool**
실크 *sseel•ku* **silk**

심각한 *seem•gah•kahn* **serious**
심장 *seem•jahng* **heart**
심장마비 *seem•jahng•mah•bee* **heart attack**
심장 질환 *seem•jahng jeel•hwahn* **heart condition**
싸다 *ssah•dah v* **pack, wrap**
싸움 *ssah•oom* **fight**
싼 *ssahn* **cheap**
쌍안경 *ssahng•ahn•gyuhng* **binoculars**
쑤시는 *ssoo•see•nun* **sore**
쓰다 *ssu•dah* **spend, write**
쓰러지다 *ssu•luh•jee•dah* **collapse**
쓰레기 *ssu•leh•gee* **trash [rubbish BE]**
쓰레기 봉투 *ssu•leh•gee bohng•too* **garbage bag**
쓰레기통 *ssu•leh•gee•tohng* **trash can**
쓴 *ssun* **bitter**
쓸다 *ssul•dah* **sweep**
씨름 *ssee•lum* **Korean wrestling**

ㅇ

아기 *ah•gee* **baby**
아기 놀이울 *ah•gee noh•lee•ool* **playpen**
아기용 물휴지 *ah•gee•yong mool•hyoo•jee* **baby wipe**
아기용 침대 *ah•gee•yong cheem•deh* **crib [child's cot BE]**
아내 *ah•neh* **wife**
아니다 *ah•nee•dah* **not**
아니요 *ah•nee•yo* **no**
아래 *ah•leh* **under**
아래층 *ah•leh•chung* **downstairs**
아로마테라피 *ah•loh•mah•teh•lah•pee* **aromatherapy**
아름다운 *ah•lum•dah•oon* **beautiful**
아마 *ah•mah* **perhaps, maybe**
아무 것도 아님 *ah•moo guht•ttoh ah•neem* **nothing**
아버지 *ah•buh•jee* **father**
아세트아미노펜 *ah•seh•tu•ah•mee•noh•pehn* **acetaminophen**
아스피린 *ah•su•pee•leen* **aspirin**
아이스 스케이트 *ah•ee•su su•keh•ee•tu* **ice skating**
아이스 스케이트장 *ah•ee•su su•keh•ee•tu•jahng* **ice skating rink**
아이스 하키 *ah•ee•su hah•kee* **ice hockey**
아일랜드 *ah•eel•lehn•du* **Ireland**
아주 작은 *ah•joo jah•gun* **petite**
아직 *ah•jeek adj* **still**
아침 *ah•cheem* **morning**
아침식사 *ah•cheem•seek•ssah* **breakfast**
아파트 *ah•pah•tu* **apartment**
아픈 *ah•pun* **sick [ill BE]**
아프다 *ah•pu•dah* **hurt**
악단 *ahk•ttahn* **band**
안개 *ahn•geh* **fog**
안경 *ahn•gyuhng* **glasses**
안경점 *ahn•gyuhng•juhm* **optician**
안내 *ahn•neh* **information**
안내 데스크 *ahn•neh deh•su•ku* **information desk**
안내 책자 *ahn•neh chehk•tzah* **guide book**
안내원 *ahn•neh•wuhn* **guide (tour)**
안녕하세요 *ahn•nyuhng•hah•seh•yo* **hi, hello**
안녕히 가세요 *ahn•nyuhng•hee gah•seh•yo* **bye, goodbye (to someone leaving)**
안녕히 계세요 *ahn•nyuhng•hee geh•seh•yo* **bye, goodbye (to someone staying)**
안다 *ahn•ttah* **hug**
안에 *ah•neh* **inside, within**

안전 *ahn·juhn* **safety**
안전 벨트 *ahn·juhn behl·tu* **seat belt**
안전핀 *ahn·juhn·peen* **safety pin**
안전한 *ahn·juhn·hahn adj* **safe**
앉다 *ahn·ttah* **sit**
알다 *ahl·dah* **know, understand**
알레르기 *ahl·leh·lu·gee* **allergy**
알레르기가 있다 *ahl·leh·lu·gee·gah eet·ttah* **allergic**
알약 *ahl·lyahk* **pill, tablet**
암 *ahm* **cancer**
앞 *ahp* **front**
애 봐주는 사람 *eh bwah·joo·nun sah·lahm* **babysitter**
애인 *eh·een* **boyfriend**
애프터셰이브 로션 *eh·pu·tuh·syeh·ee·bu loh·syuhn* **aftershave**
야구 *yah·goo* **baseball**
야생 *yah·sehng* **wildlife**
약 *yahk* **medicine**
약국 *yahk·kkook* **pharmacy [chemist BE]**
약물 *yahng·mool* **medication**
약속 *yahk·ssohk* **appointment**
약혼한 *yah·kohn·hahn* **engaged**
양동이 *yahng·dohng·ee* **bucket, pail**
양말 *yahng·mahl* **socks**
양모 *yahng·moh* **wool**
양보 *yahng·boh* **concession**
양보하다 *yahng·boh·hah·dah* **yield**
양복 *yahng·bohk* **suit**
양식 *yahng·seek* **form**
양초 *yahng·choh* **candle**
얘기하다 *yeh·gee·hah·dah* **speak, talk**
어깨 *uh·kkeh* **shoulder**
어댑터 *uh·dehp·tuh* **adapter**
어두운 *uh·doo·oon* **dark**
어디서 *uh·dee·suh* **where**
어딘가 *uh·deen·gah* **somewhere**
어떤 *uh·ttuhn* **any, which**
어떻게 *uh·ttuh·keh* **how**
어려운 *uh·lyuh·oon* **difficult**
어린이 *uh·lee·nee* **child**
어린이 수영장 *uh·lee·nee soo·yuhng·jahng* **kiddie pool**
어린이용 메뉴 *uh·lee·nee·yong meh·nyoo* **children's menu, children's portion**
어린이용 의자 *uh·lee·nee·yong u·jah* **child seat**
어머니 *uh·muh·nee* **mother**
어제 *uh·jeh* **yesterday**
어지러운 *uh·jee·luh·oon* **dizzy**
언덕 *uhn·duhk* **hill**
언제 *uhn·jeh* **when**
얼굴 *uhl·gool* **face**
얼굴 마사지 *uhl·gool mah·ssah·jee* **facial**
얼리다 *uhl·lee·dah* **freeze**
얼마나 *ul·mah·nah* **how much**
엄지손가락 *uhm·jee·sohn·kkah·lahk* **thumb**
없어진 *uhp·ssuh·jeen* **missing**
없이 *uhp·ssee* **without**
에 *eh* **at, in, on, per**
에나멜 *eh·nah·mehl* **enamel**
에메랄드 *eh·meh·lahl·du* **emerald**
에스컬레이터 *eh·su·kuhl·leh·ee·tuh* **escalator**
엑스레이 *ehk·ssu·leh·ee* **x-ray**
엘리베이터 *ehl·lee·beh·ee·tuh* **elevator [lift BE]**
여권 *yuh·kkwuhn* **passport**
여기 *yuh·gee* **here**
여분 *yuh·boon* **extra, spare**
여자 *yuh·jah* **female**
여자 형제 *yuh·jah hyuhng·jeh* **sister**
여자애 *yuh·jah·eh* **girl**
여자친구 *yuh·jah·cheen·goo* **girlfriend**

여자 종업원 *yuh•jah johng•uh•bwuhn* **waitress**
여행 *yuh•hehng* **tour, trip, travel**
여행 가방 *yuh•hehng kkah•bahng* **suitcase**
여행 가이드 *yuh•hehng gah•ee•du* **tour guide**
여행사 *yuh•hehng•sah* **travel agency**
여행 안내소 *yuh•hehng ahn•neh•soh* **tourist office**
여행자 수표 *yuh•hehng•jah soo•pyo* **traveler's check [traveller's cheque BE]**
역사적인 *yuhk•ssah•juh•geen* **historical**
연결 *yuhn•gyuhl* **connection**
연결하다 *yuhn•gyuhl•hah•dah* **connect**
연극 *yuhn•guk n* **play**
연락하다 *yuhl•lah•kah•dah* **contact, reach**
연료 *yuhl•lyo* **fuel**
연못 *yuhn•moht* **pond**
연습하다 *yuhn•su•pah•dah v* **practice**
연주하다 *yuhn•joo•hah•dah* **play (music)**
연주회장 *yuhn•joo•hweh•jahng* **concert hall**
열 *yuhl* **fever**
열다 *yuhl•dah* **open**
열쇠 *yuhl•ssweh* **key**
열쇠고리 *yuhl•ssweh•goh•lee* **key ring**
염증 *yuhm•tzung* **inflammation**
엽서 *yuhp•ssuh* **postcard**
영 *yuhng* **zero**
영국 *yuhng•gook* **United Kingdom**
영국인 *yuhng•goo•geen* **British**
영사관 *yuhng•sah•gwahn* **consulate**
영수증 *yuhng•soo•jung* **receipt**
영어 *yuhng•uh* **English**
영업 *yuhng•uhp* **sale [BE]**
영업시간 *yuhng•uhp•ssee•gahn* **office [opening BE] hours**
영화 *yuhng•hwah* **film, movie**
영화관 *yuhng•hwah•gwahn* **movie theater [cinema BE]**
옆에 *yuh•peh* **next to**
예 *yeh* **example**
예배 *yeh•beh* **service (religious)**
예쁜 *yeh•ppun* **pretty**
예약 *yeh•yahk* **reservation, appointment**
예약 접수처 *yeh•yahk juhp•ssoo•chuh* **reservation desk**
예약하다 *yeh•yah•kah•dah* **reserve**
오늘 *oh•nul* **today**
오늘밤 *oh•nul•ppahm* **tonight**
오다 *oh•dah* **come**
오두막집 *oh•doo•mahk•tzeep* **cabin**
오락 안내 *oh•lah gahn•neh* **entertainment guide**
오래된 *oh•leh•dwehn* **old (things)**
오류 *oh•lyoo* **error**
오른쪽 *oh•lun•tzohk* **right**
오븐 *oh•bun* **oven**
오직 *oh•jeek* **only**
오케스트라 *oh•keh•su•tu•lah* **orchestra**
오토바이 *oh•toh•bah•ee* **motorcycle**
오페라 *oh•peh•lah* **opera**
오후 *oh•hoo* **afternoon**
온도 *ohn•doh* **temperature**
온도계 *ohn•doh•geh* **thermometer**
옮기다 *ohm•gee•dah* **move**
옷가게 *oht•kkah•geh* **clothing store [clothes shop BE]**
옷걸이 *oht•kkuh•lee* **hanger**
왕복표 *wahng•bohk•pyo* **round-trip [return BE] ticket**
왜 *weh* **why**
외국의 *weh•goo•geh* **foreign**

외부 전화 *weh•boo juhn•hwah* **outside line**
외에 *weh•eh* **except**
왼쪽 *wehn•tzohk* **left**
요금 *yo•gum* **charge**
요리하다 *yo•lee•hah•dah v* **cook**
요인 *yo•een* **factor**
요트 *yo•tu* **yacht**
우기다 *oo•gee•dah* **insist**
우산 *oo•sahn* **umbrella**
우체국 *oo•cheh•gook* **post office**
우체통 *oo•cheh•tohng* **mailbox [postbox BE]**
우편요금 *oo•pyuhn•nyo•gum* **postage**
우편환 *oo•pyuhn•hwahn* **money order**
우표 *oo•pyo* **stamp**
운동 *oon•dohng* **sport**
운동화 *oon•dohng•hwah* **sneakers**
운전 면허증 *oon•juhn myuhn•huh•tzung* **driver's license**
운전사 *oon•juhn•sah* **driver**
운전하다 *oon•juhn•hah•dah* **drive**
운하 *oon•hah* **canal**
움직이지 않는 *oom•jee•gee•jee ahn•nun adj* **still**
웃기는 *oot•kkee•nun* **funny**
웅장한 *oong•jahng•hahn* **magnificent**
원 *wuhn* **Won (Korean currency)**
원시 *wuhn•see* **far-sighted [long-sighted BE]**
원조 *wuhn•joh* **original**
위 *wih* **top, stomach**
위층 *wih•chung* **upstairs**
위험한 *wih•huhm•hahn* **dangerous**
윈드브레이커 *wihn•du•bu•leh•ee•kuh* **windbreaker**
윈드서핑 *wihn•du•ssuh•peeng* **windsurfing**
유당 불내증 *yoo•dahng bool•leh•tzung* **lactose intolerant**
유대교 음식 *yoo•deh•gyo um•seek* **kosher**
유대교 회당 *yoo•deh•gyo hweh•dahng* **synagogue**
유람선 여행 *yoo•lahm•suhn yuh•hehng* **cruise**
유로 *yoo•loh* **euro**
유로체크 *yoo•loh•cheh•ku* **Eurocheque**
유리잔 *yoo•lee•jahn* **glass (drinking)**
유명한 *yoo•myuhng•hahn* **famous**
유모차 *yoo•moh•chah* **stroller [push-chair BE]**
유스호스텔 *yoo•su•hoh•su•tehl* **youth hostel**
유원지 *yoo•wuhn•jee* **theme park**
유적 *yoo•juhk* **ruins**
유제품의 *yoo•jeh•poo•meh* **dairy**
유효한 *yoo•hyo•hahn* **valid**
으로 *u•loh* **to (place), by (route)**
은 *un* **silver**
은퇴한 *un•tweh•hahn* **retired**
은행 *un•hehng* **bank**
은행 수수료 *un•heng soo•soo•lyo* **bank charge**
음료수 *um•nyo•soo n* **drink**
음성 안내 *um•suhng ahn•neh* **audio guide**
음식 *um•seek* **dish, food**
음식점 *um•seek•tzuhm* **restaurant**
음악 *u•mahk* **music**
음악회 *u•mah•kweh* **concert**
의료 보험 *u•lyo boh•huhm* **health insurance**
의무적인 *u•moo•juh•geen* **mandatory**
의사 *u•sah* **doctor**
의식을 잃은 *u•see•gul ee•lun* **unconscious**
의식하는 *u•see•kah•nun* **conscious**

이다 *ee•dah* **be**
이동식 주택 *ee•dohng•seek joo•tehk* **mobile home**
이륙하다 *ee•lyoo•kah•dah* **take off (plane)**
이름 *ee•lum* **name**
이메일 *ee•meh•eel* **e-mail**
이메일 주소 *ee•meh•eel joo•soh* **e-mail address**
이미 *ee•mee* **already**
이발소 *ee•bahl•soh* **barber**
이부프로펜 *ee•boo•pu•loh•pehn* **ibuprofen**
이빨 *ee•ppahl* **tooth**
이사 *ee•sah* **director**
이상 *ee•sahng* **over (more than)**
이상한 *eee•sahng•hahn* **bizarre**
이슬람교 식용육 *ee•sul•lahm•gyo see•gyong•nyook* **halal**
이십사 시간 약국 *ee•seep•ssah see•gahn yahk•kkook* **all-night pharmacy**
이용할 수 있는 *ee•yong•hahl ssoo een•nun* **available**
이유식 *ee•yoo•seek* **baby food**
이인용 *ee•een•nyong* **double**
이인용 방 *ee•een•nyong bahng* **double room**
이코노미석 *ee•koh•noh•mee•suhk* **economy class**
이혼 *ee•hohn* **divorce**
인기있는 *een•kkee•een•nun* **popular**
인도하다 *een•doh•hah•dah v* **lead**
인슐린 *een•syool•leen* **insulin**
인터넷 *een•tuh•neht* **internet**
인형 *een•hyuhng* **doll**
일 *eel* **day, work**
일하다 *eel•hah•dah v* **work (job)**
일광 화상 *eel•gwahng hwah•sahng* **sunburn**
일광욕하다 *eel•gwahng•nyo•kah•dah* **sunbathe**
일기 예보 *eel•gee yeh•boh* **weather forecast**
일등석 *eel•ttung•suhk* **first class**
일방통행 *eel•bahng•tohng•hehng* **one-way (traffic)**
일사병 *eel•ssah•ppyuhng* **sunstroke**
일어나다 *ee•luh•nah•dah* **happen**
일어서다 *ee•luh•suh•dah v* **stand**
일인용 *ee•leen•yong* **single (individual)**
일인용 방 *ee•leen•yong bahng* **single room**
일정한 *eel•tzuhng•hahn* **constant**
일찍 *eel•tzeek* **early**
일하다 *eel•hah•dah v* **work**
일회용 (카메라) *eel•hweh•yong (kah•meh•lah)* **disposable (camera)**
읽다 *eek•ttah* **read**
잃어버리다 *ee•luh•buh•lee•dah* **lose**
잃어버린 *ee•luh•buh•leen* **lost**
임신한 *eem•seen•hahn* **pregnant**
임자 있는 *eem•jah een•nun* **taken**
입 *eep* **mouth**
입구 *eep•kkoo* **entrance**
입구 경사로 *eep•kkoo gyuhng•sah•loh* **entrance ramp**
입국 비자 *eep•kkook bee•jah* **entry visa**
입금 *eep•kkum* **deposit**
입다 *eep•ttah* **wear**
입술 *eep•ssool* **lip**
입어 보다 *ee•buh boh•dah* **try on**
입장 *eep•tzahng* **entry**
입장료 *eep•tzahng•nyo* **entrance fee, cover charge**
잊다 *eet•ttah* **forget**

ㅈ

자금 *jah•gum* **funds**
자기 *jah•gee* **porcelain**
자다 *jah•dah* **sleep**
자동 *jah•dohng* **automatic**
자동차 *jah•dohng•chah* **car, vehicle**
자동차 수리공 *jah•dohng•chah soo•lee•gohng* **mechanic**
자리 *jah•lee* **place, space**
자막 나오는 *jah•mahng nah•oh•nun* **subtitled**
자명종 *jah•myuhng•johng* **alarm clock**
자물쇠 *jah•mool•ssweh* **lock**
자연 *jah•yuhn* **nature**
자연 보호 지역 *jah•yuhn boh•hoh jee•yuhk* **nature reserve**
자외선 차단 크림 *jah•weh•suhn chah•dahn ku•leem* **sunscreen**
자전거 *jah•juhn•guh* **bicycle**
자전거 도로 *jah•juhn•guh doh•loh* **bike path, cycle route**
자정 *jah•juhng* **midnight**
작은 *jah•gun* **small, little**
잔돈 *jahn•dohn n* **change**
잔디 *jahn•dee* **grass**
잘못된 *jahl•moht•ttwehn* **wrong**
잠그다 *jahm•gu•dah v* **lock**
잠수복 *jahm•soo•bohk* **wetsuit**
잠수용 튜브 *jahm•soo•yong tyoo•bu* **snorkle**
잠옷 *jah•moht* **pajamas**
잡다 *jahp•ttah* **catch**
잡지 *jahp•tzee* **magazine**
장갑 *jahng•gahp* **gloves**
장거리 버스 *jahng•guh•lee buh•su* **long-distance bus**
장난감 *jahng•nahn•kkahm* **toy**
장난감 가게 *jahng•nahn•kkahm gah•geh* **toy store**
장미 *jahng•mee* **rose**
장비 *jahng•bee* **equipment**
장소 *jahng•soh* **site**
장식 *jahng•seek* **decorative**
장애 *jahng•eh* **barrier**
장애인 *jahng•eh•een* **handicapped [disabled BE]**
잦은 *jah•jun* **frequent**
재고 정리 *jeh•goh juhng•nee* **clearance**
재다 *jeh•dah* **measure**
재떨이 *jeh•ttuh•lee* **ashtray**
재미 *jeh•mee* **fun**
재킷 *jeh•keet* **jacket**
쟁반 *jehng•bahn* **tray**
저 *juh* **me**
저녁 *juh•nyuhk* **evening**
저녁 식사 *juh•nyuhk seek•ssah* **dinner**
저렴한 *juh•lyuhm•hahn* **inexpensive**
저수지 *juh•soo•jee* **reservoir**
저울 *juh•ool* **scale**
저장하다 *juh•jahng•hah•dah* **save**
적당한 *juhk•ttahng•hahn* **suitable**
전경 *juhn•gyuhng* **panorama**
전구 *juhn•goo* **lightbulb**
전기 면도기 *juhn•gee myuhn•doh•gee* **electric shaver**
전기 콘센트 *juhn•gee kohn•sehn•tu* **electrical outlet**
전등 *juhn•dung* **light, lamp**
전망 *juhn•mahng* **view**
전망대 *juhn•mahng•deh* **viewpoint**
전망이 좋은 곳 *juhn•mahng•ee joh•un goht* **overlook**
전문의 *juhn•moo•nee* **specialist**
전염성의 *juhn•yuhm•ssuhng•eh* **contagious**
전자 *juhn•jah* **electronic**
전자레인지 *juhn•jah•leh•een•jee* **microwave (oven)**
전자티켓 *juhn•jah•tee•keht* **e-ticket**
전쟁 기념관 *juhn•jehng gee•nyuhm•gwahn* **war memorial**

전적지 *juhn•juhk•tzee* **battlesite**
전차 *juhn•chah* **tram**
전통 *juhn•tohng* **traditional**
전통춤 *juhn•tohng•choom* **traditional dance**
전형적인 *juhn•hyuhng•juh•geen* **typical**
전화 *juhn•hwah* **phone**
전화 걸다 *juhn•hwah guhl•dah* **dial**
전화 번호 *juhn•hwah buhn•hoh* **phone number**
전화 번호부 *juhn•hwah buhn•hoh•boo* **phone directory**
전화 카드 *juhn•hwah kah•du* **phone card**
전화 통화 *juhn•hwah tohng•hwah* **phone call**
절단 *juhl•ttahn n* **cut**
절벽 *juhl•byuhk* **cliff**
젊은 *juhl•mun* **young**
젊음 *juhl•mum* **youth**
점심 *juhm•seem* **lunch**
점원 *juh•mwuhn* **shop assistant**
접근 *juhp•kkun* **access**
접는 의자 *juhm•nun u•jah* **deck chair**
접속을 끊다 *juhp•ssoh•gul kkun•tah* **disconnect, log off**
접속하다 *juhp•ssoh•kah•dah* **log on**
접수 *juhp•ssoo* **reception (desk)**
접수원 *juhp•ssoo•wuhn* **receptionist**
접시 *juhp•ssee* **dishes, plate**
정류장 *juhng•nyoo•jahng n* **stand, stop**
정기권 *juhng•gee•kkwuhn* **season ticket**
정맥 *juhng•mehk* **vein**
정비공장 *juhng•bee•gohng•jahng* **garage**
정상 *juhng•sahng* **normal**
정오 *juhng•oh* **noon [midday BE]**
정원 *juhng•wuhn* **garden**
정장 *juhng•jahng* **formal dress**
정확한 *juhng•hwah•kahn* **exact**
젖병 *juht•ppyuhng* **baby bottle**
제거하다 *jeh•guh•hah•dah* **remove**
제과점 *jeh•gwah•juhm* **bakery**
제산제 *jeh•sahn•jeh* **antacid**
제안하다 *jeh•ahn•hah•dah* **suggest**
제충제 *jeh•choong•jeh* **insect repellent**
제한 속도 *jeh•hahn sohk•ttoh* **speed limit**
제한 초과 수하물 *jeh•hahn choh•gwah soo•hah•mool* **excess luggage**
조각 *joh•gahk* **piece, slice**
조금 *joh•gum* **few**
조심 *joh•seem* **caution**
조심하다 *joh•seem•hah•dah* **beware**
조용한 *joh•yong•hahn* **quiet**
조직하다 *joh•jee•kah•dah* **organize**
족집게 *johk•tzeep•geh* **tweezers**
졸린 *johl•leen* **drowsy**
졸음 *joh•lum* **drowsiness**
좀 *johm* **please**
좁은 *joh•bun* **narrow**
종교 *johng•gyo* **religion**
종류 *johng•nyoo* **type**
종양 *johng•yahng* **tumor**
종이 타월 *johng•ee tah•wuhl* **paper towel**
종종 *johng•johng* **often**
좋다 *joh•tah* **OK**
좋아하는 *joh•ah•hah•nun* **favorite**
좋아하다 *joh•ah•hah•dah* **like**
좋은 *joh•un* **good, nice, fine**
좌석 *jwah•suhk* **seat (on train, etc.)**
주다 *joo•dah* **give**
주류 *joo•lyoo* **alcoholic (drink)**
주류 판매점 *joo•lyoo pahn•meh•juhm* **liquor store [off-licence BE]**

주말 *joo•mahl* **weekend**
주말 요금 *joo•mahl lyo•gum* **weekend rate**
주문하다 *joo•moon•hah•dah* **order**
주방 시설 *joo•bahng see•suhl* **cooking facilities**
주방용 세제 *joo•bahng•nyong seh•jeh* **dishwashing liquid**
주사 *joo•sah* **injection**
주소 *joo•soh* **address**
주요한 *joo•yo•hahn* **main**
주유소 *joo•yoo•soh* **gas [petrol BE] station**
주인 *joo•een* **owner**
주일 *joo•eel* **week**
주차 금지 *joo•chah gum•jee* **no parking**
주차 미터기 *joo•chah mee•tuh•gee* **parking meter**
주차 서비스 *joo•chah ssuh•bee•su* **valet service**
주차 위반 딱지 *joo•chah wih•bahn ttahk•jee* **parking ticket**
주차장 *joo•chah•jahng* **parking garage, parking lot [car park BE]**
준비된 *joon•bee•dwehn* **ready**
줄이다 *joo•lee•dah* **reduce**
중간 *joong•gahn* **medium**
중심가 *joong•seem•gah* **downtown**
중요한 *joong•yo•hahn* **important**
즐거운 *jul•guh•oon* **pleasant**
즐기다 *jul•gee•dah* **enjoy**
증상 *jung•sahng* **symptom**
지갑 *jee•gahp* **wallet**
지금 *jee•gum* **now**
지나다 *jee•nah•dah v* **pass**
지나서 *jee•nah•suh* **after**
지도 *jee•doh* **map**
지도자 *jee•doh•jah* **leader (group)**
지방 *jee•bahng* **local**
지불 *jee•bool* **payment**
지붕 *jee•boong* **roof**
지속하다 *jee•soh•kah•dah v* **last**
지역 *jee•yuhk* **region**
지역 번호 *jee•yuhk ppuhn•hoh* **area code, code**
지연 *jee•yuhn* **delay**
지점 *jee•juhm* **spot (place, site)**
지친 *jee•cheen* **exhausted**
지퍼 *jee•puh* **zipper**
지하실 *jee•hah•seel* **basement**
지하철 *jee•hah•chuhl* **subway [underground BE]**
지하철 노선도 *jee•hah•chuhl noh•suhn•doh* **subway [underground BE] map**
지하철역 *jee•hah•chuhl•lyuhk* **subway [underground BE] station**
지휘자 *jee•hwih•jah* **conductor**
직업 *jee•guhp* **job, profession**
직원 *jee•gwuhn* **staff**
직접 만든 *jeek•tzuhp mahn•dun* **homemade**
직행 *jee•kehng* **direct, non-stop**
진공 청소기 *jeen•gohng chuhng•soh•gee* **vacuum cleaner**
진열장 *jee•nyuhl•tzahng* **display case**
진정제 *jeen•juhng•jeh* **sedative**
진주 *jeen•joo* **pearl**
진짜 *jeen•tzah* **genuine, real, authentic**
질 *jeel* **quality, vagina**
질긴 *jeel•geen* **tough**
짐 *jeem* **luggage [baggage BE]**
짐꾼 *jeem•kkoon* **porter**
집 *jeep* **home, house**
짓다 *jeet•ttah* **build**
짧은 *tzahl•bun* **short**
짧은 여행 *tzahl•bun yuh•hehng* **excursion**
쯤 *tzum* **around (time)**
찢다 *tzeet•ttah* **tear**
찢어진 *tzee•juh•jeen* **torn**

ㅊ

차가운 *chah•gah•oon adj* **cold**
차고 *chah•goh* **garage (parking)**
차선 *chah•suhn* **lane**
착륙하다 *chahng•nyoo•kah•dah* *v* **land**
참가하다 *chahm•gah•hah•dh* **join**
창문 *chahng•moon* **window**
창문석 *chahng•moon•suhk* **window seat**
찾다 *chaht•ttah* **find**
채식주의자 *cheh•seek•tzoo•ee•jah* **vegetarian**
채우다 *cheh•oo•dah* **fill**
책 *chehk* **book**
책임 *cheh•geem* **responsibility**
처방 *chuh•bahng* **prescription**
천 *chuhn* **fabric**
천식 *chuhn•seek* **asthma**
철 *chuhl* **steel**
철물점 *chuhl•mool•juhm* **hardware store**
철자하다 *chuhl•tzah•hah•dah* **spell**
첫 *chuht* **first**
청각 장애인 *chuhng•gahk tzahng•eh•een* **hearing impaired**
청바지 *chuhng•bah•jee* **jeans**
체크아웃 *cheh•ku•ah•oot* **check out**
초대하다 *choh•deh•hah•dah* **invite**
최고 *chweh•goh* **superb**
추가 *choo•gah* **supplement**
추천하다 *choo•chuhn•hah•dah* **recommend**
축구 *chook•kkoo* **soccer [football BE]**
축소 모형 *chook•ssoh moh•hyuhng* **miniature**
축하합니다 *choo•kah•ham•nee•dah* **congratulations**
출구 *chool•goo* **exit**
출금 *chool•gum* **withdrawal**
출금하다 *chool•gum•hah•dah* **withdraw**
출발 *chool•bahl* **departures**
출발하다 *chool•bahl•hah•dah* **depart**
춤 추다 *choom choo•dah* **dance**
충격 *choong•gyuhk* **shock**
충분한 *choong•boon•hahn* **enough**
취미 *chwih•mee* **hobby, interest (hobby)**
취소하다 *chwih•soh•hah•dah* **cancel**
층 *chung* **floor (level)**
치과의사 *chee•kkwah•u•sah* **dentist**
치료 *chee•lyo* **treatment**
치마 *chee•mah* **skirt**
치수 *chee•soo* **measurement**
치실 *chee•seel* **dental floss**
치약 *chee•yahk* **toothpaste**
치통 *chee•tohng* **toothache**
친구 *cheen•goo* **friend**
친절한 *cheen•juhl•hahn* **kind**
침 *cheem* **acupuncture**
침구 *cheem•goo* **bedding**
침낭 *cheem•nahng* **sleeping bag**
침대 *cheem•deh* **bed**
침대차 *cheem•deh•chah* **sleeper car (train)**
침실 *cheem•seel* **bedroom**
칫솔 *cheet•ssohl* **toothbrush**

ㅋ

카누 *kah•noo* **canoe**
카드 *kah•du* **card**
카메라 *kah•meh•lah* **camera**
카시트 *kah•ssee•tu* **car seat**
카운터 *kah•oon•tuh* **counter**
카지노 *kah•jee•noh* **casino**
카페트 *kah•peh•tu* **carpet**
카트 *kah•tu* **cart [trolley BE]**
칼 *kahl* **knife**
칼로리 *kahl•loh•lee* **calorie**

캐나다 *keh•nah•dah* **Canada**
캠핑장 *kehm•peeng•jahng* **campsite**
캠핑하다 *kehm•peeng•hah•dah* **camp**
캡슐 *kehp•syool* **capsule**
커브 *kuh•bu* **curve**
커튼 *kuh•tun* **curtain**
컨디셔너 *kuhn•dee•syuh•nuh* **conditioner**
컴퓨터 *kuhm•pyoo•tuh* **computer**
컵 *kuhp* **cup**
켜다 *kyuh•dah* **turn on**
코 *koh* **nose**
코르크 마개뽑이 *koh•lu•ku mah•geh•ppoh•bee* **corkscrew**
코스 *koh•su* **course (meal)**
코트 *koh•tu* **coat**
콘돔 *kohn•dohm* **condom**
콘텍트 렌즈 *kohn•tehk•tu lehn•ju* **contact lens**
콘텍트 렌즈 용액 *kohn•tehk•tu lehn•ju yong•ehk* **contact lens solution**
콜밴 *kohl•behn* **van taxi**
쿠킹 호일 *koo•keeng hoh•eel* **aluminum [kitchen BE] foil**
큰 *kun* **large, big**
클럽 *kul•luhp* **dance club**
키 *kee* **height (person)**
키 큰 *kee kun* **tall**
키스하다 *kee•ssu•hah•dah* **kiss**
키카드 *kee•kah•du* **key card**

ㅌ

타이어 *tah•ee•uh* **tire**
타일 *tah•eel* **tile**
탈의실 *tahl•ee•seel* **fitting room**
탈취제 *tahl•chwih•jeh* **deodorant**
탐폰 *tahm•pohn* **tampon**
탑 *tahp* **tower**
탑승 수속 *tahp•ssung soo•sohk* **check in**
탑승 수속대 *tahp•ssung soo•sohk•tteh* **check-in desk**
탑승 카드 *tahp•ssung kah•du* **boarding card**
탑승구 *tahp•ssung•goo* **gate**
탑승하다 *tahp•ssung•hah•dah* **board**
태어난 *teh•uh•nahn* **born**
태우다 *teh•oo•dah* **tan**
택시 *tehk•ssee* **taxi**
택시 승차장 *tehk•ssee sung•chah•jahng* **taxi stand**
터널 *tuh•nuhl* **tunnel**
터미널 *tuh•mee•nuhl* **terminal**
턱 *tuhk* **jaw**
턱받이 *tuhk•ppah•jee* **bib**
텅 빈 *tuhng been* **empty**
테니스 *teh•nee•su* **tennis**
테니스 코트 *teh•nee•su koh•tu* **tennis court**
테이블 *teh•ee•bul* **table**
텐트 *tehn•tu* **tent**
텐트용 기둥 *tehn•tu•yong gee•doong* **tent pole**
텐트용 쐐기 *tehn•tu•yong ssweh•gee* **tent peg**
텔레비전 *tehl•leh•bee•juhn* **TV**
토박이 *toh•bah•gee* **native**
토하다 *toh•hah•dah* **vomit**
토할 거 같은 *toh•hahl kkuh gah•tun* **nauseous**
통로 *tohng•noh* **aisle**
통보하다 *tohng•boh•hah•dah* **notify**
통역 *tohng•yuhk* **interpreter**
통조림 따개 *tohng•joh•leem ttah•geh* **can [tin BE] opener**
통해서 *tohng•heh•suh* **through**
트럭 *tu•luhk* **truck**
트레일러 *tu•leh•eel•luh* **trailer**
특급 우편 *tuk•kkup oo•pyuhn* **express mail**
특별한 *tuk•ppyuhl•hahn* **special**
특징 *tuk•tzeeng* **feature**

틀니 *tul•lee* **denture**
티셔츠 *tee•syuh•chu* **T-shirt**
티스푼 *tee•su•pun* **teaspoon**
팀 *teem* **team**
팁 *teep* **tip**

ㅍ

파도 *pah•doh* **wave**
파운드 *pah•oon•du* **pound, pound sterling**
파이프 *pah•ee•pu* **pipe**
파티 *pah•tee* **party**
판매세 *pahn•meh•sseh* **sales tax**
판매용 *pahn•meh•yong* **for sale**
팔 *pahl* **arm**
팔다 *pahl•dah* **sell**
팔찌 *pal•tzee* **bracelet**
패스트 푸드 *peh•su•tu poo•du* **fast food**
팩스 *pehk•su* **fax**
팩스 번호 *pehk•su buhn•hoh* **fax number**
팩스기 *pehk•su•gee* **fax machine**
팬티스타킹 *pehn•tee•su•tah•keeng* **panty hose**
팸플릿 *pahm•pul•leht* **brochure**
페니실린 *peh•nee•seel•leen* **penicillin**
페디큐어 *peh•dee•kyoo•uh* **pedicure**
펜 *pehn* **pen**
편도표 *pyuhn•doh•pyo* **one-way ticket**
편두통 *pyuhn•doo•tohng* **migraine**
편지 *pyuhn•jee* **letter**
편지 보내다 *pyuhn•jee boh•neh•dah* *v* **mail**
편지 봉투 *pyuhn•jee bohng•too* **envelope**
평상복 *pyuhng•sahng•bohk* **informal (dress)**
평일 *pyuhng•eel* **weekday**
평평한 *pyuhng•pyuhng•hahn* **flat**
폐 *peh* **lung**
포도밭 *poh•doh•baht* **vineyard**
포크 *poh•ku* **fork**
포함하다 *poh•hahm•hah•dah* **contain, include**
폭포 *pohk•poh* **waterfall**
폭행 *poh•kehng* **attack**
폴리에스테르 *pohl•lee•eh•su•teh•lu* **polyester**
표 *pyo* **ticket**
표백제 *pyo•behk•tzeh* **bleach**
표본 *pyo•bohn* **specimen**
표준 *pyo•joon* **standard**
표지 *pyo•jee* *n* **sign**
품목 *poom•mohk* **item**
프로그램 *pu•loh•gu•lehm* **program**
프린트하다 *pu•leen•tu•hah•dah* *v* **print**
플라스틱 *pul•lah•su•teek* **plastic**
플러그 *pul•luh•gu* **plug**
피가 나다 *pee•gah nah•dah* **bleed**
피곤한 *pee•gohn•hahn* **tired**
피부 *pee•boo* **skin**
피시방 *pee•ssee•bahng* **internet cafe**
피임약 *pee•eem•nyahk* **contraceptive**
피크닉 *pee•ku•neek* **picnic**
피크닉 구역 *pee•ku•neek kkoo•yuhk* **picnic area**
필기 용지 *peel•gee yong•jee* **writing paper**
필수 *peel•ssoo* **required**
필수적인 *peel•ssoo•juh•geen* **essential**
필요하다 *pee•lyo•hah•dah* **need**
필요한 *pee•lyo•hahn* **necessary**
필터 *peel•tuh* **filter**

ㅎ

하게 하다 *hah•geh hah•dah* **let**
하고 같이 *hah•goh gah•chee* **with**
하다 *hah•dah* **do**

하이킹 *hah•ee•keeng* **hike**
하이킹 장비 *hah•ee•keeng jahng•bee* **hiking gear**
하이힐 *hah•ee•heel* **heels**
학생 *hahk•ssehng* **student**
한 번 *hahn buhn* **once**
한 쌍 *hahn ssahng* **pair**
할인 *hah•leen* **discount**
할인매장 *hah•leen•meh•jahng* **discount store**
합법적 *hahp•ppuhp•tzuhk* **legal**
합성 *hahp•ssuhng* **synthetic**
합치다 *hahp•chee•dah* **merge**
항공기 편명 *hahng•gohng•gee pyuhn•myung* **flight number**
항공사 *hahng•gohng•sah* **airline**
항공우편 *hahng•gohng•oo•pyuhn* **airmail**
항구 *hahng•goo* **port, harbor**
항상 *hahng•sahng* **always**
항생제 *hahng•sehng•jeh* **antibiotics**
해 *heh* **sun**
해발 *heh•bahl* **sea level**
해변 *heh•byuhn* **beach**
해안 *heh•ahn* **coast**
해안 거리 *heh•ahn guh•lee* **seafront**
해야 하다 *heh•yah hah•dah* **must**
핸드백 *hehn•du•behk* **purse [handbag BE]**
행복한 *hehng•boh•kahn* **happy**
행사 *hehng•sah* **event**
허락하다 *huh•lah•kah•dah* **allow, approve**
허용한도 *huh•yong•hahn•doh* **allowance**
헐렁한 *huhl•luhng•hahn* **loose**
헤드라이트 *heh•du•lah•ee•tu* **headlight**
헤어 브러시 *heh•uh bu•luh•see* **hair brush**
헬멧 *hehl•meht* **helmet**
헬스클럽 *hehl•ssu•kul•luhp* **gym**
혀 *hyuh* **tongue**
현금 *hyuhn•gum* **cash**
현금 인출기 *hyuhn•gum een•chool•gee* **ATM**
현대 *hyuhn•deh* **contemporary**
현상하다 *hyuhn•sahng•hah•dah* **develop**
혈압 *hyuh•lahp* **blood pressure**
혈액 *hyuh•lehk* **blood**
호수 *hoh•soo* **lake**
호텔 *hoh•tehl* **hotel**
혼자 *hohn•jah* **alone**
화랑 *hwah•lahng* **gallery**
화상 *hwah•sahng* **burn**
화장 *hwah•jahng* **make-up**
화장실 *hwah•jahng•seel* **bathroom, restroom [toilet BE]**
화장실 휴지 *hwah•jahng•seel hyoo•jee* **toilet paper**
화장지 *hwah•jahng•jee* **tissue**
화장품 *hwah•jahng•poom* **cosmetic**
화재 경보 *hwah•jeh gyuhng•boh* **fire alarm**
화재 비상 계단 *hwah•jeh bee•sahng geh•dahn* **fire escape**
화재 비상구 *hwah•jeh bee•sahng•goo* **fire exit**
확대하다 *hwahk•tteh•hah•dah* **enlarge**
확실한 *hwahk•sseel•hahn* **sure**
확인하다 *hwah•geen•hah•dah* **check, confirm, validate**
환불 *hwahn•bool* **refund**
환영 *hwah•nyuhng* **welcome**
환율 *hwah•nyool* **exchange rate**
환자 *hwahn•jah* *n* **patient**
환전소 *hwahn•juhn•soh* **currency exchange office**
회교 사원 *hweh•gyo•sah•wuhn* **mosque**
회사 *hweh•sah* **company**
회원 *hweh•wuhn* **member**

회의 *hweh•ee* **conference, meeting**
회의실 *hweh•ee•seel* **meeting room**
회의장 *hweh•ee•jahng* **convention hall**
회의 장소 *hweh•ee jahng•soh* **meeting place**
횡단보도 *hwehng•dahn•boh•doh* **pedestrian [zebra BE] crossing**
후라이팬 *hoo•lah•ee•pen* **frying pan**
훔치다 *hoom•chee•dah* **steal**
훨씬 *hwuhl•sseen* **much**
휠체어 *hwihl•cheh•uh* **wheelchair**
휠체어 진입로 *hwihl•cheh•uh jee•neem•noh* **wheelchair ramp**
휴가 *hyoo•gah* **vacation [holiday BE]**
휴게소 *hyoo•geh•soh* **rest area**
휴대 변기 *hyoo•deh byuhn•gee* **chemical toilet**
휴대폰 *hyoo•deh•pohn* **cell [mobile BE] phone**
휴대품 보관소 *hyoo•deh•poom boh•gwahn•soh* **coat check**
흡연석 *hu•byuhn•suhk* **smoking area**
흥정 *hung•juhng* **bargain**
힘 *heem* **power**